THE LAWS OF THE SPIRIT

THE LAWS OF THE SPIRIT

A HEGELIAN THEORY OF JUSTICE

SHANNON HOFF

SUNY PRESS

Published by State University of New York Press, Albany

Printed in the United States of America

For information, contact State University of New York Press, Albany, NY
www.sunypress.edu

Production by Eileen Nizer
Marketing by Michael Campochiaro

Library of Congress Cataloging-in-Publication Data

Hoff, Shannon.
The laws of the spirit : a Hegelian theory of justice / Shannon Hoff.
pages cm
Includes bibliographical references and index.
ISBN 978-1-4384-5027-8 (hc : alk. paper) 978-1-4384-5028-5 (pb : alk. paper)
1. Hegel, Georg Wilhelm Friedrich, 1770–1831. 2. Spirit. 3. Justice (Philosophy) I. Title.

B2949.S75H64 2014
193—dc23 2013014432

10 9 8 7 6 5 4 3 2 1

for John Russon, whose many words echo through the pages of this book and whose commitment to philosophy and to aspiring philosophers is unparalleled

CONTENTS

PART 3
HEGEL AND CONTEMPORARY POLITICAL LIFE

ACKNOWLEDGMENTS

I believe that there is a singular tradition of Hegel scholarship in Canada, one by which I have been guided as long as I have been studying Hegel, and I am indebted to new and old figures in that tradition for their commitment to clarifying Hegel's powerful capacity to illuminate the nature of human experience. I am also indebted to John Russon's Toronto Summer Seminar and its various extensions, both for support in the development of a philosophical voice and for the gift of a philosophical community; I would like to express my appreciation for, among many important others, Kym Maclaren, Greg Kirk, Whitney Howell, Jeff Morrisey, Susan Bredlau, Ömer Aygün, Eve Rabinoff, Greg Recco, Karen Robertson, Patricia Fagan, David Ciavatta, Kirsten Jacobson, Eric Sanday, and Scott Maratto, with whom I hope for many more years of conversation and merriment. To the many junior members, senior members, and staff of the Institute for Christian Studies, who together make ICS the incomparable educational institution that it is, I owe many years of support and partnership in the pursuit of knowledge and the good life. I am grateful to Kelly Oliver, and to Lambert Zuidervaart, Eduardo Mendieta, and Robert Bernasconi, for their persistent support throughout the years, to Chad Kautzer and Senem Saner for their camaraderie and commitment both to the just and to the early stages of this work, and to Jonathan Weverink. I am also grateful for the hospitality of the various "offices" in which this manuscript was produced, offices with names like Ideal, Holy Oak, Manic, and Jet Fuel. Finally, I am grateful to my family—to my parents, Elly and Bram Hoff, for the uniquely powerful ways in which they have carved out a place in the world for me; to my brother, Marcel Hoff, for his unfailing while inadvertent support of this project; and to Aron, Rachel, Ben, Zoë, Kristin, Antoine, Julie, Peter, Jacqueline, Norah, Jaden, Asher, Rowley, Mies, Finn, and, I must add, Little and Hussein, for the "ethical life" they continue to provide.

Chapter 1 is based on an essay published in *Philosophy Today*; chapter 2 is based on an essay published in *The Owl of Minerva*; chapter 5 is very loosely based on an essay published in *Philosophy Today*; and most of what is now chapter 8 was published in an article in *Philosophical Forum*.

NOTE ON THE TEXT

The focus of this study is G. W. F. Hegel's *Phänomenologie des Geistes* of 1807. References to this text will be to *Phänomenologie des Geistes*, hrsg. v. Eva Moldenhauer u. Karl Markus Michel (Frankfurt am Main: Suhrkamp Verlag, 1970), and to *Phenomenology of Spirit*, tr. A. V. Miller (Oxford: Oxford University Press, 1977). References to the Miller translation will be given as M followed by the paragraph number, and references to the Moldenhauer and Michel edition will be given as S followed by the page number.

References to the *Grundlinien der Philosophie des Rechts* of 1821 will be to *Grundlinien der Philosophie des Rechts*, hrsg. v. Eva Moldenhauer u. Karl Markus Michel (Frankfurt am Main: Suhrkamp Verlag, 1970), and to *Elements of the Philosophy of Right*, ed. Allen W. Wood, tr. H. B. Nisbet (Cambridge: Cambridge University Press, 1991). These references will be given as *PhR* and the paragraph number; paragraph numbers are the same in the German and English versions.

References to "The Spirit of Christianity and Its Fate" will be to *Early Theological Writings*, tr. T. M. Knox (Chicago: Chicago University Press, 1948) and will be given as *ETW*.

References to the third section of the *Encyclopaedia of the Philosophical Sciences*, "The Philosophy of Spirit (§§377–577), will be to G. W. F. Hegel, *Enzyklopädie der philosophischen Wissenschaften III*, hrsg. V. Eva Moldenhauer u. Karl Markus Michel (Frankfurt am Main: Suhrkamp Verlag, 1970), and to G. W. F. Hegel, *Hegel's Philosophy of Spirit*, tr. William Wallace (Oxford: Oxford University Press, 1971).

References to Remarks will be given as paragraph or page number followed by R, and references to Additions will be given as paragraph or page number followed by A.

I have used the translations noted above as a general guide, but I have made modifications to them when necessary. These modifications are not noted in the text.

INTRODUCTION

Human beings appear in the world as single, circumscribed bodies that seem to operate on their own initiative, separable from every other being and every environment with which they come into contact. On the surface, they seem both fully formed and simply present—a determinate collection of relatively stable physical, mental, and psychological attributes. They seem to be a fully actualized part of reality; they seem complete, with all of their qualities enumerable and describable.

But these bodies speak, move, and change. They communicate with other such beings and move themselves through space in various ways, merging with other parts of the world in order to exist and to develop. The human being is not simply the body that appears, present and complete, in the world; it is also that which has cultivated it, and who it will become, elements that are not present and describable in the same way as the qualities it carries with it are. It is composed of the things and people around it, the history and future before and beyond it, that enable it to take a particular form. The human being is the home it makes for itself in the world, the earth that sustains its life, the force of gravity that allows it to exist on a surface and to interact with other bodies, the technological "prostheses" by which it extends the scope of its activity, the other people who enable its development, the laws, customs, and regulations by which this life with others is organized. It extends beyond itself; it is not simply itself, not simply given, not circumscribed by its own physical and psychological boundaries. Its functions as an individual body are supplemented in various ways: by its environment, by technology, by social life, by language. Thus is it both a natural and a technological being, a given and a made being. And its extensions are not merely added onto an already-existent entity; there is no fully formed human being who simply adds to herself, taking the initiative to make her capacities more sophisticated, to supplement her already-formed functions. The bearer of prostheses, so to speak, comes into being through them. Human individuals are as if slowly carved out of their extensions in the world and slowly develop more or less conscious and reflective extensions into it.

In the *Phenomenology of Spirit*, Hegel takes up the challenge of explaining the forces and extensions that cultivate and constitute individual human beings—the challenge, that is, of thinking through the massive historical, interpersonal, and political realities to which human identity, activity, and thought are indebted. His name for this reality that is our ground and the arena of our becoming, but that is simultaneously beyond us, is *Geist*, "spirit." It is difficult to comprehend this "spirit," since it requires that we resist thinking of identities as abstract and thinking of "objective" and "subjective" reality as clearly distinct. Thus, in addition to its task of describing "spirit," Hegel's *Phenomenology* takes on the task of cultivating in its readers the tools with which to conceive of it or the ways of thinking that will do justice to the nature of individual identities and to the nature of reality.[1]

Hegel's philosophy is a careful delineation of all the ways in which human identity is most significantly not in simple possession of itself, but emerges out of a process of dynamic interaction with what is spatially and temporally outside and beyond its self-presence. To say this is, on the one hand, to do so from the point of view of that human identity—from the point of view of that being that is dispossessed of itself. But Hegel also tracks another "point of view" as well, and that is the point of view of the reality that is the site of the development of human identity—the reality that essentially *is* human identity, in the form of its multiple extensions—namely, what he calls "spirit." In this way he witnesses to the extent to which that reality is essentially human, and not simply the external arena of human development. The ways in which our bodies, agency, and identities are extended into the world, the ways in which individuality is formed out of the plaster and fabric of homes, families, social interaction, technology, law, and language, are indications of the way in which such "external" spaces are alive with subjectivity.

These "external" sites, however, have a significance that is ambivalent: they are not simply occasions for human development and the fulfillment of human possibility, but they can also be occasions for risk, vulnerability, and the thwarting of human possibility. Human beings live only by extending themselves into space, but they often have little control over that space. We are thrust into a world that can trap us, that can violate or damage the parts and limbs we extend into it, that can frustrate, disregard, or amputate our humanity. Our environments and the tools of our development are ambivalent: they both develop and inhibit flourishing. By making them our agents and allies, by realizing ourselves through them, we give them power, and this power can then be wielded against us.

In such a context, the issue of justice—of concern and care for necessarily extended and vulnerable human beings—becomes relevant. In their attempts to act on behalf of justice, institutions, laws, communities, and practices organize human reality and human spaces in such a way as to shelter the vulnerability of extended, self-dispossessed beings. The challenge for justice is to organize and protect human extensions into the world—to organize the human world in such a way that it is safe for beings who live, so to speak, outside of themselves.

Hegel's exploration of the different shapes that the organization of social life has historically taken—the various ways in which it has extended and housed human beings—is an exploration of the historical elaboration of this concern for justice. He identifies the ways in which this concern has been exercised institutionally, culturally, socially, legally, and morally, pointing out the successes and failures of these ways as well as the tensions among them. He describes the external spaces of human development and the principles and concerns on the basis of which they are organized, illuminating the kinds of human lives that are made possible by specific kinds of worlds, or, we could say, the kinds of human beings that are enabled by specific kinds of prostheses.

The pivotal task of this book is to identify and explore what I see to be the results of Hegel's investigation of the different forms of social organization oriented toward the satisfaction of the demands of justice. It is to show that justice has been elaborated according to the three priorities of community, law, and conscience, that each of these priorities is significant, and that historical forms of social organization differ in relation to the different degrees to which they value these priorities. To do justice to the way in which individuals are cultivated, vulnerable, and transformable, that is, social forms of organization must respond to all three oft-conflicting aspects of human identity: first, our formation by particular communities; second, our organization of a stable social reality differentiated in terms of universal laws, norms, and institutions; and third, our necessarily singular perspective on and outworking of those communities and universals—a singularity that is irreducible to both law and community. Communities in their various forms shelter the vulnerability of extended beings by providing them with environments in which to develop the capacities that will allow them to extend farther into the world supporting their formation as individuals. Law organizes space and expresses our reliance on and recognition of each other. But, further, the organization provided by both community and law must indeed be an *open* organization in order to be a place for singularity—a place for the recognition, and hence forgiveness, of conscience.

Hegel's philosophical method involves equipping his readers to develop the kind of thinking that could do justice to that to which it is indebted, or that would allow us to be able to comprehend the strange and complex reality behind our appearing in space and time as seemingly individuated and self-enclosed beings. The challenge of doing philosophy with Hegel involves the challenge of employing one's individual capacity for thought to make these extraindividual forces and extensions visible, to think as an individual in a way that pays homage to all that which is beyond the scope and powers of individuality, to bring to reflection issues, things, and contexts in which we are always already involved. I will follow Hegel in trying to develop better ways of talking about identities that are fundamentally not present to themselves or not exclusively self-contained. I will focus mostly on the "Spirit" chapter of the *Phenomenology*, in which Hegel describes the basic ingredients and characteristics of human social reality, though I will also turn to other parts of the *Phenomenology*, as well as to the *Philosophy of Right*, the "Philosophy of Spirit" in the *Encyclopaedia of the Philosophical Sciences*, and an early essay, "The Spirit of Christianity and Its Fate." I will make my argument by talking through many of the major texts in which Hegel develops insight into community, law, and conscience, since it is not possible to understand the full significance of Hegel's position if his explicit discussions of these matters are abstracted from the larger context of his philosophical analysis of human life and action. I will be primarily oriented by this trio of primary dimensions that define our intersubjective reality in the studies that follow, which, in addition to being ingredients of a coherent theoretical analysis, also stand on their own as independent studies of different parts of Hegel's work. This trio of primary dimensions can be given several names: From the point of view of principles of political organization, I will speak in terms of ethicality, law, and forgiveness. From the point of view of individual experience, I will speak in terms of cultivation, organization, and transformation. From the point of view of ontological principles, I will speak in terms of particularity, universality, and singularity.

Because of its contemporary predominance as a category in terms of which justice is articulated, law—its nature, its significance, and its limitations—is the single most important notion guiding this study and the primary concept that organizes the analysis. Law, human rights, legal protection, and equality are the terms we most often hear when people speak about justice, and to a certain extent rightly so; law is essential to us for both ontological and political reasons. Ontologically, law speaks to the unique kind of being that the human is, a being that operates in relation to principles and in relation to others and a being that relies on recognition. Law institutionalizes the need for recognition; in obeying law, human beings essentially indirectly express their recognition of all of those who are protected and enabled by law. The political accomplishment of law is that through it the individual person can assume her inherent universality and be recognized as inherently universal—that is, as ultimately irreducible to any one of her particular characteristics and, given her capacity to determine herself, fundamentally free from external determination.

Despite the significance and necessity of law with regard to our human fulfillment, however, it is merely one ingredient of justice, and Hegel is ultimately ambivalent with regard to it; on its own it is inadequate for the production and protection of just personal, social, and political relationships. The recognition of human beings as inherently universal by means of law is equally an *erasure* of their singular significance, inasmuch as they become interchangeable, under law, with any other member of their law-governed society. Additionally, law requires expression and execution and thus cannot be exercised in purely universal ways but relies on the judgment of singular agents. Further, law protects and presumes already formed and determinate individuals, and in so doing does not recognize the work of "ethical life" or the work of transformation—that is, it *fails* to adequately recognize both the intimate relations of nurture in which individuals immediately find themselves and are cultivated and the possibility that individuals will become different and come to have different priorities.

We are *already*, however, the kind of beings that are constituted by law and shaped by its accomplishments. What this means is that we have to approach the issue of law from the inside, so to speak, describing, as Hegel does, the lived and presently valid reality of legal selfhood with all of its essential importance for human life and allowing that description itself to show us the incoherent or problematic aspects of this reality—the ways in which legal validity and value can also operate as obstacles to human life and fulfillment.[2] What we will find is that law can never completely do justice to, first, our status as belonging to communities that define us in certain ways and, second, our singularity or uniqueness, our capacity for newness. I will identify *ethicality* and the *forgiveness of conscience* as the other significant ingredients of justice, as they essentially respond to the problems encountered by law and the individuals and societies it protects and structures.

Ethicality or *ethical life*—Hegel's term for the phenomenon of belonging to a community that immediately generates and informs one's way of relating ethically to a world—is one aspect of any human being's ontological makeup. Of ultimate significance to us are the roles we play in these communities, the fates we have as members of them, and their revelation to us of the nature of responsibility in general and our responsibilities in particular—as mother, husband, son, Muslim, teacher, preacher, Kenyan, female. This phenomenon of belonging—belonging before having a choice about it, and in a way that motivates the choices we make—must be given *political* recognition; a society needs mechanisms by which to ensure recognition of the import of such identifications to human life.

Conscience—and the attendant value of forgiveness—also has both ontological and political import. Ontologically, we must recognize the dependence in principle of all human affairs upon the irreducible initiative of the individual in the attempt to do what is right in the absence of guidelines that are specific enough so as to eliminate the need for interpretation and judgment. Conscience must be recognized, on Hegel's account, because the singularity that is effaced by law and concealed by ethical life is *ultimately the real source of the meaning and initiative that engender the social world*, and this singularity, while insistently nonuniversal, demands recognition, in the form of forgiveness. Politically, a society needs to have mechanisms by which to address the injustice that comes from recognizing the worth of its members exclusively in terms of those aspects of their identity that are interchangeable with other members of that society (a recognition performed by law), or exclusively in terms of those aspects that are interchangeable with members of their communities of cultivation. It requires mechanisms by which to address or recognize the unjust character that specific laws can take or the injustice that comes from the specificity (of judges, for instance) that contaminates the execution of law. And it requires mechanisms by which to acknowledge that human beings can never be finalized or finished, that their constant interaction with other human beings, with other things, and with a history and future that are themselves dynamic brings about constant transformation to which the formulas of social life will always be inadequate. We are always faced with the question of what it is to be human, and we are always called to responsibility for answering it ourselves, because we always have situations of action and interaction in front of us. The answer to this question is always yet to be resolved; it is irreducible to our formulas and formulations, even while it relies on them.[3] The principle of conscience and its forgiveness, thus, represents in various ways the demand for concrete recognition of singularity at the level of actual political life and practice.

Law, ethicality, and conscience are not simply opposed to each other, even though each in a sense operates where the others leave off; they are *all* of significant value, even in their tensions with each other. Law and the relations of universality it inaugurates, conscience and the forgiveness of human singularity, and ethicality and the particular communities of cultivation are all differently necessary dimensions of human life and fulfillment and share an orientation toward that human life and its fulfillment. Justice must work itself out in universal laws *and* in respect for traditions and cultures *and* in respect for the unique singularity of human beings that is neither captured by law nor by tradition.[4] Further, while there is an irreducible tension between the demands of law, of conscience, and of ethicality, this tension makes ethical and political responsiveness and responsibility possible, since because of it human beings are prevented from resting content with given formulas for their shared life and interaction.

In these conclusions from Hegel's analysis of "spirit," we find a powerful contribution to contemporary discussions of justice, a way of negotiating the insights and shortcomings of predominant, differing views of justice in dominant contemporary approaches to politics. In liberal political philosophy, the idea of justice is based predominantly on the idea of right; in some critical theories of society, and of race, gender, and colonialism, the idea of justice is developed in response to the significance of discourse and recognition; in what is often called poststructuralist or Foucaultian thinking, the idea of justice is expressed as a matter of concern for the unceasing character of human becoming and thus is opposed to the reification of any particular shape of human being; and, in a thinker such as Derrida, justice is responsive to and torn, as in Hegel's work, among these different priorities. While oriented toward the development of a better understanding of Hegel, the following work is also dedicated to illuminating the force of his insights for these contemporary discussions of the nature of justice. In fact, it will be evident throughout the book that my understanding of Hegel places him very close to Derrida, and, while this connection between the two cannot be explicitly demonstrated here, the reader should keep it in mind and will be reminded of it regularly.[5]

In part 1, "Law, Ethicality, and Forgiveness," I defend the thesis described above, that justice as Hegel construes it is fundamentally responsiveness to the diverse priorities of ethicality, law, and forgiveness, and I explore these priorities one by one. To do so I follow his sustained development of these three elements and his indirect identification—through discussion of actually existing social frameworks that prioritize merely one of these elements—of a social framework that could house all of them. Since each chapter is oriented toward discussion of a different part of Hegel's work, the analyses of the nature and limitations of each of these three elements also vary: they are at times specific, but at other times broad and merely suggestive.

The first two chapters of part 1 are motivated primarily by an analysis of the phenomenon of ethicality or the bonds and relations among people that are logically prior to relationships of positive law and that are a fundamental source of value, meaning, and judgment in human life, and hence they put into relief the inadequacies of law. The first chapter treats the nature of ethicality as it is described in "The Spirit of Christianity and Its Fate," an early work in which Hegel challenges law in the name of the relations of love that foster and sustain moral agency. The second chapter extends the discussion of Hegel's notion of ethicality to the section of the *Phenomenology* called "True Spirit, Ethical Life," in which Hegel further discusses the relations by which ethical agency is generated in the context of a particular ethical community or how individual ethical agency is an extension of the "we" and its "way of doing things." Here I begin to elaborate Hegel's critique of the employment of "natural" determination in ancient Greek society, which renders it one sided and incapable of speaking adequately to the creative and self-making nature of human existence. Taking the authority of intimate relationships to be natural and immediate, this ethical life suppresses the reality of human interpretation and mediation. We will derive two conclusions from this reading: first, that the compulsion of immediate identification is a real and significant aspect of human life, and second, that the "artificial" production of law is a fundamental and necessary aspect of human social organization.

The third chapter turns to the significance of the accomplishment of legal order, as the universal framework by which each human being is construed as significant independently of, and protected from being reduced to, her particular characteristics and forms of identification—that is, the framework that allows each person freedom to take up new and different forms of identification and ethical bonds. It does so by discussing Hegel's analysis of the Roman "condition of right" or "legal status" and its accompanying conception of the rights-bearing person.[6] I consider both the significance and the limitations of this form of personhood and the law that protects it, specifying the accomplishments of such a society as well as the problems it incurs due to its one-sided reliance on law.

Because Hegel's discussion of legal order in the *Phenomenology* is, first, largely critical, and second, connected to his analysis of specific ancient societies, in the fourth chapter I take a detour through the *Encyclopaedia* for his discussion therein of the basic principles behind modern law. The *Encyclopaedia*'s treatment of law allows us to have in mind a full account of the nature of law and its operation in the modern world. In the chapter I discuss the ways in which posited law is a "nonlimiting limitation" or the ways in which the laws are the condition of human agency, its freely produced ends, and its substance, even though the individual agent may perceive them to be impositions on her freedom.

The fifth and last chapter of part 1 discusses the third element of justice, that of conscience and its forgiveness, as the principle of respect for singularity or for that which is effaced by law in its representation of human beings in their formal identity and effaced by ethical life in its emphasis on communal belonging. Elaborated in the discussion of conscientious action in the "Morality" section of the *Phenomenology*, conscience and forgiveness are the concepts by means of which Hegel identifies the ontological and political significance of singular, transgressive action in opposition to both customary and posited forms of social order. This third moment of justice is the aspect the impact of which is least acknowledged in the stereotype that Hegel's "absolute spirit" represents some kind of final reconciliation or end. What this moment entails is that, if it is to be just, the organization of reality cannot stifle but must support the unending process of interaction and transformation that defines human human personal and social life. Human social and cultural life must take shape in such a way as to allow dynamic human beings to take up their futures with a sense of openness to possibility and transformation, of their irreducibility to the past and the present.

The goal of part 1 is the production of a coherent theory of justice, one that makes various demands. For a political framework to be just, ethical bonds and relations and their agency in the construction of ethically capable human beings must be recognized; law and the irreducibility of human beings to their ethical bonds and relations must be upheld; and the unique singularity of human beings and the centrality of conscience, often concealed by law and by ethical bonds and relations, must be identified. In exploring these elements of justice and the tensions between them, this section will provide a theoretical framework for parts 2 and 3.

Part 2, "The Actuality and Practice of Law," traces the notion of justice as ethicality, law, and conscience in the context of the "nation," an important site in and by which the pursuit of justice is enacted. This section explores the constitution of the nation (chapter 6) and its reaction to wrongdoing (chapter 7), illuminating the ways in which the paradigm of ethicality, law, and conscience makes itself manifest in these domains as well. Chapter 6 explores the relation between justice and the nation-state—namely, the reliance of justice, democracy, and universal law on relations of specificity and singularity represented by our principles of ethicality and conscience, or the dependence of law on singular political judgments and a particular political terrain—relying on Hegel's discussion of the absolute freedom and terror of the French Revolution in order to do so. Through Hegel's analysis in this section I explore the alternative to the problematically construed, ideal nation of the French Revolution—namely, real nations enacted by real individuals who are linked to each other in response to the determinate, localized demands that arise in the context of a shared spatial and temporal life.

Chapter 7 treats the analysis in the *Philosophy of Right* of the transgression of such shared life through crime and the attempts to restore this shared character through punishment and through pardon. I show how Hegel's defence of punishment as required by law is, like law, circumscribed by the operation of ethicality and of forgiveness: the *Philosophy of Right* defends the rationality of law and of punishment, but it also shows their limitations; law, like crime, can lead to a violation of the ethical conditions of agency. In the text, Hegel arms the monarch, as the highest representative of the law's authority, with the power of pardon, further exposing the limits of legal authority. Unlike law, the power to pardon and the authority of ethicality cannot be systematically defended and elaborated, but the possibility of genuine responsibility is located in their very unjustifiability.

In part 3, "Hegel and Contemporary Political Life," I show how this theory of justice, with its expression in ethicality, forgiveness, and law, can both challenge and embolden contemporary philosophical attempts to articulate and put into practice the nature and demands of justice, whether through rights, recognition, protection of the possibility of transformation, or attempts to determine the nature and operation of democracy. The two chapters of this third and final section of the book take their orientation from dominant political paradigms of our time, illuminating various ways in which these paradigms could be productively reoriented on the basis of Hegel's insights.

The first chapter of this section, chapter 8, treats the contemporary philosophical and political project of liberalism, and its attempt to delineate justice mainly in terms of law and rights. Here I critically investigate the liberal strategy of avoidance by which certain issues are relegated to the private realm, the "universal moral consensus" so undermined by the deep-seated conflicts of political life, a politics of the individual that precludes a politics of participation and the presumed neutrality of the state as the executor and arbiter of rights. I develop my critique of liberalism in tandem with those of critical theory, feminist philosophy, communitarianism, and (for lack of a better term) poststructuralism. While the chapter is critical of liberalism, it could also be cast as an articulation of a fundamentally transformed version of liberalism—one that recognizes the need for plasticity in the legal order that would allow it to be more properly responsive to the conscientious individuals it protects and one that, more generally, develops ways in which to philosophically and politically recognize the political weight of the elements of ethical life and conscience.

Chapter 9 addresses the rhetoric of recognition—the demand for recognition of distinctiveness that is made in light of a dialogical model of identity—at work in critical theory and in discussions of cultural, racial, and sexual difference. I demonstrate how the theory of recognition has strayed from its Hegelian roots and must be understood in relation to the tripartite structure of justice Hegel advances. What demands recognition is the human as dynamic possibility and agency, as oriented toward a future—that is, the qualities held sacred, in different ways, by law and by forgiveness. What also demands recognition, however, is the self as defined by its outside, the self that is constituted as a self by a world already structured in a certain way—that is, the qualities captured in the notion of ethicality.

In the conclusion of the book I review the political consequences of thinking of law and ethicality through the lens of forgiveness. This chapter addresses the dependence of both tradition or ethical life and law on singular, transgressive action, exploring various concrete ways in which that action could be housed in contemporary political life. For a sociopolitical framework to be just, it needs mechanisms by which to address the injustice that comes from a) the failure to protect legal recognition and free self-determination, but also b) the failure to recognize the import of ethical bonds and relations toward human life, and c) the failure to recognize and protect the unique singularity of different human beings. It is necessary that these mechanisms be filled out and defined in relation to actual political and legal practice, and this final chapter begins to explore how that can be done.

The issues of law and justice can be approached from many different angles—from a consideration of the nature of action, a consideration of the nature of society, a consideration of the nature of history, and so on. Hegel himself approaches the study of law and justice from many such angles, and each of the chapters of this book is attuned to one of these various "roots." Hence, while I aim to present something like a systematic theory of justice, the presentation, though orderly, is not a systematic development from first principles, and neither is it a systematic presentation of the different kinds of law. Instead, I unfold the various stages of the analysis of law and justice by responding in each chapter to a specific text of Hegel and, correspondingly, to the "root" that Hegel there analyzes. Thus, in addition to presenting a relatively unified theory of justice, the book also stands as a set of independently defined chapters, each of which is dedicated to close study of a central and specific idea in Hegel, such as the phenomenon of action, the problem of crime, the issue of sexual difference, or the idea of revolution. Finally, as a close treatment of several of Hegel's specific texts, the book guides the reader into an ability to work with the material available in these texts, independently of the overarching thematic framework that this work provides.

Hegel himself does not ever *argue* that there are determinate mechanisms of justice that will reveal themselves to our perception if we carefully consider the nature of human life, but this is in effect what close observation of his own text allows us to see. His work enables its readers to more accurately perceive the assumptions and patterns of their own social contexts and to more adequately respond to the issues and demands they pose. In this work I invoke his careful observations for the sake of responding to the central issue of political organization and prioritization in this era: that of rights, legal order, and the legal organization of institutions. It is my belief that Hegel's work speaks powerfully to this issue, and it is my hope that this book will provide those who are familiar and unfamiliar with Hegel the resources with which to begin to address it.

PART 1

LAW, ETHICALITY, AND FORGIVENESS

1

THEMES FROM "THE SPIRIT OF CHRISTIANITY AND ITS FATE"

In an early essay, "The Spirit of Christianity and Its Fate," Hegel provides a preliminary account of issues that will continue to occupy him in later texts such as the *Phenomenology of Spirit* and the *Philosophy of Right*. In this brief text we find both a concise critique of law and an introduction of the moral and political significance of both human relations of love, which give us a sense of belonging and by which we feel immediately obligated, and the power of forgiveness, which restores relations when they have been disrupted. While his essay is critical of the idea of making law the basis of political and moral life and reasoning, Hegel's introduction of the significance of both forgiveness and affective relations in fact requires not a simple abandonment of law but also its reconfiguration—that is, the situating of law as a single element in a more complex conception of political and moral justice and as answerable to and motivated by a fundamental human embeddedness in and orientation to ethical experience. What remains after Hegel's critique of law in this early essay is not the privileging of forgiveness and affective relations over law but the identification of a constitutive tension between these three phenomena, all of which are essential to justice and morality. By investigating this introductory essay, we can begin to develop a sense of the dynamic relationship between what I will call the three elements of justice—ethicality, law, and forgiveness—and a sense of the significance, to the existence of law, of our immediate ethical attachments.[1]

This chapter begins by identifying Hegel's criticisms of law as he introduces them in this essay, and by exploring his account of the phenomena—relations of affect and forgiveness—in the name of which he develops these criticisms. It then investigates the way in which Hegel redescribes punishment in light of his criticism of law and concludes by suggesting that the operation of affective relations and forgiveness show on their own terms why a specific kind of operation of law is necessary, Hegel's critique notwithstanding, and that the tension between law and the other two elements of justice in fact energizes political and morality responsibility instead of immobilizing it.

This chapter will serve as an introduction to issues that we will be working with throughout the book, but most importantly to the significance of what Hegel later calls *Sittlichkeit*—that is, "ethicality" or "ethical life." While Hegel does not use this term in "The Spirit of Christianity and Its Fate," his critique of law is made on the basis of the ideas that he will later unite under the term "ethical life"—namely, the ideas of a "reconciliation in love," a "living bond," a "spirit of love and mutual faith" (*ETW* 241), the affective "human relations" (*ETW* 212) by which individual lives are oriented and made meaningful, the "united life" (*ETW* 229) by which individual self-isolation and legal judgment are implicitly condemned. "Ethical life" essentially refers to the human relations that are prior to and more substantial than relations governed by law and obedience; it is Hegel's term for the fact that we are always already captured by a way of life or a sense of connection with particular people and situations and communities, which endows us with commitments even before we develop the capacity to formulate them ourselves. Not something we actively and reflectively choose, ethical life stands for a way of life that we relate to as simply "the way things are" or "the way things are done." Ethical life names the way in which we take up our relation to the world initially, primordially, and powerfully in an unreflective way, a way that orients and colors all consequent reflection and is itself deeply resistant to reflective insight. This substantial life generates us as individuals—only on its basis do we become individuals capable of critically and reflectively defining our own lives—but the history of this generation can never be made a transparent object for reflection. We have already *been committed* to it. While in various parts of his work Hegel denotes different things with the term "ethical life" (in the *Phenomenology*, for instance, it is the name for the way of life of the world of ancient Greece, whereas in the *Philosophy of Right* it is the name for the social and institutional organization of free modern life), it can always be understood as that to which we are already committed and by which we already feel called, that reality greater than ourselves as individuals that makes it possible for us to be individuals, the "we" through which the "I" is and to which the "I" is irrevocably and to a certain extent unreflectively attached.[2] Our discussion of "The Spirit of Christianity and Its Fate" serves as an introduction to this important reality, and our treatment of it will be continued in the second chapter in relation to Hegel's discussion of ethical life in the *Phenomenology*. Now let us turn to discussion of how Hegel uses the notion of "ethicality" or the "spirit of mutual love and faith" found in affective relations to identify problems with the operation of law.

THE CHALLENGE TO LAW

Hegel's aim in "The Spirit of Christianity and Its Fate" is to expose and criticize the commitments shared by the two paradigms of Judaic legalism and Kantian morality. Hegel presents the life and legacy of Abraham, whose story is told in the book of Genesis, as representative of Judaic legalism. According to the book of Genesis, Abraham is called by God to leave his people and be led to the land that God promised him, where he will be blessed and become a great nation. But Hegel argues that Abraham's legacy, far from being of moral or social value, is one of obedience to a life-denying, wrathful God who demands that Abraham abandon the life and love that nourished him for the sake of the establishment of a community that is fundamentally hostile to all those who do not recognize its divine law-giver and that finds its source of unity outside of itself, outside of its social bonds. Hegel argues that Abraham "steadily persisted in cutting himself off from others" (*ETW* 186) and that the Jewish people of the Old Testament "had committed all harmony among men, all love, spirit, and life, to an alien object . . . [T]hey had put nature in the hands of an alien being. What held them together were chains, laws given by the superior power" (*ETW* 240). According to Hegel, the Old Testament tells the story of a people who posited an alien ideal over against their own reality and renounced beauty for themselves, replacing the substantial ethical ties of community with shared obedience to an alien law (*ETW* 241). The people led by Abraham operated with "an impassable gulf between the being of God and the being of men," not recognizing that "spirit alone recognizes spirit" (*ETW* 265) or that the separate being of God and man was in fact the diversification or modification of one life (*ETW* 261–62).[3]

Hegel's criticism of what he views as Judaic legalism and his extension of this criticism to Kant's moral philosophy present a powerful and dramatic account of the shortcomings of law and crystallize the core philosophical commitments that guide his later work. According to Hegel, in making respect for the law the motivation of moral action and in proscribing the motivating force of inclination, Kant's philosophy manifests an opposition to life similar to that exhibited by Judaic legalism. Both the relationships that inspire and sustain moral agency and the aspect of the self that exhibits attachment to those relationships are rejected: the developmental and motivational ground of moral agency and the richness of human life not captured by law are completely eclipsed. In defining morality in terms of respect for the law and in denying inclination any moral value, Kant demands that the life and love that bring ethical agents into being as such be explicitly disregarded and that only one aspect of the human agent—the rational aspect—be the site for moral identity and agency. Hegel says that the spirit of Jesus, on the contrary, is "a spirit raised above Morality" (*ETW* 212). His critique is partly captured in the following paragraph:

> [B]etween the Shaman of the Tungus, the European prelate who rules church and state, the Voguls, and the Puritans, on the one hand, and the man who listens to his own command of duty, on the other, the difference is not that the former make themselves slaves, while the latter is free, but that the former have their lord outside themselves, while the latter carries his lord in himself, yet at the same time is his own slave. For the particular—impulses, inclinations, pathological love, sensuous experience, or whatever else it is called—the universal is necessarily and always something alien and objective. (*ETW* 211)

Thus what in Kant's terms is the expression of my essential core—the law that I identify by means of my capacity for reason—becomes, in Hegel's view, that by which essential and valuable aspects of my being and of reality are subordinated.

The ideas that Hegel introduces here are not as fully treated in this early essay as they are in his later work, but they get a cogent and powerful expression here, and our preliminary examination of them is intended to identify the key issues that are explored in more detail throughout the book. Briefly, exclusive reliance on law does at least three things: first, in making obedience to universal law the ultimate moral value, it downplays the significance of the fact that demands upon us are always expressed in the context of particular situations, and it impedes the cultivation of responsiveness to these situations; second, it conceals the ethical significance and value of particular ethical relations and situations, or the way in which moral agents and their impulse to moral responsiveness are cultivated and produced through relationships of love and nurture; and third, it devalues certain aspects of life and human being—for instance, those impulses, inclinations, and sensuous experiences to which Hegel refers in the above quotation. Let us look at these three issues more closely.[4]

First, law cannot include reference to the particular characteristics of any given situation, but the only thing that motivates us to act morally, that demands of us ethical attention, and in response to which we accomplish the good or not, is a particular situation with determinate characteristics. To demand abstraction from particular human needs, lives, and love is to risk the disabling of ethical concern, which must be taken up vis-à-vis actual, complex situations. It is the particularity and the insistent demand of human need in its specific forms to which we must be attentive in order to truly practice and cultivate ethical concern. To demand action for the sake of law is to demand unresponsiveness to need—Hegel says that Jesus illustrates this point when he heals people and picks fruit on the Sabbath.[5]

Second, and related, the universality of law in fact commands abstraction from the affective relationships that nurture ethical sensibility in human beings.[6] Through relationships we are cultivated as moral agents capable of making ethical decisions, and we experience the love, care, and connection that motivate us to attend to human connectivity in ethically sensitive ways.[7] To develop models of morality and justice that do not take the ethical significance of these relationships into account is to perpetuate a misguided picture of human identity and moral motivation and to disavow and perhaps even jeopardize the ethical labor such relationships perform.

Third, if the law and moral judgment must operate independently of affect, inclination, and relationality, then these will also be alienated, according to Hegel, from the transformative power of the good. According to Hegel, Kantian morality and Judaic legalism construe aspects of the self as unredeemable and underestimate the power of the good in thinking it incapable of pervading them. Need and inclination are construed as irreducibly opposed to the law and as obstacles to obedience. The moral law exists in the name of the human being as end in itself, but following it requires setting aside various "offensive" elements in that human being.[8] In this case, dutifulness essentially becomes self-hatred; as J. M. Bernstein observes, Hegel conceives of Kantian universality as a punishing superego, and the moral law as a slave morality.[9] Because the relation between the specificity of ethical situations and the universal and abstract principles of moral reasoning is identified as a relationship of disparate elements, reality itself is degraded. Reason and law are opposed to both the real self and the real conditions of its life that propelled it toward a cultivated and responsible respect for the moral law. If the Kantian moral law is already a product of life, it turns against itself in turning against elements of that life; the abstract ideal condemns the reality that gives rise to it.[10]

For Hegel, on the other hand, what is genuinely good is identification with the good on the part of the *whole* human being, whereby the universal (the good) and the individual are reconciled and their opposition overcome. Hegel argues that if human beings are inclined by love to act in the way that the law commands, if their "inclinations" lead them to do what the law also commands, then that law loses its form as law, and reality and law lose their opposition in reconciliation (*ETW* 214).[11] Kant was right, says Hegel, in saying that love cannot be commanded, but he was wrong to therefore exclude it as an inherently valuable aspect of moral life.[12] Its very "uncommandability" is its virtue, and loving for its own sake is generally better than loving for the sake of duty, since the freedom at work in such action renders it valuable above and beyond simple obedience. This could perhaps be construed as Hegel's reading of the New Testament claim that love fulfils the law: it does so because it does what the law commands without being commanded; it freely does what under law is only followed. From this perspective the human being and reality can be genuinely valued as sites of virtue and occasions for good, not simply as what must be manipulated, coerced, and combated in the name of the good. The integration of affective and rational motivations toward good, or the "correspondence of law and inclination[,] is life and, as the relation of differents to one another, love" (*ETW* 215). Let us turn now to the *disruption* of affectively charged life and relations—that is, to crime—in which context forgiveness, as the overcoming of division in the context of life, becomes relevant.

PUNISHMENT AS LAW AND PUNISHMENT AS FATE

Hegel's description of moral agency and the life through which it is cultivated also has consequences for the way in which crime is understood—the reasons why crime is wrong, the ways in which it does damage, the consequences it has for society and the criminal, and the appropriate response to its destructive force. If the focus on law is displaced (or fulfilled) by the life, love, and relations that inspire and cultivate agency, then first, crime must similarly be construed as wrong not merely because it breaks the law but for its transgression of the affective and ethical conditions of agency, and second, the kind of punishment that avenges the law fails to resonate with the real reasons that crime is criminal and thus fails to adequately respond to the crime. Here the concept of forgiveness becomes relevant, as a second aspect of Hegel's identification of law's inadequacy, and as a response to crime that is different from the purportedly automatic, neutral, and indifferent response of law.

Hegel says here that what makes crime criminal is the fact that it destroys the life and relations in and by which human beings are bound together. He calls the kind of punishment that accompanies crime understood in this way "punishment as fate." That is, the life that the criminal transgresses with her crime is in fact the ground for her own life, and thus her crime transgresses the ground that sustains her own agency. In this context, fate is, as H. S. Harris notes, "the actual experience of reciprocal action and reaction in the abiding equilibrium of a living whole."[13] The criminal is generated as a self in interaction with the social resources around her and is not merely her own agent but a site of the agency and accomplishments of that society. Her crime against that society is, then, a crime inflicted upon herself, and that society's punishment is also her punishment of herself, an attempt to redress her self-destruction. She sets the fate of this kind of punishment in motion with her crime.

With the concept of forgiveness, Hegel incorporates this consideration of the social conditions of agency into a response to crime. Transgressive, criminal action tears the fabric of social life and damages the conditions of agency, both that of the criminal and that of any victims, and no legal restitution can restore the original condition; the loss can in a sense only be grieved. If we think of criminal action as tearing the fabric of social life and damaging the conditions of agency, however, then we can formulate a different response to it that specifically targets these problems—constructing a new basis for a shared life upon the remains of the old by means of forgiveness and reconciliation. Ideally, forgiveness allows a commitment to be made to renewing the terms and resources of agency, to bringing about a new order that allows for a different future, one detached from the damage the criminal unleashed. The event of forgiveness can recover the integrity of that substance from which the criminal separated herself, but in a new form. It is a dismissal of the law for the sake of the ethical life out of which law emerges, to which it responds, and to which it is subordinate. It is a witnessing to the life that extends beyond the penal system and the law; "life in its integrity is above the law which governs it in its disruption."[14]

Hegel says various things that are worth repeating in this context. First, against a principle of universal legislation

> Jesus sets the higher genius of reconcilability (a modification of love) which not only does not act counter to this law but makes it wholly superfluous; it has in itself a so much richer, more living, fullness that so poor a thing as a law is nothing for it at all. In reconcilability the law loses its form . . . but what reconcilability thereby loses in respect of the universality which grips all particulars together in the concept is only a seeming loss and a genuine infinite gain on account of the wealth of living relations with the individuals . . . with whom it comes in connection. (*ETW* 215)

Reconciliation is not a refutation or rejection of law; it simply does the same thing that law does, but in a way that more powerfully contributes to the singular richness of human life. The "spirit of Jesus" is "a spirit raised above morality" that strips the laws "of their legal form" (*ETW* 212). Hegel also writes that under penal law "the law is a power to which life is subject," whereas "in the case of punishment as fate, however, the law is later than life and is outranked by it . . . life can heal its wounds again" (*ETW* 230). And further: "The punishment inflicted by law is merely *just*. The common character, the connection of crime and punishment, is only equality, not life . . . Before the law the criminal is nothing but a criminal. Yet the law is a fragment of human nature, and so is the criminal; if the law were a whole, then the criminal *would* be only a criminal" (*ETW* 238–39). On its own, law does not express the full extent of human life and interaction, and, if it were assumed to do so, that life and interaction would lose their fullness and significance. Forgiveness points explicitly to the mismatch between law and life, and the subordination of law to life. It cannot itself become *general*, however, or *prescriptible*, in the way that the law is; to truly be forgiveness and the recognition of life by life, it cannot be programmed or prescribed. Hegel's discussion of forgiveness, then, should not be understood as a recommendation that forgiveness become the principle by which the legal system is oriented. Prescription, systematicity, and regularity are the terrain not of forgiveness but of law. As we shall go on to see in subsequent chapters, the stability and prescriptibility that law provides are important and valuable in their own right, even given Hegel's characterization of the impoverished nature of law in relation to life.

CONCLUSION

Hegel's critique of law in this early writing is a bit one-sided; he later develops equally emphatically the other side of the issue—that is, the nature, necessity, and positive significance of legal order. Hegel does not advocate exclusive moral and political reliance on the ethical relations that cultivate us as ethical subjects or on the order of forgiveness that exceeds law and witnesses to these originary ethical relations. Instead, he seeks to highlight the necessary responsiveness and tension between affective relations and forgiveness, on the one hand, and law and moral reasoning, on the other.[15]

To summarize what we have seen so far, Hegel's view is that exclusive reliance on law cannot do justice to the ethical sensibilities fostered and practiced in relations of ethical life, nor to the power of forgiveness, which can restore the ground upon which to cultivate those sensibilities and relations. The formal relations of law disregard, and must disregard, the significance of the particular affective relations by which we are brought into existence as beings capable of being moved to act in accordance with law. Further, the fact that law must be stable and fixed can prevent the appearance of new relations and new ways of being human individually and together.

While "The Spirit of Christianity and Its Fate" shows the insufficiency of formal relations of law for organizing and understanding social interaction, and identifies the significance of immediate relations of affect and of the singularity testified to by the practice of forgiveness, Hegel's treatment of these elements in the *Phenomenology* further defines and elaborates them, and we shall turn to that text now. In his treatment in the *Phenomenology* of ancient Greek ethical life, Hegel explores the reality of ethicality and also exposes its specific shortcomings, which show on their own terms the corresponding need for law. In his discussion of the Roman "condition of right" or "legal status" (*der Rechtzustand*), Hegel shows the significance and irreducibility of law and the formal relations it enables, but he also identifies the limits to law, limits similar to those discussed in "The Spirit of Christianity and Its Fate." In his discussion of conscience, Hegel explores the significance of forgiveness and its relation to ethicality and law. We will systematically work through Hegel's treatment of each of these elements—ethicality, law, and the forgiveness of conscience—with the help of an additional discussion, in chapter 4, of his account of law in the *Encyclopaedia*. By means of this route, we will come to find that each of them—ethicality, law, and the forgiveness of conscience—is a significant element of a dynamic, intricate, and multifaceted *system of justice* that is just insofar as it is responsive to the variegated complexity of human life. Hegel's analysis of each element brings us to the limit of each, a limit at which the others are shown to be necessary complements. Ethical life, which could be understood as Hegel's explanation of how justice relies on the affective relations that motivate and nurture ethical concern, brings into relief the need for posited law. The condition of right brings into relief the need for meaningful ethical relations and an account of the social aspects of individual agency. Conscience and its forgiveness bring into relief the need for posited law and witness to the ethical relations that are irreducible to law. Let us move, then, to Hegel's *Phenomenology*.

2

THE IMMEDIACY OF ETHICAL LIFE

Hegel's focus in his treatment of what he calls '*Der Wahre Geist, die Sittlichkeit*'—that is, "True Spirit, Ethical Life—is the idea of a society that works because its members feel compelled immediately by a sense of ethical obligation, because they consider their very being to include an immediate fidelity to specific roles and responsibilities in this society. In this reality, which Hegel describes in the *Phenomenology* by invoking the example of ancient Greek society, responsibilities are taken to be natural or simply given, and agents do not conceive of themselves as authorities who decide upon and judge the legitimacy of these responsibilities, for to do so would be to fail to respect their absolutely compelling character. Hegel's discussion here, as we have also seen in the previous chapter, has significance beyond its insight into a particular ancient society. That is, the immediacy of ethical obligation *does* found and enable human agency; we do not emerge in the human world as already fully functioning adult human beings independent of any particular community, but are characterized fundamentally and substantially by our *belonging* to a particular world with a particular self-understanding, one that we can never completely leave behind. Ethical life or ethicality is one of the essential factors that define the nature of human life, experience, and selfhood. As we shall see, however—both in the context of Greek ethical life and in our thinking through the issue in its significance to us—the ways in which we feel immediately attached to a particular world, and feel its identity enacted through our very sense of ourselves and of our own obligations, do not constitute the whole story of obligation and responsibility. The moment of decision, of reflection, and of conceiving oneself as a self-determining author of one's own actions is inevitable, and social life must change to take shape around this reality. There must be more to human life than ethicality, than community, than a sense of belonging, and more to justice than responsiveness to these forceful and formative aspects of human life.

In this chapter I discuss the specific form of ethical life portrayed in the *Phenomenology*, identifying the factors that necessarily interrupt the ease and serenity of the Greek world of immediate ethical determination: that is, the inevitability of human decision and reflection, and, further, the inevitability of the human *production* of law and social organization, beyond mere acquiescence to what is given by nature and "the gods," a production that in turn carries with it a diversity in human values that motivates the detachment of institutions of social life from specific values.[1] Because there is a developed feminist discourse around Hegel's discussion here—a discourse that I consider to be, while correct in its philosophical motivations, sometimes significantly mistaken in its interpretations of Hegel's text—I will regularly engage with it, both implicitly and explicitly.[2] Unlike most feminist interpreters, I argue that Hegel's reading of Greek ethical life should not be understood as advocating an authoritarian political order hostile to the familial conditions of its emergence, nor as permanently answering the question of the significance and roles of women in social life. The key to this alternative reading is Hegel's claim that ethical life's immediacy "has the contradictory meaning of being the unconscious tranquillity of nature, and also the self-conscious restless tranquillity of spirit" (M476, S354, W/C260). I do not abandon, however, the feminist impulse behind interpretations of this section; rather, I seek to establish a basis upon which to construct a more promising and productive framework for feminist, legal, and political philosophy's engagement with Hegel.

HEGEL'S CRITIQUE OF "NATURAL" SOCIETY

Feminist readings of Hegel's account of ethical life in the *Phenomenology* have mostly taken issue with his interpretation of the figure of Antigone as represented by Sophocles in the play *Antigone*. It recounts the tale of how Creon and Antigone disagree about what should be done with the dead body of Polyneices, Antigone's brother and Creon's nephew, who brought an army against a Thebes ruled by his brother Eteocles because Eteocles refused to give up the throne to Polyneices for a year, as had been agreed. Creon, made king after both Polyneices and Eteocles die, orders that Polyneices, a traitor to Thebes, not be buried, and Antigone, who as Polyneices' sister sees her responsibility to be that she bury him, resists Creon's order and buries Polyneices. Creon condemns her to death, and by the time he changes his mind she has already killed herself.

It has almost become standard, for feminist readings of Hegel's account of ethical life, to suggest that the figure of Antigone does not simply disrupt the peaceful harmony of this Greek ethical life, but also the coherence and legitimacy of Hegel's entire project. The victim of Creon and Hegel's tyranny has her revenge, so to speak, by rendering the system itself a victim of its attempt to exploit her singularity; in failing to incorporate Antigone's singularity, its systematicity is jeopardized. This line of reasoning, however, which has been perhaps most notably developed in different ways by Luce Irigaray, Patricia J. Mills, and Judith Butler, is based upon a misunderstanding of Hegel's assessment of Antigone's agency in the undoing of ethical life. It not only fails to recognize its own affinities with what I will show to be a more plausible account of Hegel's position, but also the critical resources available in his system. If the alternative account given here is convincing, Antigone's supposed "inadmissibility"[3] must be read differently—that is, as something that Hegel himself identifies as a problem and as key to understanding his evaluation of Greek society and the instability of its sex-based identifications. The account of ethical life in the *Phenomenology* results in a decisively negative judgment concerning the organization of sexual difference and social life in Greek society, on the basis of *its* fundamental incompatibility with the development of a truly human society.

What is central to Hegel's treatment of sexual difference in ethical life, and to his discussion in general, is the function of nature and the immediate relationship between nature and the laws that motivate sexually differentiated ethical agents. Hegel sets out to show that Greek society demands obedience to an inherently unstable interpretation of the meaning of sexual difference and of nature's relationship to ethical functions and responsibilities, and that this is its undoing. In considering this concrete form of social life we learn that the ethical meaning of sexual difference and of human responsibility is not immediately evident or given by nature but the result of the mediating force of human interpretation. The accomplishment of this analysis of Greek ethical life is to identify the necessary presence in human social life of artifice, or the idea that who human beings are is imagined and produced by them in collective collaboration in a human social order; further, law is recognized as an aspect of this self-production and is not itself a reality immediately and divinely given. For Hegel, the relationship between nature and spirit must be lived and described otherwise than the way this society would describe it.[4]

The basic framework of ethical life can be understood as follows. For Hegel, ethical consciousness is immediately affiliated with its particular law—the woman with divine and the man with human law. The action expected of each is action that is in accordance with these laws; the man's role is to support the self-determining, human political realm, and woman's role is to support the domestic realm, upholding the dictates of nature and the gods that defy explicit and critical reflection. In marriage the two laws and sexes attain a unified harmony and tranquil movement (M463, S250); the laws and the realities they represent are integrated into one smoothly functioning social fabric. This imagined harmony is in fact unstable, however, because whenever the single self acts its deed has the unintended consequence of interrupting this natural harmony and the simple unity of its laws; it reveals both the fact of human initiative and the artificiality of the division between human and divine, political and domestic.[5]

What has been misrepresented by some feminist attempts to clarify the logic behind Hegel's reading of ethical life, however, is the *reason* for this interruption. Such a disruption occurs, according to Hegel, because the immediacy of Greek ethical life "has the contradictory meaning of being the unconscious tranquillity of nature, and also the self-conscious restless tranquillity of spirit" (M476, S260). That is, Greek society has a fundamentally contradictory relationship with nature; it exists in tension with itself by its assertion of two opposing values or aspects. On the one hand, it takes itself to be naturally determined; "nature, not the accident of circumstances or choice, assigns one sex to one law, the other to the other law" (M465, S252).[6] Each ethical "character" identifies with the immediate dictates of this ethical substance, which she or he takes to be naturally and divinely given, and cannot do otherwise, since individual reflection on this immediate identification is inappropriate.[7] I will call this aspect "natural determination." On the other hand, however, the ethical action that these characters perform always moves beyond mere natural determination, beyond the limitations of natural life and death, and as such gets to be "counted" as of ethical import.[8] In other words, while each ethical character is naturally or immediately determined by his or her law to perform a certain kind of ethical action, each in effect "spiritualizes" nature by these acts, or is required on the basis of his or her role to transcend the immediacy of nature for the sake of the spiritual identity of the human community over time. The result of ethical action in this world is a life after death, so to speak—an overcoming of the naturalness of death and a commemoration of the spiritual contribution of the dead, which endures in the identity of familial and political generations. To act on ethical principles is inevitably to distinguish oneself from the immediacy of nature; ethical characters accomplish this self-distinction in obeying ethical laws.[9] This wrestling with and transcendence-through-interpretation of the limitations of nature and death I will call "ethical aspiration."

Let us now state what the specifically ethical actions are, so as to understand how they are both naturally determined and transcendent of nature. In the context of Greek ethical life, man and woman have different ethical responsibilities, which are construed as their natural and immediate responsibilities and to which they relate in a nonquestioning way. The woman's task is to give spiritual meaning to nature through burial and commemoration, restoring the male to his familial genealogy, which in its continuity over time and in its spiritual commemoration defies mortality. She transcends nature by resisting through her action the notion that nature will consume the dead body and leave no remainder.[10] The woman's performance of funerary rites is intended to spiritualize both death and the earth; Hegel says that she transforms the dead body into a spiritual universal (that is, irreducible to a mere body destined for natural deterioration), and the earth into a community that receives the spiritualized male body (that is, irreducible to a mere conglomeration of natural substances that will indifferently consume the natural body).[11] The man's task, on the other hand, is to contribute to the existence of a human community that is irreducible to a moment in natural history, in that it becomes through its members' contributions a tradition sustained beyond the ebb and flow of natural life and death. Collective principles of social organization are maintained over time in memory and practice, and the man's participation in this timeless tradition transforms his finite, natural life into an eternally and universally significant one. Such mechanisms have "the negative significance of elevating the single individual [*der Einzelne*] above confinement in the natural community to which he belongs as an *actual* individual" (M453, S334).

Nature, therefore, is on the one hand taken to be the foundation of and determining force behind identity, action, and ethicality, but on the other that which ethical action must confront and transcend in order that it be truly ethical. The tragic conclusion of ethical life, however, shows these two approaches to nature's significance to be fundamentally contradictory, and its agents acknowledge this contradiction in assuming their tragic fate. This social reality gives way to a new reality by virtue of its agents' inability to act, as they claim to, according to its principle—the immediacy and naturalness of their determination. On the one hand, the first characteristic (natural determination) finds its contradiction in the second (ethical aspiration); that is to say, the laws of ethical life, taken to be natural and assigned to agents by virtue of a natural determination, are *also* the result of particular customs and traditions that have come into existence by virtue of human practice, and their status as such is brought to light. Human ethical practice, as apparent in the phenomenon of ethical aspiration, is always already engaged in and motivated by the appropriation and transformation of nature. The division of ethical tasks according to sexual difference, therefore, cannot simply be the "reading" of something that is naturally given. On the other hand, however, the ethical aspiration defining ethical life is frustrated by natural determination. In the actual experience of ethical life and the attempted fulfillment of its laws, *nature* throws in the wrench of contingency that compromises the ethical deed. In this way Hegel shows that nature cannot in fact be taken to be the foundation of ethical life; on the contrary, it frustrates ethical action and social organization.

Let us look more closely at the idea that natural determination is problematized by ethical aspiration. The inevitable infiltration of sociocultural, interpretive significance into the laws of ethical life is evident in Hegel's description of guilt. Hegel interprets this guilt as a self-conscious acknowledgment on the part of the ethical character of the infiltration of her *own* perspective on things, and the accompanying assumption of her tragic fate. Guilt is the acknowledgment of the way in which human action disrupts the natural given. Guilt brings with it a moment of spiritual hesitation, a division between self and context, that interrupts forever the immediacy of ethical certitude. The presence of this hesitation and division, however, is what makes ethical agents particularly *ethical.* It reveals that the task of ethical agents is to recognize this division as their own such that it is no longer accidental or surprising, and to recognize that it grants them freedom to identify with a variety of ethically significant spheres in any particular form of social organization—and that their identification with these spheres cannot be immediate.

Antigone's ethical deed, the burial of her brother Polyneices, is performed in the context of a community—that of the family—in which natural determination is operative.[12] The woman is associated with the "unconscious tranquility of nature" (M476, S354) in her ethical affiliation with the family, but inadvertently enters the realm of self-conscious spirit—the domain of humanly determined customs and practices—in acting. In other words, Antigone exhibits the interference of spirit in nature, since she is an exemplar of a natural community yet acts politically in a sphere that is supposed to be inaccessible to her. Her transgression shows the inevitability of the spiritual transformation of nature, the impossibility that human practice could ever leave nature as it is, or the obstacle that spirit presents to a community that takes itself to be purely naturally determined.

Creon, on the other hand, acts in the realm whose law and organization are conscious and publicly operative, and his action is frustrated by nature; this realm and its agent find their greatest obstacle in nature. What is shown through his action is the contradiction of this way of life: it is presumed to be naturally determined, to be in an alliance with nature, but natural elements in fact disrupt and challenge it. Nature in fact itself "shows" this society that it, nature, is not a feasible foundation of social life. Hegel writes that "this determination of immediacy means that nature in general enters into the action of ethical life . . . On account of this naturalness, this ethical people is generally an individuality determined and thus limited by nature, and so finds its sublation [*Aufhebung*] in another" (M476, S354, W/C260). The second operative principle and goal of ethical life—that true spirit must transcend the limitations of nature in order to show itself as spirit—is frustrated by nature, and this contradiction is played out most explicitly on the terrain of humanly determined customs and practices—that is, Creon's terrain. Either what seems naturally contingent (or, not in conformity with natural law) interferes with the attempt to "spiritualize" nature, or nature becomes the *means* by which the transcendence of nature as such is attempted, and thus is the attempt undermined.

Nature interferes with the attempt to act ethically in a couple of ways. The foremost operative condition of this tragic conflict is a naturally contingent condition—that there are *two* brothers with a legitimate claim to leadership, Eteocles and Polyneices. Their birth shows that nature does not operate in a way that is consonant with the needs of the laws of the community (that is, the need to have a single ruler who is determined by heredity). As Derrida writes, in his discussion of this section of the *Phenomenology*, "because of this contingency (*Zufälligkeit zweier Brüder*), naturalness stays"[13]; this society's ethical rationality cannot accommodate this natural fact. Further, Creon violates the law of burial, taken to be natural, because of the fact of this problem of having two brothers where there should have been only one. Second, Creon's vehement opposition turns out to be radically uncivilized, as Martha Nussbaum notes, and devastatingly so; it undermines the very possibility of human community.[14] Creon fails to adequately acknowledge the importance of family ties and commitments, destroying the possibility of community by denying the social significance of the family as a form of social organization that has natural aspects. The dependence of the realm of human organization on the "natural" element that is the family asserts itself in the form of the death of Creon's own family. What this means is that Creon does not adequately juggle the relation between immediate and reflective forms of social organization. He opposes nature; he attempts to deny and eradicate its ethical force; and it asserts itself through the destruction of the elements that give his personal life meaning. The principle of ethical life was the harmonious coexistence of divine and human law (M463, S250), but this harmony is shattered; ethical aspiration and natural determination are fundamentally in conflict.

Hegel construes nature, therefore, as the cause of turmoil in this ethical world. *Nature* eradicates the individual by making it into a thing, and the power of divine justice, in the hands of the woman, must overcome *this*. The community's justice must struggle against the injustice of nature's arbitrariness in providing two men capable of ruling the community. Social disequilibrium does not emerge merely from the opposition between the two laws, in neither female nor male ethical action; it is nature that initiates it. Nature is thus two conflicting things; it is the source of strife and the frustration of ethical action, on the one hand, and the source of the laws and obligations of Greek ethical life, on the other. In finding its ethical action *frustrated* by that action's rootedness in nature, this society experiences contradiction and its own incoherence.

It is the way in which sexual difference is represented in ethical life that is the most ethically and socially definitive "natural" determination, or the most concrete existential consequence of nature's presence in social relationships. If Hegel shows the incoherence of a society that takes nature to be authoritative with regard to ethical action, then he also shows the incoherence of taking sexual difference to be ethically determining and authoritative—that is, he shows the *ineluctable self-destruction* of a community constituted on the basis of this interpretation of sexual difference, and the correspondent demand for a different form of negotiation between nature and culture. What this means is that Hegel is *unveiling* the intrinsic instability of the organization of Greek society; his assessment of Antigone's agency in the destruction of ethical life is due to Greek society's inability to deal with sexual difference (among other things), and not his own such inability. To divide ethical tasks according to what one perceives to be an ethically significant natural difference is already an interpretation of nature, and hence already an interruption of it—that is, unnatural. Greek ethical life fails to understand its interpretation of the natural, which denies the spiritual breadth of the individuals who constitute it and denies the contingencies of that nature that is understood to make ethical demands of it, *as an interpretation*. In short, self-identification according to natural determination is actually the work of spirit—that is, of social self-determination.[15]

In various ways, Antigone disrupts the smooth operation of nature in ethical life; the events around her death challenge the idea that nature can be ultimately authoritative with regard to the ways in which human beings live together. First, she fails to develop into her "natural" roles as a wife and a mother—indeed, precisely *because of* the fact that she obeys the given, divine law that orders her to bury her brother. Antigone never becomes a wife, a participating member in the "syllogism" that unites male and female in the ethical world.[16] Second, her death and the death of Creon's family members in fact leave Creon, the man, in mourning, a role that is not "naturally" his to fulfill. Third, she ends her life *unnaturally*, through suicide, thus withholding her ethical contribution as wife and mother from the society that has opposed her.[17] Because of the misbegotten structure of this society, her fulfillment of one "natural" obligation leads to her failure to fulfill others, a tension that introduces the need for, and implicit presence of, human discernment.

Hegel's purpose, quite simply, is to record the inevitability of and the reasons for this society's destabilization.[18] Laws, social values, spiritual roles—such phenomena cannot be presumed to be naturally determined and given; they are the results of habits, customs, and a tradition that has always already distinguished itself from nature. By enacting her identity with and carrying out her obedience to law, Antigone initiates the unraveling of the fabric of this world. Through her ethical act, which inevitably spills over into the public realm of human law, ethical life and its "natural" division show themselves to be unsustainable.[19]

THE AMBIVALENCE OF ETHICALITY

In the first chapter I discussed the significant role of the ethical bonds and relations that are logically and experientially prior to relationships defined by positive law, and that are a fundamental source of meaning and value (and of the capacity and motivation to judge meaning and value) in human life. In this chapter, however, we see the problems with taking a way of life to be immediately given, to have direct and unquestionable authority with regard to ethical decision and action; these are the problems Hegel highlights in his account of ethical life. While, as the first chapter shows, the ethical bonds and relations prior to relationships defined by positive law are a significant aspect of personal and social human development, they must be lived in such a way that they can exist in *tandem* with the need for a society to consciously take up its role in its own formation—to recognize itself as *artifice*, as a human production. Social life is lived in the tension and relation between what seems to be given (the "natural") and what seems to be made, and this tension and relation can be negotiated in better and worse ways.[20] While any society must recognize and acknowledge the bonds and relations that provide persons with meaning and value, with content and contexts for their self-production, as Creon fails to do (and as the society of ancient Rome also fails to do, as we will see in the next chapter), Greek society fails to fully recognize the artificial aspect of its laws. It refuses the task of negotiation of the *tension* between given and made, and refuses to own up to the responsibility of its *self*-production.

The disavowed dependence of this society's organization on "nature," the insistence on the naturalness of legal determination and identification, Antigone and Creon's vulnerability to this divided society—these are the reasons that Hegel gives for ethical society's demise. Through his interpretation of Antigone's action and of the society around it, Hegel gives us the resources with which to diagnose representations of nature that do not acknowledge the fluidity of human identity, the multiplicity of its aspects, and the diversity of human commitments. The conflict between the characteristics of natural determination and ethical aspiration in ethical life contributes to its destruction, which Hegel records, but it could also contribute to contemporary attempts to analyze the codetermination of "natural" and legal identification, the relevance of "natural" identity to political agency and representation, and the "nature" of "woman." Hegel's resistance to Greek society's representation of the "natural," his acknowledgment of the necessity of its negotiation, and his critical treatment of Antigone and Creon's forms of legal identification—all of these considerations constitute very good reasons for feminist and political theory to reconsider the terms of their engagement with Hegel and to redeploy this engagement in challenging those who *would* ally against all the Antigones our laws have displaced.

While the given, particular, and circumscribed forms of social reality into which we are inducted (simply by virtue of the fact that they represent to us what it means to be human before we can discern what that means) are determinative of our actions, self-understanding, and responsibility, human fabrication and human interpretation have the capacity to carry us beyond these particular shapes that social reality takes, and human sociolegal orders also *must take guidance from and be shaped in response to this capacity*. There are diverse human realities at stake in this tension: the immediacy of the communities and commitments by which we find our ethical concern oriented, and the production and transformation of those communities and commitments that occur on the basis of our capacity to reflect on them. The institutions of social life can be effective institutions only on the basis of their responsiveness to *both* of these aspects of human life, and this Greek ethical life could not do.

Through Hegel's discussion in "Spirit of Christianity" and the *Phenomenology*, we see the significance and power of ethicality made manifest, but we also see its inadequacies revealed. We have seen the need for the positing of law to become self-conscious, for the structure and shape of society to be understood as a human accomplishment, for the contradictions of human life to be self-consciously confronted and negotiated by actual human beings. Now we will turn to Hegel's discussion of a society fundamentally based on this self-conscious assertion of the significance of human self-governance and the rule of human law, to see what kind of world such an assertion supports. We will find that, just as an investigation of ethicality led to insight into its incapacity to be the ultimate and exclusive ground of human social life, so too law, and the artificial and self-conscious construction of human society, will manifest this incapacity. Having determined, however, that the conscious taking up of human society as something to be fashioned is ultimately necessary, we will also have to find a way to deal with the incapacity of law without sacrificing the true and undeniably valuable elements it provides.

3

THE RIGHT OF PERSONHOOD

In the "Condition of Right,"[1] Hegel discusses the attempt to detach the mechanisms of social organization from tradition and attach them to single individuals, such that the individual capacity for creation and production can be formally and officially recognized. If human beings are producers of significance and not just recipients of it, then the mechanisms that govern their relations and interaction must be faithful to that productivity and oriented to individuals as a political priority. That requires, in effect, that these mechanisms be prevented from taking shape prior to and independently of the articulation of that will and that they be detached from particular, inherited values.

Hegel identifies the site of the development of this political recognition—the development of a *world* around this principled commitment to the *individual*—as ancient Rome, and identifies its most central mechanism of political organization as "right." The person's acquisition of right is supposed to reflect universal recognition of his individual authority over his own life and over the path that his life takes.[2] Authority is transferred from nature, from the divine, and from social roles predetermined on their basis (all that is operative in "ethical life") to the self. But Hegel's assessment of this accomplishment is also critical: in attaining this authority, the person loses it. While "the actuality of the self . . . has been attained by its return to the *person*," what in ethical life "was unified now emerges as developed, but as alienated from itself" (M483, S359). The self is asserted as significant, but it is fundamentally impoverished, unable to meaningfully develop any significance for itself. The price of the gain of the self turns out to be too high; attaining the power to determine the shape of one's life in this way in fact entails the foreclosure of meaningful and effective agency and personal fulfillment.

Like his discussion of ancient Greek society, Hegel's discussion of the Roman world is relevant not simply on the basis of its historical insight but also on the basis of its import for our political thinking.[3] What he illuminates here is the import of the legal protection of individuals *as* individuals and also the problem with developing a *world* that is constructed solely on the basis of this priority, or solely oriented by it. There is an important similarity between this problem and that seen in ethical life. Each world, the world of the Roman Empire and the world of ancient Greek society discussed in the previous chapter, is oriented by a priority or a commitment that is real and significant, but each tries to found and orient itself solely on the basis of that single, fundamental commitment. The timeliness of insight into these ancient issues, for us, is found in the fact that such insight aids in the development of a mode of social organization that avoids the single-minded or one-sided construction of a world on the basis of a mere part or aspect of what it means to be human and to live together, a form of social organization that is capable of responding to each of these priorities in a way that works to reconcile them to each other.

There exists relatively little scholarly treatment of the condition of right. For that reason, and because Hegel's discussion is quite compressed, I focus in the first section on simply explaining Hegel's account of the condition of right, and in the second on explaining his critique thereof, showing how agency is only meaningfully attained in relation to that which is apparently external to the self—namely, nature, God or the gods, other human beings, and social institutions, roles, and practices. I explain his account and critique of the condition of right by exploring the distinction between it and ethical life (the social reality and set of social priorities discussed in the previous chapter), since what is counted as meaningful or valid in the condition of right can be understood most clearly in contrast to this ethical life. The discussions of the first and second sections will lead us, in the third, to a more robust account of the nature of ethical and political self-authorship and responsibility than that envisaged in both the condition of right and in contemporary political contexts structured around right.

THE SELF AS SUBSTANCE

The Roman world is representative of an important criticism of the nature of human agency and social reality in ethical life. Greek ethical life takes itself to be determined by nature and by divine will, such that the destinies and choices of individuals are immediately wrapped up in the destiny and self-understanding of the social world; or, the individual is only an authoritative and meaningful self by virtue of her identification with her social world and the role it immediately associates with her. The incoherence of this social reality is found in the fact that this external determining authority relies on individuals to carry out its commands; it depends on those whose significance it denies. In the context of conflict (such as the conflict between Antigone and Creon) it becomes apparent that human initiative *is* necessary for the operation and sustenance of what is substantial or meaningful, that human action is necessary to the efficacy of laws and custom. The laws of ethical life are in fact incoherent if they apply to beings that are purely determined, since laws are only meaningful as laws for beings capable of choosing to act otherwise, and they depend on human agents to recognize their authority and carry them out, to the extent that this human obedience and execution are essentially constitutive elements of the law.[4] Thus is the significance of individual initiative, singularity, and difference introduced into the homogeneous ethical world, and authority is seen as needing to be fashioned, asserted, and recognized, not merely given.

What is reflected in Hegel's analysis of the condition of right reflects acknowledgment in relation to this particular problem with ethical life. The condition of right is acknowledgment of the fact that, without the individual's recognition of and consent to the authority of "substance," the latter *has* no authority; hence it is an identification of external authority as something that does not occur naturally but instead exists only in being recognized. For anything to be authoritative, it must be taken up as authoritative by individuals, and thus is it the case that individuals have an ultimacy that must be recognized by law. In the condition of right, right is invoked in response to recognition of the centrality of human agency to the existence and authority of the social order and recognition of the undeniable capacity for self-determination—indeed, recognition of the *demand* that human beings determine themselves, insofar as it is impossible that available rules and guidelines would be able to speak to every diverse human situation.

In his discussion of the religion of the Greeks later in the *Phenomenology*, in the section called "Art-Religion," we find another mention of this theme of distantiation between substance and subject. Hegel explains here the difference between ethical life and the condition of right as akin to what happens in the development from tragedy and comedy, in which the gods, hallowed in the tragic context, become in comedy "clouds, a vanishing mist," whose "contingent determination and superficial individuality" are recognized (M746, S543).[5] As the comic actor recognizes the fact that he is unbeholden to the limiting conditions that set in stone the tragic character's fate, so the self perceives the distance between himself, on the one hand, and his social substance and the role it demands of him, on the other, and experiences his "artistic" and "expressive" control—his capacity for self-expression and creation.

Right is explicitly the protection and endorsement of the simple, infinitely determinable capacity of self-determination on the part of the person. In the condition of right, the "I" (or the "*actual*, *acknowledged* independence of consciousness" (M479, S355) assumes centrality; it takes the place of what was substantial and authoritative and so becomes what is substantial. The person "is that substance" (M477, S355) because he has ultimate authority in deciding on what is meaningful and important and what is not, and because without his acknowledgment nothing has authority or meaning.

Since what is recognized is the simple capacity of self-determination, the rights-bearing individual is not perceived as inhabiting a role or station that requires particular actions, behaviors, or ways of life. This simple capacity, inasmuch as it decides what is substantial, is not inherently shaped by anything substantial and is therefore inherently empty. The law that protects the person does not demand that he inhabit a particular life sphere and exercise a particular kind of participation in it; rather, it enshrines his capacity to freely determine these things on his own. This is not a law whose logic is obedience, but right (*Recht*), through which the person himself makes a demand on his world for individual freedom and authority with regard to self-determination, through posited laws (*Gesetze*). The conflict between Creon and Antigone represents, for Hegel, the revelation of the irreducible introduction of singular human initiative into a social reality previously understood as absorbing and directing individual agents, and the condition of right emerges as the sociopolitical structure that is structured around a commitment to that singular human initiative above all else. This is a society based on the principle of discrete individual identity, agency, and right—a society in which the person, a self-possessed locus of freedom, is the proper subject of law. The Roman world, which institutionalized the legal status of individuals, is the exemplar.[6]

Personal right, according to Hegel's elaboration of it, has three predominant characteristics: it is universal; its exercise requires no predetermined, specific content; and it relies on the bolstering of a certain kind of worldly authority. First, right exists as predicated of all, is universally recognized as such, and only as such does it function smoothly; thus the legal independence of any one person depends on the legal independence of the many. Because the purpose of right is to recognize the person's authority for self-determination independent of any particular quality he has, it cannot be granted on the basis of particular qualities, and hence cannot discriminate among persons. Second, and related, the content that the rights-bearing individual is free to will or attain, "whether it be an external possession or the inner wealth or poverty of spirit and character" (M480, S357), is indeterminate. The direction that each will takes is insignificant and arbitrary from the perspective of the formal freedom of that will, which is central. This means, however, third, that the world of independent persons requires some measure against the unlimited and indeterminate acquisition of content and exercise of right. There are no habitual, instituted, and collectively coordinated measures available that would inwardly compel persons to some sort of orderly behavior or that would express their internal commitment to such behavior; hence something external must be invoked to constrain the potentially chaotic consequences of unrestrained and unlimited personal self-determination. Further, if there is no already existing agreement about what constitutes legitimate authority, then the initial establishment of authority takes the most immediate shape authority could take—that is, it is asserted, by force, as force. As Terry Pinkard writes, "since authority is not a natural feature of human beings, it must be something achieved, and thus where there is no antecedent agreement about who or what has authority, one or the other of them will simply have to establish authority; thus, without any further authoritative principles for doing so, the initial establishment of authority will have to be done by fiat, by an act of will."[7] It is only a central and forceful authority that can guarantee this collective independence and make decisions regulating the diverse content willed by all—this is the rationale behind the rise of the Roman emperor. The guarantor of the law must come from within the unity of this realm of persons, since all authority other than that which stems from the universality of personhood has been cast as suspect. He must be a person like all others, one point in the multiplicity, an authority present in this world, and not of order of the "blood," the "earth," or the "divine," since only persons are recognized as authoritative. The Greek city-states and the laws of the hearth and the city, or the divine and human laws, thus become integrated into a single universal empire and a single universal law.

It should be noted, also, that Hegel's observations as to the rationale behind the rise of the emperor are again not simply relevant for their historical insight; rather, there is an important truth about the general nature of right being articulated here. When there is no *prior* ground, no set of shared, common commitments out of which might emerge a standard by which people could determine for themselves a common authority, then authority emerges haphazardly from out of the collection of individuals, with no other reason for being than that it *happened* to be able to make the claim to authority and happened to be able to sustain it in the face of possible opposition. This authority will almost inevitably make use of force, for it has no widely accepted *reasons.* One final point about the contrast between ethical life and the condition of right that is relevant for understanding this new world should be mentioned, and it involves the "character" that Hegel introduces in his discussion of ethical life who emerges from ethical "non-actuality" into actuality in the condition of right—that is, the dead "blood-relation of the family" (M477, S355). While Hegel does not mention a name, his earlier reference to Sophocles' *Antigone* and his description of this individual make it seem that he is referring to Polyneices, that brother who rose up against his own city and for the sake of whose burial Antigone broke Creon's law. Hegel writes: "What in the world of ethical life was called the hidden divine law, has in fact emerged from its inward state into actuality; in the former state the *single individual* [*der Einzelne*] was and counted as actual merely as the universal *blood* of the *family*. As *this* single individual, he was the *selfless departed* spirit; now, however, he has emerged from out of his non-actuality" (M477, S355). Polyneices, dead, serves primarily as a resource for reaffirming, of the family that mourns him, its primacy in defining his reality and significance. It is this individual, who in ethical life is defined simply as "the blood of the family," who in the condition of right has a new significance.

I want to make four points here concerning the change in status of the individual from his position as the dead blood relation of the family to "legal person." First, Hegel writes that this individual was actual and valid merely as the "blood of the family" but has now emerged from that given, immediately authoritative substance to a position in which self-determination and singular initiative are of the essence. The development here is from membership in a meaningful, intimate whole, the family, to selfhood as meaningful in its own right and on its own solitary terms. The authority of the ground from which he emerges, the family, is exhausted and abandoned through the accomplishment of this independent selfhood. This individual now has meaning apart from the familial ground in relation to which he used to be merely a member, significant merely on the basis of its terms and not in his own right. Second, it is the person who could *not* live in the world of ethical substance—the dead one—who is resurrected in the world of right. Ethical life could not sustain the actions of people like Polyneices (or Antigone, for that matter), but the condition of right can. Indeed, Polyneices enacts a truth about this Roman world in rising up against his own substantial ground—his own city and his own brother, his political and his familial life—and that is that in this new world given substantial contexts are not authoritative for him. Third, the way of life of the ethical order was thought to be natural and given, but the condition of right allows nothing but the power of choice to occupy this position. The uptake of the dead individual into the condition of right shows the powerlessness of nature or of the mere natural fact of death in posing an obstacle to the transfer of meaning, which is essentially beyond nature and beyond what is merely given. The fourth point, finally, brings us to our next topic—Hegel's bleak assessment and critique of the condition of right. We could say, metaphorically, that the individual who is recognized as a rights-bearing person is *already dead*, and this point foreshadows Hegel's diagnosis of the incapacity of the condition of right to sustain meaningful life. Individuals can only be fully singular in death; it alone grants them freedom from the contingent and particular details of life that limit and constrain their capacity to determine themselves in unlimited ways, limits and constraints that the condition of right in a sense denies. The rights-bearing person, seeking universal recognition of his hallowed singularity, experiences no guidance in negotiating his particular life and its particular content. Such a person, in his detachment from the concrete particularities of everyday life, is in a sense already dead.

In this section we have discussed the significance of the notion of right and its extraordinary nature as a political accomplishment by exploring Hegel's discussion of it in the condition of right and contrasting it to the reality of and principles behind ethical life. We have determined what kind of persons it makes possible, what kind of way of life it makes available to them, and what kind of authority must be enacted in order for this way of life to be sustained. However, while Hegel saw in the Roman Empire an important political accomplishment—it institutionalized recognition of the individual capacity for self-determination—he considered the *world* of that accomplishment to be fundamentally unlivable. While he identified the construal of people as rights-bearing persons to be a valuable and irreversible accomplishment, he also saw that to live solely on the basis of that identification was both impossible and undesirable. This next section treats his critique of the condition of right, and, with it, his critique of the idea that any world could take as its fundamental principle of organization the priority of individual right.

HEGEL'S CRITIQUE OF THE CONDITION OF RIGHT

Hegel's central critical point with regard to the condition of right is that the link forged by right between the person and his world is insufficient for the genuine exercise of self-determination, such that the independence promised by right is in fact abject dependence and unfreedom and the world in which the person lives is fundamentally alien to that person.[8] His critique of the condition of right challenges both an individualist, rights-based account of individual agency (the person) and an account of political authority based on protecting autonomous rights-bearing selves. It illuminates the narrowness and insufficiency of a form of political organization that relies solely on the notion of right, and, insofar as that form is comparable to that of the contemporary political context, it is a powerful resource for contemporary political criticism.[9] Hegel's critique, however, also sets in relief several positive conclusions regarding individual ethical and political agency; the mediation of self-authorship and agency in fact supports a more robust account of individual agency, and, indeed, of just political authority. In this section we will explore his criticism of the condition of right and of forms of political organization comparable to it, as well as the positive conclusions it sets in relief.

Hegel's criticism of the condition of right can be expressed in terms of two basic points. First, he shows how the power of the "lord of the world," supposed to uphold the right of the person, is insecure and arbitrary and hence incapable of fulfilling its purported purpose. Second, Hegel compares the condition of right to Stoicism and shows that to withdraw into the self and identify it as the only substantial thing in an insubstantial world entails an impoverished way of life for that self and impoverished forms of interaction with others, which results in a decreased capacity for agency. Let us treat each of these points in turn.

THE LORD OF THE WORLD AND THE PROBLEM OF POLITICAL AUTHORITY

The right of personhood is undermined or destabilized partly through the arbitrariness and insecurity of those elements supposed to uphold it—namely, the lord and the Roman Empire as such. The lord of the world guarantees the rights of all, but the condition of right essentially becomes a condition of subordination to his arbitrary will. Hegel makes this point in various ways. He writes that "the lord of the world has actual consciousness of what he is—namely, the universal power of actuality—in the destructive violence he exercises against the selves of his subjects, the selves that are opposed to him" (M482, S358). Just as right takes on no content but that which is given it through the individual's self-determination, making no reference to the world as a limit or a medium, so also the lord's relationship to the world is based on the pure, abstract notion of self-determination, in which the world acts neither as a limit nor as a resource. The lord's power is simply pure, brute, immediate force—power in its most immediate form. Also, since the lord's power in securing the existence of the empire depends on persons perceiving that power as absolute and not to be crossed, the lord must parade it and exercise it arbitrarily so as to provoke fear and submission in his subjects and to have evidence of that power manifested in their submission. Further, since the person's expression of freedom is manifested in the acquisition of property (a point to which I will return), the lord's authority must be used to limit what could in principle be unlimited, and in having this as its central task his authority comes to resemble less a bulwark of freedom than a militaristic police force. Also, the right of the person is insecure in that the power of the empire, that which secures and ensures right, is essentially insecure. The arbitrariness of the lord's power, and the extent to which it can be personally advantageous to have such power, can provoke rebellion in the military and in other would-be tyrants; hence the empire is prone to upheaval, which in turn undermines the particular content and the reliability the lord gives right. Finally, the security of right is also challenged by virtue of the essential contradiction inherent in the nature of the lord's power. The lord of the world lays waste to that which is needed to recognize and reflect his authority—that is, to persons—and in so doing disables and undermines his authority. As Hegel writes, "the destructive agitation in this insubstantial arena gives him . . . consciousness of his dominion over all, but this self is simple devastation and is thus external to itself, and even the rejection of its own self-consciousness" (M482, S359). In sum, the fact that the Roman world relies on such an external authority for its sustenance renders its right inherently unstable and the freedom it protects fragile and insubstantial. The lord's exercise of lordly power is shown to be essentially *outside* of the scope of the will of the person and a threat to it, even though the condition of right is premised on the essentiality of this personal will.

Hegel's critique of Roman political authority speaks to the more general question concerning what form political authority should take in order to be responsive to the way that individuals actually become persons and experience their agency. Any given society needs mechanisms by which issues of organization and governance can be decided; what Hegel shows here is that legal personhood, the governing principle of this society, cannot on its own provide such mechanisms. To be sure, the recognition of individual right is a political accomplishment with enormous significance, but the fact that there is a *society* of such individuals, and that the right of each has to be reconciled with the rights of the others, demands a form of organization that cannot *simply* be derived from the idea of individual right. Indeed, while the right of persons is supposed to protect against the abuse of authority, Hegel shows in his analysis of the Roman Empire that the very construal of individuals as atomistic rights-bearers renders them powerless against such abuse from political authority, because this kind of right in fact indirectly achieves, for political power, the freedom to function outside of individual control. If right and the power of self-determination are defined as inhering merely in individuals, and if the delegation of genuine power to particular persons and institutions is ignored, then the operation of this power is essentially outside of individual control, and persons have few real reasons to participate in collective action and institutions designed to keep it in check.

If human agency is fundamentally social and responsive, then to construe it as individual and self-determining and to protect it in those terms is in fact to deter and discourage its effective exercise. In individualizing its recipients through granting them right, this kind of political authority conceals the sociality of human agency and thereby disempowers it; it prevents the articulation and development of the specifically social aspects of this agency and disconnects individuals from the social resource of solidarity. When individuals are characterized as free autonomous beings whose import lies in their capacity to choose for themselves, and when political power is mobilized to protect only that capacity, then the social, cultural, psychological, and economic human flourishing possible with the aid and support of healthy social and material conditions is undermined.[10] Human agency develops out of and in relation to a particularly human context, in which that context is as important to the individual's growth as the individual's own initiative is, or in which any separation of the two is an abstraction. When political power is invoked to defend the right of the individual, and when individual empowerment is expressed in and by right, various other forms of mediated power and empowerment are lost: that found in the greater power of collectives, in traditional and customary means of constructing, elaborating, and communicating meaning, and in the historically sedimented agency of the entire domain of social institutions and practices.

The question of what form political authority and institutions responsive to the social character of human agency should take, and what kind of access to that authority and those institutions should be advocated, remains open. But one point can be made here, based on the idea that we rely for our agency on already given and meaningful contexts. This point is that political authority and institutions are similar to individual agency in this regard; they operate only as or in the context of an already given set of meanings. They too are a specific aspect of "ethical life" and take their guidance from a particular, already given content, not from the arbitrary will of an ultimate lord. They too, like individual agents, are not at any moment self-founding and self-legitimating, but they have the shape and the prerogatives they do in response to a particular history and set of needs and demands, and those who act to sustain them do so with a kind of blindness as to their origin. The authority of such institutions and governance structures is mediated, just as the person's is, by the conditions out of which they emerged. What this means is that it should be possible to reflect on their particularity and thus on the partiality of their attempts to satisfy the demand for justice. That is, there must be room and opportunity for genuine reflection on the ways in which these institutions and structures actively and determinately shape social reality, delimit possibilities for social interaction and agency, and reflect the more or less just conditions of their emergence.

Agency is exercised only in responsive interaction with what is given, and without responsiveness to particular needs and demands political agency and authority will not be effective at all.[11] This authority *must* be partial to be responsive, and in answerability to what is given, in its limitation by what is given, it becomes effective and meaningful *as* authority. It must be partial and particular in order to be able to enact justice. It must not conceal its partiality by pretending to be adequate to the universal, and it must not discourage the operation of other partial, mediating social institutions and practices by construing the individual it "protects" as fully individuated and fully universal, as though it were not reliant for its very being on the assistance and support of these mediating forces.

Ultimately, the abstraction of the individual from her social context does not simply increase the scope and effect of her power but also in significant ways decreases it, in that such an abstraction allows the purportedly objective and external world to function outside of her control and affords her none of the resources in that world for the exercise of her agency. The externalization of her own authority and agency—

its mediation by forces and agents apparently outside of the scope of her will—can in fact operate as a check on the illegitimate exercise of authority on the part of external agents. Similarly, the elaboration of political authority and institutions beyond the protection of individual rights can be the occasion for the real satisfaction and exercise of these rights. The acknowledgment of the partiality of this authority and these institutions makes room both for the more active operation of other mediating institutions and for the elaboration of the human beyond the constraints of existing definitions and the activity of the human beyond the scope of her single, isolated self. If such an elaboration is to occur, right cannot be the fundamental principle to which all forms of social organization are ultimately reduced.

The Meaninglessness of the World and the Problem of Individual Agency

While right is ineffective for the reason that the power that protects it is arbitrary and insecure, it is also ineffective in that its assertion results in the impoverishment of the world. This second point of criticism presented in "The Condition of Right" can be illustrated by reference to the comic figure with which Hegel concludes his treatment of art-religion in the *Phenomenology*.[12] Like the rights-bearing person, the comic figure is certain of his own selfhood and his independence from the gods, laws, and practices that used to be taken as authoritative. He celebrates the capacity to follow whatever whim demands or the circumstances allow and achieves thereby a state of "well-being and repose . . . such as is not to be found anywhere outside of this Comedy" (M747, S544), for he can laugh at the gods and feel the power of his own will. But this reality is essentially impoverished, in a way that has consequences for his individual agency. As Hegel describes it,

> trust in the eternal laws of the gods has vanished, and the oracles . . . are dumb. The statues are now only stones from which the living soul has flown, just as the hymns are words from which belief has gone. The tables of the gods provide no spiritual food and drink, and in his games and festivals man no longer recovers the joyful consciousness of his unity with the divine. The works of the muse now lack the power of the spirit, for the spirit has gained its certainty of itself from the crushing of gods and men." (M753, S548)

In fact, the comic figure is unhappy, since what it has attained is an awareness of the loss of all essentiality (M752, S547). What is lost here is any social ground and spiritual meaning that might fill out and give content to this empty self. The outlook on relationships with others is similarly bleak. When the comic figure disparages all that is external to him, he simultaneously forecloses the opportunity to create connections with that externality in the various forms it takes. In casting himself as that which ultimately determines and delegates meaning, but in simultaneously divesting everything else of meaning, he has immobilized and disempowered his own meaning-making capacity.

Hegel explains this problem by describing the condition of right as Stoicism in the shape of a world, since, just as the Stoic withdraws into inwardness and strives to be impervious to the agency and influence of the external world, so the legal person has stepped out of "substance" and has marked himself, as the only substantial thing, to be essentially independent from the world.[13] Stoical inwardness takes itself to be essentially impenetrable by anything external and construes this impenetrability as freedom. Similarly, the person, free of determination by anything outside of himself, takes the measure of what is substantial to lie solely in himself. Right is formal; it does not depend on or require external occurrences, accomplishments, or things. As such, with it the person is protected from intervention and influence by external forces; right is supposed to render him impervious to them.

The problem the stoical person encounters, however, is the same as that which the legal person encounters: if he is the location of all that is substantial, then all that is external to him ceases to have an intrinsically meaningful connection to his identity and will, and he is compelled neither for nor against it.[14] Withdrawing into the certainty of his own thinking, his relation to the world is undefined and indeterminate. Further, if all that is external is held at bay from this self, and only his initiative is imbued with value, nothing external can be essentially valuable to him. The actual world of Stoicism is in fact an isolating and meaningless one. If the stoical self is the one who picks and chooses what matters, and only in so doing creates value, then nothing essentially matters in its own right and on its own terms. The value of things relies on the person's whim, which, because it takes itself to be independent of formation and cultivation, is more or less underdeveloped and arbitrary.

We can further explore the consequences of this self-isolation by developing the parallel between the person of the condition of right and

Hegel's presentation of the development from Stoicism to Skepticism. In the context of his treatment of the condition of right, Hegel says that the abstract independence of Stoicism "passes over into the sceptical confusion of consciousness, into a raving of the negative, which wanders aimlessly from one contingency of being and thinking to another, dissolving them in its absolute independence but just as much creating them anew; it is in fact simply the contradiction between the independence and dependence of consciousness" (M480, S356). The stoical self takes itself to be ultimately authoritative and independent and chooses on its own what will count as valuable or substantial, removing itself from the world of already-existent value. The skeptical self, which is a kind of temporary solution to the problems the stoical self confronts, attempts to demonstrate its freedom in relation to all that is external by taking up particular content and showing its inessentiality thus *enacting* the stoical conclusion that there is nothing substantial. The skeptic demonstrates that all of reality is a senseless, contingent collection of serial experiences (M202, S159–60).

But the skeptical self, Hegel shows, does in fact rely upon something it takes to be certain: its *own* capacity to show the insubstantiality of the diverse content of experience. While it proclaims everything to be insubstantial, it is in principle committed to the presumption of the unity and authority of its own consciousness, for which this collection of experiences *is* a collection. It demonstrates itself as unified and authoritative *through* interaction with the manifold it encounters. Its assertion of the insubstantiality of everything is problematic, then, in two ways: a) it presumes its own authority to declare this and to operate as the center around which reality is organized; and b) it relies upon that which it negates, which must exist for skeptical consciousness in order that this consciousness be able to show the insubstantiality of what it negates and therefore its own substantiality.

The condition of the legal person is similar to that of the skeptical self: first, the legal person presumes the authority of his *own* self in a world in which nothing is supposed to be substantial; second, he is dependent in fact upon that which he negates in principle. As formally free, the person demonstrates his freedom by calling his own whatever he finds before him, making arbitrary things his property and in so doing manifesting his right. In order to make his independence manifest, he engages all kinds of random things in the world, none of which has any substantial value in comparison with his free will. He experiences his freedom by entering into proprietary relations with things the value of which is undermined by the very fact that he is the only thing of value, and which are essentially at odds with his will because of their relative lack of value. This constant, dizzying "skeptical confusion" has the consequence, as in skepticism, of dependence (M480, S356). The content willed and the achievements accomplished in the world are the result of mere arbitrary decision in the face of contingent situations and resources—or, as Hegel says, the content of the person's world is set free and unordered (M480, S356). In appropriating any particular content that happens to come his way, the person in fact demonstrates the essential contingency of his supposed independence, his incapacity to define and fill out his selfhood meaningfully and in accordance with his substantial will. The freedom of the person is nothing more, it turns out, than the insubstantial thing he owns and with which he has no essential relation. Right without the capacity to meaningfully appropriate it, or without the capacity to exercise it in substantial ways in an ordered and meaningful world, does not in fact substantiate the person but renders him insubstantial—does not free but impoverishes him. If nothing in the world is valuable, then the right of personhood protects an agency that is made meaningless. If everything in the world with which he could interact is cast as meaningless, then the person in fact degrades himself in his interaction with that world.

Another aspect of the impoverishment of the world is the impoverishment involved in relations with others. When the atomic, isolated self becomes the most substantial thing or the linchpin of all meaning, and when the occasion for the expression of independence is taking possession, then the self is essentially opposed to social continuity and interaction with others. Disparaging of all that is external to him and convinced of his own independent authority, the person's apparent independence would be threatened by any meaningful social interaction; all others, after all, are effectively obstacles to his taking possession and to his authority over his own life. The community here is merely a collection of parts, a random multiplicity; it has no logic of its own, and persons have no reason to identify with it. The alien character of their connection is symbolized by the fact that the lord, the authority that integrates them into one body, has no connection to their character *as* a body or a whole. Additionally, persons have no essential reason to engage in social interaction, since they are all essentially the same. That is, what is formally recognized as valuable by right is the empty self that is capable of taking on any content and making anything meaningful; as mere potential, this capacity is equal and identical in each.

Relations with others so conceived also contribute to the perversion of independence into dependence. With others understood as obstacles to his personal development, the person is more restricted than enabled, since the help they could offer in the formation, cultivation, and satisfaction of his free will is precluded, as is the support they could offer in collaboration against the potential rise of oppressive power. The formal opposition between self and others precludes the concrete exercise of agency on the basis of collectively achieved and negotiated practices. Also, since other selves experience *themselves* as the sole sources of meaning, in the face of each of these others the person is in fact meaningless and vulnerable to the arbitrary exercise of their arbitrary wills.

The promise of agency and freedom granted in this way involves the thoughtless transformation of the world into a devastated wasteland devoid of meaning, a "chaos of spiritual powers that, unleashed, move madly and destructively against each other, as elemental beings in wild debauchery" (M481, S358). The world is ultimately incapable of supporting human life, and the "self is simple devastation" (M482, S359). All that the self does not choose, all that she does not shape, is essentially outside of the scope of the meaningful and the rational. Further, nothing the person does or owns has any inherent meaning in its own right; hence, while agency is formally recognized by right, it has no rationally determinable content. If the world is inherently meaningless and irrational, then anything the self does in it will be arbitrary. All that she has received, all that provides for her objects of choice and makes her capable of choosing, is made imperceptible or removed from the scene. Through the individualization of agency and authority, the possibility of true agency and authority is lost. The price of choice is the loss of an already meaningful social world, such as the one described in ethical life.

What this analysis puts into relief is the idea that genuine agency involves responsiveness to and support by that which lies outside of the individual and has been removed from the scene by insistence on personal right; it is agency as inspired by and indebted to already compelling and given contexts of meaning; it is freedom as embodied in determinate things, people, and institutions. This analysis shows that the person cannot construct and organize a meaningful and independent experience without deep collaboration with the already meaningful material the world offers—be it in the form of objects, practices, institutions, others, and so on. We develop, exercise, and interpret our identities as persons only through interaction with our environments, which are themselves cultivated and charged by the perspectives and agency of others. Agency is had only on the basis of the nontransparent and given material and environment by which it is invoked and supported. It is exercised insofar as individuals have access to this external material and environment—

access to public goods, political practices, the products of nature and of cultural activity, and so on. And agency is had on the basis of given and developed relations with others, whether these relations be originally given and nourishing or self-consciously adopted.

In the context of these relations, the person is formed as a being by significance that she does not give or choose herself. She interacts with things, contexts, and other people on the basis of a significance that is prior to her reflection and creative power, and her agency arises on the basis of their authority over her, their capacity to inspire her to action, their lending her their substantiality for her substantiation. Without this already existent environment and connection, the agency of the individual person would have nothing essentially to do with the world and would therefore be of little significance in relation to it. Assuming the authority of this given world in fact entails rendering more effective and substantial the authority of the self.

What this means for right, then, is that, instead of being conceived merely as right *against* an alien world and others, it must be conceived as right *through* and *with* this world and these others. If right is the occasion of separation and individualization, if it alienates the individual from her environment, its force is undermined, and the "condition of right" turns into a condition of rightlessness. What Hegel has shown to be necessary here is: a) explicit identification and acknowledgment of the world as already meaningful in ways that we do not individually determine; b) the development of interaction with that world that is constituted by more than just legally instituted property relations; c) the acknowledgment of essential and meaningful dependence on others; and d) the development of a political authority that is well suited to the way in which agency and self-determination are a matter of collaboration.

ETHICALITY AND RIGHT

We have elaborated Hegel's description and critique of the condition of right, illuminating the kind of agency it makes possible for both individuals and political authority and proposing some ways in which we might think of such agency and authority differently. My goal in this last section is to process the observations made at the beginning of this chapter, and indeed in these first few chapters in general, as to the nature of both ethicality and right. We now have an account of the significance of and problems with a world organized in terms of ethicality and a world organized in terms of right, and hence we can begin to articulate the significance of each in a way that is responsive to the significance of the other.

The relationship between the two ways of life and sets of priorities can be illuminated by discussing two issues facing ethical life and the condition of right: first, the way the authority of law is construed as absolute and immediate, and second, the issue of the opposition between natural determination and human convention. First, both the ethical order and the Roman order construe their laws to be ultimate and unmediated or unaccompanied by any other commitment or principle. Ethical life is organized by *customary* law; the human beings who live in it feel themselves immediately obligated by customs that they see to be absolutely given and that dictate appropriate actions in the familial and political arenas. The condition of right is organized by *posited* law, law that is made by human beings in a way that is appropriate to their capacity to determine and govern themselves. The "characters" of ethical life, Antigone and Creon, take their social order and its laws to be immediately authoritative; their obedience is, as it were, an immediate consequence of the existence of laws and social life. The "person" of the condition of right takes *himself*—his self-authorship and self-determination—to be immediate, and his centrality is protected by right. But the problem here is that each denies the authority of a significance *corresponding* to the significance of its law. The structure of ethical life institutes a denial of the way in which law exists *for* human beings and thus in response to their singularity, and the structure of the condition of right institutes a denial of the way in which law enables and relies on social forms of recognition, institutions, and authority.[15] Thus, whereas in ethical life the self is eclipsed by the claim on the part of the social order to immediacy and authority, in the condition of right the social order is eclipsed by the self's claim to immediacy and authority. Neither is seen to be mediated by or dependent upon the other.

In reality, however, law is mediated by the nature and demands of the human beings whom it protects, *and*, conversely, the identity of these beings is achieved by law and other institutional accomplishments. I mentioned above, in the first section of this chapter, the contradiction inherent in the laws of ethical life—that, if individuals immediately and necessarily do what they should, then no law is in fact necessary. In the condition of right we see a different contradiction: law or right is a *social* accomplishment engaged to protect and enshrine the right of an individual who in turn denies any such agency to the social, or who is construed by right in such a way as to render such social agency invisible and ineffective. We see here again that while the principle of the right of personhood is an important accomplishment, the *world* of that accomplishment is unlivable. The principle of personality, for Hegel, is insufficient as the basis of a world and establishes a world the person cannot inhabit, since the operation of this right leads to a denial of the reality and efficacy of this world as a world.

A similar problem can be identified if we look at the operation of natural determination, on the one hand, and human convention, on the other. The collapse of ethical substance reveals nature's powerlessness in providing the norms by which social life is lived and organized. It is not nature that names and determines individuals in a certain way; on the contrary, who and what human beings are is envisioned by them in collaboration with each other in a human social order—indeed, *this* is their nature, to make themselves and to make forms for their interaction.[16] This conclusion is expressed explicitly in the condition of right, in which all authority with regard to norm construction is established in this world and claimed by the human as such. Persons are construed as identical by a single, shared authority that speaks to all of them equally; this is not an achievement of nature but of human convention and agreement. But as the failures of ethical life revealed nature's powerlessness, so also do the failures of the condition of right reveal the powerlessness of human convention in providing norms by which social life is lived and organized, when the *social* nature of convention is denied and the individual is asserted as its own "miraculous," spontaneous achievement. That is, right is a *human* accomplishment, but not that of an *individual* human being. The ultimate authority of the person over his own life does not translate immediately into social norms or norms for social interaction. The significance of human convention and agreement is undermined by right's actual operation, which denies the significance of the shared domain and the authority of the social order in naming, defining, and shaping personality. The social world is not nature, but it is not simply chosen by each human individual; it is like a *second* nature, given in the way that only something human can be given—by already having been made by human beings and by shaping our capacity to make.[17]

Hegel identifies the reason for the downfall of ethical life as its denial of human agency in constructing ways of life, worlds, social practices, and so on. The problem with the condition of right, in turn, is that in embracing the notion of human agency it individualizes it. In the condition of right, authority, while construed as internal to the human world, is not conceived as had by this world as such but by the individuals who constitute it. The designation of social roles and responsibilities is discovered to be a human determination, but the condition of right conceives of human powers of determination not as collective but as individual. Hegel's account of the condition of right is in fact an account of the maturation of a substance, world, or way of life, but one that conceals itself as such; the configuration of the right of the person makes it seem like a fundamentally individual, private, or personal accomplishment. The world and the social nature of the accomplishment and exercise of right are denied any reality.

In both ethical life and the condition of right, human agency and responsibility are stifled and frustrated, but for what seem to be opposite reasons: it is too much to demand of the individual that he be the source of all meaning, and too much to demand of the individual that she live only according to already existing meanings. Both models fail to institute recognition of the fact that meaning is the result of an interaction between individuals and their social reality, individuals and others. Genuine agency and responsibility could be conceived, therefore, on the basis of some kind of compromise between the two principles by which each world is organized. The person gains her own capacity to make meaning by living out of given or received meanings, and the task facing her is to recognize the extent to which her agency is situated by what is so given and received and the extent to which it is reliant on the healthy functioning of that which is "external" to her. It is equally necessary to live in a way organized by and responsive to law and to live in a way organized by and responsive to the reality of ethicality (or customary law). And these are transformed, of course, if they are construed not simply as the sole, basic principle by which a world is organized, but as *co-existent aspects of its organization.*

CONCLUSION

What Hegel shows in his terse, critical treatment of the Roman condition of right is that if right is articulated in such a way that it effectively posits agency as purely individual and presumes that the sole prerogative of political authority is the protection of such individual agency, what results is a world without meaning and a self without agency. In order to be authoritative and effective, the person must recognize and reflectively integrate into his life the authority and efficacy of that which lies outside of him and accept the essentially mediated nature of agency and authority. He relies for his own agency on a rational authority and a well-developed social structure—or, in Bernstein's words, an ethical geometry that runs both vertically and horizontally.[18] In order to develop a meaningful relation to the content of his will, the person must submit to a process of cultivation—the cultivation of the empty and atomistic self—*and* he must acknowledge that in fact he has been cultivated already. In order to experience an increase in his agency through continuity with other persons, the person must be open to his outside, to the determinations of substance, to the authority and meaning of the external world. Without the mediation of these various "outsides," any authority or agency the self has will be ineffectual, underdeveloped, and insignificant. Without responding to and living in the context of the claims articulated by his world, the self cannot freely articulate his own.

Right as such, however, is not inconsistent with agency; Hegel's critique here is of right articulated in abstraction from other significant aspects of social life, right as misconceived and misconstrued. In the condition of right, Hegel's analysis of posited law in a political context is brief and highly critical, and the *Phenomenology* in general has no isolated treatment of posited political laws. Hence, to round out our account of his understanding of posited law, we will now take a detour through a context in which Hegel treats in more detail the important operation of law in a diversified modern context, the "Objective Spirit" of the *Encyclopaedia*.[19] Up to this point we have been exploring the historical contexts within which law functions in a particular way, contexts that are more or less one-sided and problematic while being simultaneously revelatory of important aspects of the operation of law and the operation of individuals in human society. We have seen the necessity of posited law emerge out of our analysis of ethical life, and we have explored Hegel's critical analysis of right in "The Condition of Right," so we have an account of the significance and shortcomings of the notion of ethical life and an account of the shortcomings of law, but we have not yet had the opportunity to unveil and delineate the importance and positive significance of law—the way it, in its proper functioning, operates as an empowering extension of human agency. Because law is such a pivotal figure in this book, given its centrality to contemporary theories of justice, it calls for this kind of fair and detailed consideration.

4

THE LEGAL CONDITIONS OF ACTION

In this chapter we turn to examine Hegel's discussion of law in the *Encyclopaedia*, and in so doing we will move from a closed and problematic world governed autocratically and based primarily on an unfulfillable commitment to individual right to a world filled out politically by other supplementary commitments, the justice of whose legal order is confirmed and stabilized by a variety of complex political arrangements and institutions. We will further explore the idea that law, properly understood, is an extension of human identity, a mechanism of organization and regulation that precedes and conditions action, and an organization of physical space and intersubjective interaction that responds powerfully to the fact that human beings live in a sense "outside of" themselves. In all of these ways we will see that law is not an external limitation but an internal, "nonlimiting" limitation. I will show again, however, that even law in this ideal form allows for only the partial operation of justice and must be supplemented by mechanisms of justice that lie outside of its determining power.

I will begin by discussing the notion of posited law, or law as explicitly posited rule, and the mechanisms of its actualization in the world. I will discuss the ways in which posited law becomes internal to human experience, no longer a limitation but a condition of it, even though its operation can continue to inspire the misperception that it is merely external. I will differentiate and discuss the different elements of law and corresponding attitudes toward it that Hegel delineates in section 538 of the *Encyclopaedia*:

> The laws express the determinate content of objective freedom. First, for the immediate subject, they are barriers to his

> independent freedom of choice [*Willkür*] and particular interest. Second, however, they are an absolute *final aim* and the universal *work*; thus are they generated through the functions of the different estates [*Stände*] that distinguish themselves further with regard to the general particularity, and through all the activity and private concern of *single individuals* [*der Einzelnen*]. Third, they are the substance of the willing of these individuals—which is thereby *free*—and of their disposition, and so are portrayed as valid *custom* [*Sitte*]. (§538)

That is, I will be exploring *how*, instead of being restrictions on human agency, laws are its conditions, its freely produced ends, and its substance, and I will be exploring *why* the "immediate subject" may fail to see them as such. Finally, however, I will show the ways in which, even in this more stable and diversified context, law is limited in its operation, and thereby lay the groundwork for the exploration, in the next chapter, of the third ingredient of Hegel's theory of justice, the recognition and forgiveness of conscience.

I will begin this chapter with a consideration of the nature of freedom and the way in which it must externalize itself in property, an externalization that in turn announces the necessity of law for freedom. Second, I will discuss posited law, showing why it should be understood as an "absolute final aim" and "the universal work." Third, I will discuss how, as an extension of the human being, law is the kind of extension that is not merely added on to an already-existent human being, but is that through which she comes into being as such. In this context, law comes to appear, as Hegel says, as "valid custom," preceding and sustaining the willing and the dispositions of individuals. Let us begin, then, by pursuing Hegel's identification of the avenue that leads to law—the expression of freedom in the ambiguously internal and external phenomenon of *property*.

THE ESSENTIAL EXTERNALIZATION OF THE PERSON IN PROPERTY

In his discussion of property in the section of the *Philosophy of Spirit* called "Law," the section with which "Objective Spirit" begins, Hegel says that the "subjectivity of intelligence and of freedom of choice [*Willkür*]" gets its particularity and fulfillment by making a thing into *possession*, the "external sphere of its liberty" (§488). Its "self-knowledge of freedom," as described in section 488, is "abstract and empty" without becoming particular and fulfilled in an external thing; through such fulfillment, personality becomes existent (§489); hence freedom requires property (an argument also well-rehearsed, in various ways, by John Locke, Adam Smith, and J. G. Fichte, among others). Let us explore more thoroughly why this is true, keeping in mind that more than just self-assertion in property will follow from this basic proposition.

Agency is not simply the abstract power of a self-determining will, a "subjectivity of [pure] intelligence and volition"; rather, it is *bodily*, *thingly*, and *worldly*. To be active, to freely engage in projects and have actual purposes, human beings have to be able to take up the world as their material, and indeed, to take it up in such a way that others are prevented from having access to it. Free agency is agency that has a physical presence in the world, that has access to and works with things, that develops projects and pursuits in relation to things and a world, and so on. The individual is not simply its inwardness, but it is what it does; it is its activity in a world and with things; it is filled out in the objects and contexts with which it interacts. Subjectivity is formed and performed through these things, objects, and contexts.

If freedom is essentially activity that is engaged with things and spaces, then to be free requires access to the things that are the ingredients of activity and access to a space in which to be active—or, freedom requires property. The identification of property as a primary ingredient of human freedom is the acknowledgment that we are determinate, bodily beings who live in and on the basis of things and a world; Hegel says that "in property the person is united with itself" (§490). Property is no longer solely or strictly a thing, but a vehicle of subjectivity, internal to it, bearing its significance. In the thing, the character of the I as "infinite relation" of itself to itself is manifested: "I . . . am as a person the repulsion of me from myself" (§490). To be an I is to be myself even in the context of my self-repulsion, my being outside of myself, in things, defined by "external" contexts and expressed in "external" products.

But the simple reality of freedom as property has many additional corollaries and consequences; appropriation of property, and self-determination and self-expression in property, is not the end of the story of freedom. Hegel continues with reference to the fact that the thing is merely an abstractly existing thing, and thus the person is abstractly external in it. This means that while my freedom needs this external reality—while to be an agent requires a fundamental alliance with and commitment to things—freedom is always more than its expression in property. He writes: "The *essence* of spirit is . . . *freedom*, the absolute negativity of the concept as identical with itself. According to this formal determination it *can* abstract from all that is external and from its own externality, from its very existence; it can . . . preserve itself affirmatively and be identical with itself in this negativity" (§382). While freedom requires externalization, it is not dependent on any specific form that such externalization could take, but it maintains a fundamental independence with regard to it. What it is to be me is to take up things *and* have my significance be inexhaustible by them, to be able to make myself determinate differently.

The freedom I have in the thing also extends beyond the thing in a different way, insofar as in it I also encounter others. Let us turn again to section 490, in which Hegel writes that "the thing [*Sache*] is abstract and external, and in it I am abstract and external. The concrete return of me into myself in externality means that I, the *infinite* self-relation, am as a person the repulsion of me from myself, and have the existence of my personality in the *being of other persons*, in my relation to them and in my recognition by them, which is mutual." When I express my will in the thing, I encounter others, and I encounter, in a sense, *their* wills, since I encounter in my possession of the thing their *permission* or allowance of that possession. They see me as a freely active and capable being in my possession of things, *and* their acknowledgment of me and of my appropriation of the thing makes that appropriation possible. Hegel writes in section 491, "The thing [*Sache*] is the *middle* through which the extremes, i.e., persons, in the knowledge of their identity as free and simultaneously mutually independent, are united. For them my will has its *determinate discernible existence* in the thing through the immediate bodily taking of possession, or through the formation of the thing, or even through the simple identification of it." My personality exists—I have property—because other people permit me to; they allow my *claim* to the thing to have standing; they *acknowledge* the existence of my will in the thing. Individual private property can exist because our wills are in agreement about it, because we *share* a commitment to it. The site of the realization of my freedom—the world of things—is also that for others, and hence my realization relies on their permission; our wills are mutually dependent. Thus is my freedom supported by them; thus is freedom an intersubjective matter.

While I find myself in a sense in control of objects and their meaning in my taking possession of them, however, I do not have the same capacity with people. Rather, I am *dependent* on them in that if they do not recognize my property, it does not exist. But this dependence on them, like my appropriation of objects, gives me the capacity to be a person, capable of taking possession and being an agent, and I have a rich world and meaningful occasions for self-expression in the domain of things because this domain has been extensively cultivated and developed by these others. My relation to and recognition by others is not the occasion for the eradication of my personality but for its existence, sustenance, and meaningful development; hence this dependence is also intrinsically connected to and required for independence, for freedom.[1]

These two issues—externalization in property and the reality of recognition that we encounter in that externality—point, finally, to our central point of focus: the organization of the intersubjective world, the establishment of mechanisms by which both our taking possession and our mutual recognition can be honored, mechanisms that we can collectively endorse as appropriately responsive to our individual ownership and our intersubjective existence. How do we *arrange our affairs in the world* such that our exercise of freedom through possession in the same shared world can occur without disturbance, without doing injustice to our mutual dependence—or, as Hegel calls it (indicating that independence is something we develop *together*), our "mutual independence" (§491)? Instead of allowing our social environments to haphazardly take shape around the random whims of their members, we institute (or live by already-instituted) principles that formally express our mutual recognition; we establish (or live by already-established) institutions that carry it out. The reality of recognition and of freedom as property takes formal, instituted, and organized shape.

Thus far we have moved from the idea that freedom requires property to the fact that property impinges on others, and hence to the fact that freedom relies on the wills of others; now we have in front of us the idea that the cooperative communication of wills requires organization. In other words, we have moved from the basic idea of freedom as property, through the meeting in the thing of mutually recognizing persons, to the organization and structuring of this social reality by shared mechanisms, principles, and institutions. Let us turn in this next section to further exploration of law and of how it, rather than being a restriction on our activity and existence, is a *product* of our action and the substance behind our volition (§538).

LAW AND ITS MEDIATION OF HUMAN ACTION

"Nothing has become more familiar," Hegel writes, "than the notion that each must restrict his freedom in relation to the freedom of others, and that the *state* is the condition of this reciprocal restricting and the laws are restrictions. In such notions freedom is regarded merely as contingent pleasure and freedom of choice [*Willkür*]" (§539). However, while laws are experienced as restrictions "for the immediate subject . . . to his independent freedom of choice and particular interest," they are in fact "an absolute *final aim* and the universal *work*" generated by various groups and individuals and taking shape as "the substance of their willing . . . and their disposition" (§538). In this section we will investigate laws, exploring the way in which they are "the final aim and the universal work."

Action always requires a *context*, a physical space in which to transpire, and this space or context must be meaningfully articulated and organized for action to be successful. For us to be able to have the impact on reality that we intend, the contexts in which we act must be more or less stable.[2] Thus, while we may explicitly desire to act on our specific intentions and our specific individuality, the implicit desire concealed in that explicit one is the desire to live in a coordinated context that will allow us to act successfully in our individual ways. A coordinated social context is implicitly willed as the condition of possibility of any explicitly willed individual project. Further, this organized and coordinated social context is an organization and coordination of individual wills in relation to each other; or, the context is a stable one if other people allow it to be so or actively make it so. What we will in willing an organized social context is shared standards and expectations and the implicit and explicit support of others.

Some of the primary terms of this organized context, this system of intersubjective support and cooperation, are *laws*. They are the mechanisms that sustain this cooperation, this social order, this supportive context. This cooperation, this order, and this context allow us to pursue the demands and desires presented to us by our individuality; hence we will the existence and maintenance of laws. Laws therefore are properly understood as the "universal work" produced alongside our individual "activity and private concern" (§538)—something we all work on producing.

We can see an example of the implicit willing of rules and rule following in the phenomenon of a soccer game. Rules permeate this form of organized interaction, such that the significance of almost every action and occurrence is attributable to a rule—the length of the game, the presence of a referee, the number of people on the field, the size and nature of the ball, the size of the field and the placement of lines, the reaction to a high kick or a foul, the characteristics of the items of clothing, and so on. Because of these rules and conventions, it is possible for players to be oriented competitively against other people without having their interaction become fighting; without these rules, something like soccer could not exist at all, since it would be too dangerous. Because of the rules, the structure of the game does not need to be arranged every time, so players have the opportunity over time to develop the skills appropriate to such an activity. The presence of a highly organized context allows for a highly complex and developed form of action and interaction; because of our shared development of skills and our shared, articulated context, we can individually come to act in very sophisticated ways. The coherent and sophisticated action of individuals depends on a structure of rules; hence in willing that action we implicitly will these rules.

While this is true for soccer games, it is even truer for the complex and heavily mediated activities of everyday life. Law operates like the rules of a soccer game in the organization of space, for instance, and of individual movement in it. Space is divided into streets, sidewalks, pathways, bicycle lanes, fields, meadows, forests, and public and private property; it is zoned as residential, agricultural, commercial, and industrial. Rules govern these spaces, rules that take the form of speed limits, traffic lights, building regulations, and zoning laws. These rules that govern space demand a certain kind of movement from people and dictate what kinds of things belong in what spaces; the ordering of space and of movement are systematically integrated. In demanding certain kinds of movement in space, rules make it such that the movement of one individual can be made compatible with that of another individual. Hence spaces are made accessible and useable by the regulation of movement in them. Because of laws that exclude certain kinds of vehicles from the highway, for instance, or laws that require communicative behavior in the form of turn signals, that dictate certain levels of speed, that separate the "passing lane" from the "slow lane," and that demand taxes for the sake of the upkeep of roads, people in cars can easily fulfill their independent ends, in a highly unobstructed and efficient way.

This situation of regulated traffic is an example that shows that successful action requires the cooperation of others, but this cooperation takes on a particularly interesting form—that is, it does not *appear* as cooperation. The rules of traffic organize and coordinate human beings in relation to each other and bring about cooperative interaction among people with different intentions, but while this highly organized world of motion is characterized by an extreme degree of cooperation among people with different intentions, what it looks like is noninteraction. The support we extend to each other in the interaction involved in driving a car is the support involved in *leaving each other alone*. The way we take others into account while driving is by following the rules—which allow us not to take others into account explicitly. The rules allow us to communicate our intentions to each other without explicitly taking on the project of communication; at a four-way stop sign we have implicitly agreed that you, as the first on the scene, will go first; at an intersection, you, by using your left turn signal, tell me that you will turn left, and I, approaching the intersection from the other direction, have received your permission to go through first. The rules have accomplished this communication for us; as the condition of successful interaction, they produce the *experience* of noninteraction.

It should be clear now why Hegel says that law is the "universal work"; action depends on an organized social context articulated in terms of principles or laws—that is, on shared and shareable truths. Because action *depends* on these principles or laws, they are also the implicit *goal* of all action, in principle, and they are such a goal for *everybody*. Because of our mutual adoption of law, we make accessible to ourselves the activities and pursuits we consider essential to the enactment of meaningful human lives. With law, we have all those things the absence of which Hobbes evocatively describes in the *Leviathan*; without law there is, he says, "no place for Industry, because the fruit thereof is uncertain: and consequently no Culture of the Earth; no Navigation, nor use of the commodities that may be imported by Sea; no commodious Building; no Instruments of moving, and removing such things as require much force; no Knowledge of the face of the Earth; no account of Time; no Arts; no Letters; no Society; and which is worst of all, continuall feare, and danger of violent death."[3] With law, we can cooperate; we can be assured that our projects have a future; we can benefit from the accomplishments of others; we can engage in activities other than the desperate protection of our physical existence; we can have access to all of the riches of human culture and history.

THE WORLD OF LAW

Thus far we have explored why law is necessary and what it does; now let us look at what the world of law looks like—what forms it takes and what bodies of enactment it requires so as to be actual and effective. The first thing to observe is that there are different *kinds* of laws. There must be laws governing action and interaction, yes, but law must also account for and speak to two possible failures—the failure of people to follow law, and the failure of law to justly and effectively govern action and interaction. Hence, first, we have civil law, which designates what is appropriate and inappropriate for individuals and groups in relation to each other, and how conflicts afflicting such individuals and groups should be addressed. Second, there is criminal law, which regulates treatment and punishment of the transgression of law, articulating how political bodies may prosecute people who perpetrate illegal acts against each other and the state. Third, there is constitutional law, which identifies limits for the production of law, as well as for the activities of law-making and law-executing bodies of political power; as a kind of "law of laws," it protects individuals against the bodies that exercise a necessary kind of power over law; it ensures the justness of laws.

Law must also come into existence; hence it requires a legislative body or an agent of its creation, the regulation and production of which is performed by constitutional law. Further, for the laws this body posits to be fair and effective, it must establish procedures for the communication and promulgation of law; law must be *known* in order to be followed. There must also be lawful practices for the execution of law, or apparatuses that ensure the maintenance of law in everyday life and ensure that laws actually function. These "agents of law," so to speak, are, for instance, the police, the courts, and the military. Police forces ensure adherence to laws, preventing harm and damage to people and property by being present in what they deem to be volatile situations and by responding to calls for support. It is their task to respond to the transgression of laws by apprehending those suspected of breaking them and transferring these people to figures vested with the authority to discern guilt and innocence and decide on punishment. Courts and judges, the places and people with this kind of authority of discernment, are further agents of law; judges attempt, in the context of judicial procedure, to interpret what the law requires in the context of particular situations, especially situations of dispute. Further, the military protects the existence of the community itself, ensuring its integrity and the perpetual continuation of its capacity to regulate itself and sustain its organized reality.

Police, courts, and militaries are in a sense direct agents of law, ensuring adherence to it, its application in particular situations, and its continued capacity to exist, but there are further institutions that operate *indirectly* as agents of law. The institutions of education and social welfare, for instance, cultivate and support individuals as *members* of this organized social reality, capable of participating in it, of benefiting from and contributing to it. These institutions allow for the rich filling out of the framework that law provides, for carrying out the tasks for which it provides the groundwork: they build up the actual infrastructure that will house mutual cooperation and establish and carry out the concrete methods for its execution. Educational institutions induct human beings into the broader historical and cultural world available to them because of a certain degree of social stability. They sustain, distribute, and support further development of the insights, discoveries, and developments of human history, providing fora in which they can be shared. Institutions of social welfare provide certain basic goods and resources, such as housing, food, and access to employment, when for various reasons an individual's own attempts to secure such things have failed. They are an institutional recognition of the way in which social cooperation and social stability are goods we all will, of the way in which our individual resources are sustained collectively by a large and complex socioeconomic framework, of the way in which wealth and resources are a social production.

The services these institutions and agents of law render are like law, or are the expression and embodiment of law, insofar as they ensure a certain degree of social stability, which in turn ensures a certain willingness to be out in the world and open to risk, which in turn ensures the development on the part of people of complex and cooperative activities and projects. Ideally, I will trust that the police will ensure a certain degree of safety and security in public, and I do not have to be afraid that their force will be exercised arbitrarily, such that I, for instance, have to fear being in a world that is "secured" by them; hence my mobility and my access to diverse spaces is enabled. Ideally, I will trust that if I lose my physical abilities and can no longer perform my job, or if the world of economic exchange develops in such a way that my development of the skills and infrastructure needed to provide a particular product is no longer "valuable," I will be supported by a social welfare system; here also the idea of this potential support, this system of cooperation and its provision of context for individual action, serves to encourage my undertaking of diverse projects. Further, and again, ideally, I will trust that if I am harmed by another, the legal system will take up my claim fairly and will make a rational decision about retribution and restitution; here also the mere operation of this neutral and supportive system can be sufficient to propel my agency and to instill in me a sense of confidence that others will not harm me. For my agency to be developed in a sophisticated way, in a way that contributes to a shared social life, this social context must take a certain degree of responsibility *for me*.

These institutions and agents of law are also like law with respect to the principle of fairness. In basically liberal societies, that is, these institutions are expected to distribute their goods and services in a way that is indifferent to aspects of the recipient that are irrelevant from the point of view of the goods and services being distributed. For example, the police force is expected to "distribute order" or "force" in a way that is responsive to situations of public upheaval and crime, not to its preconceived notions about the kind of people who may be prone to upheaval and criminal activity, and public educational institutions are expected to be concerned with providing education to every person of a certain age, without regard for other factors that have been deemed irrelevant, such as ability or family background. The expectation of such institutions is that they distribute goods equally or that they not consider or address individuals in ways that are arbitrary. This fairness is ensured, at least to a certain extent, by a whole host of administrative, bureaucratic, and procedural formalities that prevent institutions from being made to answer to the demands of private interest or bias, from acting or providing their goods in a way guided by individual interest or bias.

Laws and the institutions that sustain them and carry them out in the world are in these multiple ways most properly understood, in principle, as the "universal work" and the product of individuals and socially and economically distinguished groups generated in their very activity of self-definition and self-development. They are "nonlimiting limitations," goals we have if we have the goal of self-development and self-determination. And, like the rules that make possible the soccer game, they require our cooperation, our recognition of their status as the conditions and goals of our action. Most of the time, however, the posited laws and institutions that provide the context for our free agency are not explicitly the product of our volition or action; rather, they preexist this volition and action. Hegel ends section 538 with an observation of what this means for us—that laws, for individuals, "are the substance of their willing—which is thereby *free*—and their disposition," that law comes to be simply "what is done," so to speak, or "valid custom [*geltende Sitte*]," and, finally, that law can be seen as restrictive. Let us turn now to explore these aspects of law further.

THE "BECOMING-CUSTOM" OF LAW, AND THE EXPERIENCE OF LAW AS RESTRICTION

This complex fabric of social collaboration and cooperation makes itself manifest in external laws and institutions, but it is also manifested internally, in our very characters, orientations, and desires. We are inducted into the world that law structures and differentiates with the help of people whose self-understanding and sense of propriety have already been shaped by these laws and institutions. Their expectations for us and our behavior are shaped by these existent rules and standards; hence their shaping of us is already a shaping in a particular direction, with particular values, particular modes of being human. We are taught "ways of being human" by people whose criteria of acceptable and unacceptable behavior, and whose expectations and desires for us as individuals, are already shaped by the ideas of propriety expressed by laws.[4] To become a person, then, is already to have internalized standards, practices, and expectations, such that their particularity becomes in a sense invisible; they simply are part of what it comes to mean, for us, to be human. Our individual disposition takes a certain shape *because of* the laws; our obedience of them is not due simply to our conscious acknowledgment of them and their legitimacy. Rather, it is as though we find in them acknowledgment of ourselves, confirmation of the people we have become; we feel *at home* in them, in the given order and organization of our social interaction.

This inheritance is of ancient origin; the fact that space and the agency of others are amenable to our desires, our movement, and our projects is the result of many centuries of living together. Indeed, even operative governments typically do very little to change the existing political fabric and the culture of existing institutions; while their accomplishments may seem hugely important or disastrous, they are most often small in relation to the accomplishments represented by underlying institutional arrangements and the spirit of obedience to or respect for them. As Hegel writes in the Remark to section 540 of the *Encyclopaedia*,

> The question, to whom—to which authority, and to an authority organized in what way—belongs the power *to make a constitution* [*eine Verfassung*]?, is the same as the question, Who has to make the spirit of a people? . . . What is called *making* a constitution [*eine Konstitution*] . . . has never happened in history, just as the making of a code of laws has never happened. A constitution [*eine Verfassung*] . . . is the indwelling spirit and the history—and thus is history only *its* history—from which constitutions have been and are made.

Constitutions and codes of laws do not exactly get produced; the ways we have of living together always precede our emergence as individuals into a shared and organized world. Because of the fact that our individual disposition is shaped in relation to these laws—because of the "found" character of constitutions—the way in which we feel at home in the given order and organization of our social interaction can go unnoticed, and it usually does. This has two consequences: first, we can come to see our own way of life and our social world as neutral and obvious, in a way that other ways of life and social worlds are not; this disposition-shaping that is performed by law and social organization can cause us to fail to recognize the specificity of our social environment in relation to others. Second, we can underappreciate the agency of this social world in our own agency, and, as Hegel says, experience the laws and the mechanisms of their embodiment as "barriers to [our] independent freedom of choice and particular interest" (§538), for, as we saw in our discussion of traffic laws, the successful enactment of law is a form of cooperation that conceals our interaction and leaves us experiencing ourselves as operating independently of each other.

"The more freedom is established," Hegel writes, "—as security of property, as the possibility for each to develop and exercise his talents and good qualities—the more it appears to be *a matter of course*; the consciousness and the estimation of freedom then turns principally to the *subjective* sense of it" (§539). The more freedom is protected and individuals are secured in their ability to develop, the more individuals think of freedom as something that adheres to individuals in their private subjectivity and think of their accomplishments in freedom as due to their own initiative, underestimating the agency of the laws in their development and overestimating their own. There seem to be several reasons for this. First, if a given society is well developed, with a great store of resources (educational, social, economic, etc.), then the individuals in it are likely to be highly developed. One of the characteristics one has as a well-developed person, it seems, is the capacity for independence, for taking care of one's own needs and shaping the world and one's situations to fit one's desires and goals; hence the very resources that allow for this development can be rendered invisible in its accomplishment. We can lose sight of the way in which our development is due to our cooperation with and facilitation by the complex world of social resources. Second, in such a well-developed society, I am freed to take myself up as a project, to take my own development as my sole concern, and I do not immediately experience the significance of social stability for it since I am wrapped up in the project of self-development and not brought to witness the way in which instability threatens my agency. Third, the conditions of shared life can appear to us not as accomplishments but as the way the world *is*; we tend not to see the work of human agency and freedom in making these conditions, and hence we take them for granted as the given, indeed unfree, terrain *upon which* we exercise subjective freedom. Finally, the cooperation of others—an important aspect of the objective fortification of liberty—can also make itself invisible, in the fact that it is carried out substantially by a basic following of rules, which is to say, by leaving each other alone. But to see the laws and the agents of their embodiment as in principle restrictions is to see incorrectly, to fail to recognize accurately the conditions that allow one to credit so much to one's own subjectivity.

CONCLUSION

We have seen that we are in principle wrong to interpret the laws as restrictive and wrong to think of our development as our own doing. Rather, the laws are the *conditions* of action and as such its goal, and we understand them properly if we understand them as nonlimiting limitations, as an ambiguously external and internal phenomenon. Thus, while the "immediate subject" may experience laws as restrictive of her independence and particular interest, the agent who has *overcome* her immediacy—or who has come to understand her own personal life as intensely mediated by various forms of "externality"—will generally not experience the laws in this way. To *understand* the importance of what appears to be a recalcitrant and restrictive objective reality is simply to improve one's perception—to see things as they really are, as the mechanisms of freedom.[5] To know oneself, as Hegel says in his introduction to this third part of the *Encyclopaedia*, the "Philosophy of Spirit," will be to know oneself not in terms of "the *particular* abilities, character, inclinations, and weaknesses of the individual," but with respect to what is most "truthful" and "genuine" about oneself as a human being—the reality of the mediated, articulated, and organized world, the organs, body, ground, terrain of individuality (§377). To know *oneself* is to know this external world.

This does not mean that we should simply accept law in all of its forms; rather, the analysis provides an outline of the proper way in which a critical attitude toward law can take shape—indeed, a critical attitude toward law that law itself, as the condition of individual action and the substance of individual disposition, can empower. It is not the case that laws and institutions always function as they should, but a *meaningful* criticism of them requires a proper appreciation of their role and their significance. Once we develop this appreciation, we should be better equipped to correctly identify the ways in which they do operate improperly and unjustly. Laws may *cease* to act on behalf of a social body, in support of action and interaction, and become, *like* the misguided "immediate individual," wrapped up in "independent freedom of choice and particular interest" (§538). Laws can be corrupted into the service of private interest, and their agents can foster suspicion and hostility and undermine the trustworthiness of law by developing idiosyncratic ideas about specific elements of the social body or about the nature of their responsibilities. In this vein, the action that the proper functioning of laws should ultimately make possible is the action of meaningful social criticism, or meaningful critical evaluation of the laws and its agents. The cooperative, free people that laws are supposed to cultivate could, through the agency of law, become critically responsible for shaping the laws of their own communities, for cultivating laws that are actually lawful in nature, operative *as* the condition and goal of human action and interaction, and indeed, for employing the platform laws provide for creatively envisioning new possibilities for human life that may demand the transformation of these laws.

Indeed, we continue now to Hegel's discussion of the figure in the *Phenomenology* most equipped for such social criticism, that figure who has learned the reality and significance of law and yet is capable of being meaningfully critical and responsible—that is, the figure of conscience. This discussion will develop the theme of forgiveness already introduced in the essay "The Spirit of Christianity and Its Fate"—that element which supplements, with ethicality, the formal relations of law in social life and calls attention to the creative and transformative singularity of persons, which can never be captured or predicted by ethicality or done justice by formal relations of law. Once this element is articulated, we will be better able to identify the rightful place and nature of law, in a way that responds effectively to the criticisms of it that Hegel presents in his discussion of the condition of right treated in chapter 3 and in "The Spirit of Christianity and Its Fate," the essay treated in chapter 1. The place and genuinely rightful nature of law will only be understood if its relation to that which it is not—and to that which is also necessary for justice—is elaborated.

5

LAW, RIGHT, AND FORGIVENESS

The first several chapters have treated the principle of ethicality and the principle of posited law. We have seen that each is necessary for the elaboration of a society oriented by the demand to be just, but we have also become aware of the shortcomings or limitations of each, especially when each is independently taken to be the ultimate and exclusive principle of social organization or when social worlds are constructed solely on the basis of one or the other principle. Through discussion of the principles behind the legitimate operation of law in the previous chapter, we have set the stage for an account of meaningful criticism of the law or meaningful evaluation of the shortcomings it can manifest in actual practice. In this chapter we turn for such resources to a third principle, that found in Hegel's treatment of morality, the discussion of which will complete our account of Hegel's vision of the basic nature and demands of justice.

This third principle can be identified in the following phenomenon. We typically recognize that, in addition to the customary sense of "what is proper"—the "unwritten laws" of social propriety—and in addition to the explicit rules of political life, we experience a domain of answerability in which we feel individually called to answer to an absolute and universal authority—an authority, indeed, that we may experience as *commanding* us to overrule both the customary and the posited laws of everyday life. "Morality" is the general name we typically assign to this distinctive form of experience, or, more specifically, "the call of conscience." The conclusion of Hegel's discussion of "Morality" in the *Phenomenology*, entitled "Conscience. The Beautiful Soul, Evil, and Its Forgiveness,'" is, not surprisingly, the most important site for our study of this experience, but a consideration of Hegel's prior study of the nature of action in the concluding section of his "Reason" chapter, entitled "Individuality, Which to Itself Is Real in and for Itself," will help us set the context for understanding his discussion of conscience.

Hegel's study of the conscientious self, confessing and being forgiven, is powerful and interesting especially with regard to the terms of human life we have so far explored. The conscientious agent portrayed by Hegel acknowledges the significance of the relations with others by which it has come into being (what we have analyzed under the rubric of "ethical life"), as well as the significance of the laws by which these relations are organized and structured (what we have analyzed under the rubric of "law"). The conscientious self acts only as one who is profoundly aware of the significance of these motivating and organizing forces, as one whose critical attitude has been shaped by these elements. It does so, however, from the standpoint of the recognition that the burden lies upon *it* to figure out how to responsibly respond to the demand to do what is right—that only it can determine how to do justice to both the law and its ethical relations in its response to the specific situation with which it is confronted. This domain of answerability is undeniable and irreducible to the other domains—hence the significance of forgiveness as the appropriate response to this exercise of answering. Here, in the principle of the forgiveness of conscience, we will find the third element of justice.

While the principle of the forgiveness of conscience emerges as a principle that is irreducible to the operation of given custom and posited law, it exists in the name of purposes similar to those that inspire law, and in a way that is responsive to the power of ethicality. With the concept of conscience, Hegel describes the coexistence of singular initiative and social membership; he describes the way in which a community and the universal principles of its organization exist only through their expression in and recognition by individuals, whose actions, as singular, both construct this community and the universal but at the same time subvert them and thus need forgiveness. Indeed, Hegel shows that transgression and reconciliation are both essential aspects of justice.

In order to construct the ground upon which to show the relevance of Hegel's theory of forgiveness to his theory of law as custom and law as right, this chapter, following Hegel, enacts a kind of phenomenology of action, finding out from this consideration of action what it is and what it requires for its support. The chapter treats: a) the phenomenon of individual action and the forms of social life in the *Phenomenology* that are organized in terms of custom ("ethical life") and posited law ("the condition of right"); b) the way in which the principle of the forgiveness of conscience illuminates and resolves the challenges involved in these elements of social life; and c) the transformation of law and custom suggested by Hegel's discussion of conscience and forgiveness. In this chapter I briefly describe how individual action relies on universal standards and shared social practices and how universal law can only take shape in relation and response to inherently singular action that is never adequate or identical to law—how an ongoing process of forgiveness and reconciliation between them is necessary to the existence of each. I also show that any way of conceiving of action and law that does not acknowledge and take up this truth is irrevocably flawed. For the present the discussion is limited to the internal logic of the *Phenomenology* and the significance of conscientious action and its forgiveness to social life; in later chapters I turn more explicitly to identifying the ways in which Hegel's discussion here offers an alternative to contemporary legal and political thought.

INDIVIDUAL ACTION AND LAW IN THE PHENOMENOLOGY

Before we turn to Hegel's most explicit discussions of the concepts of conscientious action, confession, and forgiveness, we will visit (and revisit) other sites in his work in which he describes the nature, specifically, of *individual action* as it takes place in the context of a community structured by principles regulating such action. "Individuality, Which to Itself Is Real in and for Itself," particularly the subsection called "The Spiritual Animal Kingdom," sets out some of the significant characteristics of action, and Hegel's discussions of ethical life and the condition of right set out two different versions of the possible legal terms by which individual action can be regulated or organized. As we have already seen in the previous chapters, Hegel articulates the nature of action and law on a trajectory that is delimited by two extremes: first, the self-asserting action of a self-interested and isolated individuality, and second, the self-asserting law of an authoritative "ethical life" or community. While action appears to be irreducibly individual and law immediately universal, Hegel shows each to be implicated in and necessary to the other. Forgiveness is the concept Hegel uses to illustrate this relation between action and law, between individual and universal, a relation by which the significance of both action and law is transformed.

ACTION IN THE SPIRITUAL ANIMAL KINGDOM

Let us begin with Hegel's initial, focused description of the phenomenon of action, in what he calls the "spiritual animal kingdom," and then move to his discussion of law, which his analysis of the "spiritual animal kingdom" shows to be necessary. In this part of the book Hegel is investigating, through a series of stages, the question of whether the individual on her own is sufficient to explain the meaningfulness of her own action. The study of the "spiritual animal kingdom" demonstrates that the idiosyncrasies of the individual's perspective cannot be relied on to explain the social mediation integral to the meaningfulness of the individual's action. In subsequent studies, Hegel investigates whether individual reason—as universal, and not idiosyncratic—is sufficient to explain the significance of social mediation. Specifically, he investigates whether reason is sufficient to create or adjudicate the laws that would define the meaningful parameters of social interaction. Just as the idiosyncrasies of individual perspective were seen to be insufficient to explain action, so is the universality of individual reason insufficient.

In his discussion of this "spiritual animal kingdom," Hegel explores a central idea that comes to the fore in the consideration of action—that in it is manifest a preoccupation with the self and an impulse to self-expression. The basic aspects of this central idea can be captured by the following: when I act, I assert my presence in the world; I mobilize my interpretation of the world's significance and of what the world requires from me; I bring what is internal to me into externality; I effect a connection between me and the world that is driven by my own conception of myself and the world. All of these motives behind action can be portrayed as belonging to the self and as responding to the self's sense of its own prerogative.

The performance of an action, however, brings to light different aspects of action than those reflected in this central idea: action has consequences that are outside of the individual's control and it invokes standards beyond that of adequacy to the self by whom they are performed. First, when the agent acts, her action becomes vulnerable to the interpretations of others, and thus the significance of her very self, which is expressed in that action, becomes different from what the agent had imagined about herself. Second, through acting the self discovers standards for action beyond that of fidelity to self-interest and self-expression. That is, the inevitable *publicity* of action gives rise to uncertainty in the individual with respect to her own nature and motives and confronts her with other realities—persons, situations, consequences, and so on—

for which she might be concerned. Action implicates the individual in the world to such an extent that the significance of this action cannot be infallibly predicted or known, and the self-interest and self-concept the individual expresses through this action are open to transformation. These factors demand a different understanding of action than the one with which the spiritual animal kingdom begins (and that reflects our own default, "individualist" assumption)—that action involves the simple self-expression and self-interest of a given individual. Action, that is, must be understood as dual in nature, as both essentially public and essentially private. It is intimately tied to the individual's interiority, but it forces the individual into contact with the social framework that ultimately "interprets" action and, it turns out, demands its integration and regulation.[1]

These two aspects of action make it an ambivalent site—the site of a certain kind of tension between what is (or seems to be) external and what is (or seems to be) internal to the individual. Some of the indicators of the significance of action lie *outside* the individual—in the interpretations of others, in other actions, in the consequences the action has in the world. Thus, in order for the individual to actually carry out *her* action effectively, she would have to be able to orchestrate and bring into harmony this bewildering multiplicity of factors, which she simply cannot do on her own, since doing so requires the cooperation of others, and their cooperation can only be offered, freely, by them. What this shows, in other words, is that the individual's own knowledge and intentions, on their own, are not competent or sufficient to establish the significance of action and that the individual does not have the vision or understanding necessary to organize and harmonize the action of multiple individuals, even though such organization is necessary in order that she be able to carry out her individual action. The question of what is right and proper is not answerable simply by the individual; it is not solely her prerogative to decide on the answer to this question. Her action does not belong solely to her as the product of her self-expression; this action implicates the individual in a world, which actively reflects back to the individual the significance of that action and herself in a way that matters to her. What to do, what is right, is a public or worldly question or issue, since the doing of it is not only beholden to the actor's interpretation; action is a uniting of individual and world.

The actor also, however, insistently and inevitably expresses her singularity, never acting in a way that is seamlessly compatible and integrated with the world and with all the action, interests, and expectations of others that essentially matter to her and that are always significant with regard to the meaning of her action. On the contrary, the action of the individual will always be essentially discontinuous with the world into which it enters, and this is the case even though in acting the actor undermines that very context that makes her action possible and lends it significance. To be an individual is to be beholden to an external world that decides upon the significance of one's action, but it is also to be persistently incapable of adequately reflecting one's indebtedness to that world in acting.

Law is the conceptual next step, since this analysis of action has shown the need for law. The invocation of law is a response to this ungoverned multiplicity of human action in the public realm, a response to the demand expressed *by* individuals in their individual action—that they be able to undertake it in the way that they want, without encountering too many obstacles in the outside world, and that they be able to more or less effectively predict what kind of significance it has. Law emerges as a response to the need for regulation and organization of these independently acting selves so that their action can be what it is. Hegel thus moves—in the section called "Law-Giving Reason"—to a consideration of the attitude of rationality that tries to compensate for these problems inherent to action by attempting to posit a law, a standard that can be public and held in common by all.[2]

It is possible for this need for law to be recognized and for individuals to take it upon themselves to respond to this need by saying, effectively, "If I simply rely upon reason, I can find a rule to follow to which we should all agree." This is an attempt to stay within the resources of the individual and to solve the problems of human sociality through appeal to the abstract universality of reason. This reason tries to regulate the "animal realm," to make it human, by a simple appeal to the norms of indifferent universality that are inherently available to all individuals.

Such an indifferent universality, however, is insufficient to address the inherent particularity of human social situations; this positing of law is also incoherent and unsustainable. Law is *of a different logic* than reason: law is a principle for determining how to make the appropriate decision in response to the concrete and specific circumstances unique to situations of human action, whereas reason is a rule for determining situations in indifference to their particularities. Whereas law must answer, "What about this?," reason in principle has nothing to say to "this" as such. Initially, then, we see that the appeal simply to the individual's self-expression is insufficient to establish a coherent realm of human action; now we see that appeal to the individual's reason is likewise insufficient to establish such a realm.

Hegel then turns to consider what he calls "law-testing reason"—that is, the stance of rationality that, rather than trying to give law, instead tries to determine whether specific, posited laws conform to the demands of rationality, even if they are not generated from them. But the problem with law-testing reason is similar to that of law-giving reason: again, there are many actions that would be conformable to the form of law, and the universality of reason is once more shown to be insufficient as a guide for particular contexts.

What is revealed through this analysis, which is essentially a *reductio ad absurdum* of the attempt to explain action and sociality on the basis of individuality, is that law and social organization are significant, but that it is never individuals who simply determine these things on their own. As we have already seen, law, custom, tradition, and all of the accompanying institutions and structures of social life bring these individual subjects *into being*, preceding and sculpting the rationality that these individuals subsequently invoke, in turn, to formulate, identify, and interpret law, custom, and tradition. Law, custom, and tradition, are given inheritances, not simply creations, that provide an *already* established and meaningful content for action. This is why Hegel makes the radical transition, in the next chapter of the *Phenomenology*, to the history that precedes the emergence of a modern "spiritual animal kingdom," the individualistic culture of Western modernity, by studying the ancient Greek ethical life and the Roman condition of right that we have already analyzed in earlier chapters. Let us revisit briefly Hegel's discussion of law-based human society, so as to discern its import for the present discussion.

Law in Ethical Life and the Condition of Right

We have explored the notion of ethical life in quite a bit of detail already; here I simply want to call attention briefly to a particular aspect of it for the sake of the specific analysis of the present chapter. Of interest here is the way in which ethical life *obligates* people, or the particular kind of power it has to give people a sense of what must be done. This ethical life is structured by certain kinds of rules about what people should do, by which they feel obliged but in an immediate and unself-conscious way. These rules are not like traffic laws or like the bylaws of an organization, which are the results of self-conscious human insight and decision into how human things should be organized so as to function smoothly, or into how to structure and organize interaction in a shared world. Rules that are consciously posited in this way may feel like an imposition, in that they are not something automatically adopted, whereas the "laws" and rules of ethical life make up the fabric of *what it is to be "us"*; they express our basic orientation to the world and our basic sense of how to interact with others.[3] They give Antigone, for instance, a sense of who she is; she can be herself in acting according to these social rules and expectations. Persons, effectively 'characters' in a script, identify immediately with the laws of ethicality, finding in these laws their meaning, their identity, and their reasons for action.

As we have seen, however, the immediacy of this identification is problematic: the priority of "the way things are done" precludes any recognition and expression of the singularity of these ethical agents, of their irreducibility to social roles and expectations. The community of ethical life is in a sense certain of itself, confirmed in its traditional beliefs and values through these agents, but these agents have no role to play in the determination of what the law is, and their singularity is unheeded by it.

In the condition of right, on the other hand, what is essential is no longer the community and its unconscious rules, but the *single person* in his self-certainty. Personal right attaches to a self-certain individual, just as customary law attached to a self-certain community. The condition of right seems to recognize the significance of individual choice in that right is mobilized to protect and secure the power of self-determination, to free the individual from any predetermined social ties, obligations, and identifications, and to do this on a *universal* basis, for everyone. This is a significant response to the limitations facing individuals in ethical life; it is the assertion of a universal principle by which to protect *each* individual in his self-determination, no matter what his "ethical" commitments or coordinates are. As we have seen, however, the priority that right gives to the individual is only artificial. The right that "protects" him affords him no means for the meaningful expression and elaboration of his unique significance, even foreclosing the avenues of such expression, and it prevents him from experiencing his continuity with others. He loses any positive or productive relationship to that which was previously essential—the "ethical substance"—or to any social contexts, relations, and practices that would give him something to choose. This kind of right, then, ultimately inhibits the very self-determination it is intended to empower.[4] Both the system of given laws in ethical life and the system of positive law in the condition of right disable individual action, for neither officially or unofficially recognizes the reality of the individual behind it.

But systems of customary law and the system of positive law, as we have discussed and will discuss further, are both significant and irreducibly necessary to human life; how singular, individual action can be reconciled with these legal systems is the question that Hegel pursues in "Conscience. The Beautiful Soul, Evil, and Its Forgiveness." The philosophical framework that concludes with forgiveness in fact reconciles the extremes represented by both formal and customary legal systems, on the one hand, and the self-interested action of the spiritual animal kingdom and the self-centeredness of the legal person, on the other. In this framework, in other words, an identification with universal humanity and with a particular way of life that subordinates singularity is reconciled with an individual self-certainty that negates or destroys the significance of universality and particularity. Hence it is the culminating shape in the *Phenomenology*'s analysis of law.[5] The framework of conscience and its forgiveness presents a model of individual action in which individuals act for the purpose of singular self-determination (which was impossible in ethical life), while simultaneously acting on the basis of shared customs and engendering active interaction with others (impossible in the condition of right) and contributing to the construction and sustenance of the universal principles that organize social life (impossible in ethical life). Let us now turn to a closer examination of this framework, beginning with a close investigation of the figure in the *Phenomenology* that leads Hegel to introduce the concept of forgiveness—the figure of the conscientious self.

"CONSCIENCE. THE BEAUTIFUL SOUL, EVIL, AND ITS FORGIVENESS"

Hegel's analysis of what it is to act morally comes to a head in the concluding section of his chapter on "Spirit," the section called "Conscience. The Beautiful Soul, Evil, and Its Forgiveness." In this section, Hegel describes first the basic experience of acting on "conviction" (*die Überzeugung*), describing in particular the ways in which such conscientious action inevitably produces conflict, as different agents experience the moral import of each other's actions differently. Hegel then describes the interplay between the experiences of *acting* conscientiously, taking upon oneself the authority for intervening in and transgressing upon the domains of others, and conscientiously *judging* or *criticizing* another's actions for their transgressive character. His study concludes with a description of the experience of mutual forgiveness in the ultimate recognition of the *necessarily* transgressive character of all action. In what follows, I will work through Hegel's discussion of the dynamic unfolding of the relationship between the "acting consciousness" and the "judging consciousness," in order to show how and why conscience in general, and the practice of mutual forgiveness specifically, presents the ultimate terms in which our human action is to be understood.

In his study of the acting and judging consciousness, Hegel continues the description of the inherent one-sidedness of action that we began investigating in his section on the "spiritual animal kingdom." Here, in his discussion of conscientious action, Hegel investigates the discovery, on the part of the "acting consciousness"—on the part, that is, of the one who chooses to intervene in the public world on the basis of its conscientiously held moral convictions—that it is not possible for human beings to perform "pure duty" (that is, to live up to the unconditioned standard of the "categorical imperative" imagined by a Kantian "law-giving reason") or to answer perfectly to the ideal of absolute goodness. Instead, this self discovers that any *conscientious* action, though intended as an unbiased fulfillment of duty, is always nonetheless a matter of acting on *its own* personal convictions and could thus only be a one-sided, contingent realization of its own subjective perspective. Its action is always in principle open to such a criticism from others. In fact, however, inasmuch as no action can be exempted from this situation, this is the *only* way that the agent—and, indeed, any others—can act. Everyone can be judged to have fallen short of the accomplishment of the good, because every actor is singular and specific, having specific and partial insight, and finding herself not in global situations but in specific ones, to which general rules can never speak exhaustively. For that very reason, however, even the act of accusing the acting self of such one-sidedness, can, *qua* act, be itself accused of being one-sided. Overcoming this one-sidedness in judgment is what Hegel argues is ultimately accomplished in the act of forgiveness, for this is the gesture that recognizes about itself that it must not hold the good apart from the one-sidedness of action, but it must instead recognize that the good has one-sidedness as its *only possible domain of realization*. To forgive is to embrace the propriety of what could always be condemned for falling short of the ideal and therefore to treat what is inherently perspectival and relative as, so to speak, "the absolute."

There are two points of principal importance that we should draw from this analysis of conscientious action, transgression, and forgiveness. First, as far as the conscientious self knows, the good has no universal or perfect being to carry it out, so if *it*, as conscientious, cares about the good it must act anyway, even in light of the many obstacles in its path that stem from its inevitable partiality. Second, since the conscientious self knows that it must act upon its own insight, and that no rule or law could dictate in every situation what it should do, then it also knows the significance of its own inward perspective in explaining its action, and that means, further, that it should recognize as well the significance of the inward perspectives of others in explaining their actions. "There is something to be understood here," says the conscientious self to itself, when faced by the sometimes mysterious character of the actions of others—simply because it knows of itself, of its own inwardness, that there is something to be understood. Let us turn now to an examination of Hegel's analysis of the experience of conscience, keeping in mind these two issues: 1) the incapacity of law to speak to us directly and to give us meaningful guidance in the singular, specific contexts in which decision and action are required, and 2) the fact that the need to rely on one's own conscientious insight is a need that is shared by *all*, to the extent that understanding another's action requires that I learn from that other her own understanding of her behavior or her own intention.

There are two figures in Hegel's analysis of this framework, because, first, there are two opposed ways to be conscientious (that is, to act and to judge an action, or to be discerning), and second, the solution to the problem each encounters singly is to be discovered in their interaction. Let us consider these two sides of conscience.

The first side of this pair, "acting consciousness," acts in the world according to its immediately held conviction about *what* is called for in *this* situation. By its action, it implicitly affirms a criticism of an abstract morality or duty ("law-giving reason"), implying that an abstract rule is insufficient to speak to the unique contingencies of *this* situation, whereas genuine duty requires that it respond immediately in a way suitable to the moral urgency of the moral demand—that is, *now*, in the context of the imperfect insight of the personal perspective of the agent.[6] To act conscientiously is to assert that one must rely upon one's own insight, which means that to act conscientiously is in fact to act "in opposition to the acknowledged universal, according to [one's] *own* inner law and conscience" (M662, S486)—according to one's own *certainty* that one does right, not according to an independently establishable "truth of the matter."[7] In doing this, acting consciousness *explicitly* does its best to be an agent of the good, taking responsibility upon itself to act on behalf of the ultimate interest of all others; and yet, in so doing, acting consciousness in fact *implicitly* wrongs others. It wrongs others in that its action is always a gesture in an intersubjective space, as we saw through analysis of the "spiritual animal kingdom," and in this space it is effectively asserting the authority of its own interpretation of the law or duty *over* that of others; making the law exist "for the sake of the self," when others know it to exist for them, and when it actually should exist for all, or for the sake of their co-existence (M639, S469); and doing all of this even though its knowledge of the full situation is incomplete. For this reason, this actor is called "evil" and is said to indulge in "hypocrisy" (M660, S485). Rather than appearing as the richest form of experience, taking responsibility in itself for embodying the "absolute," it thus appears as "consciousness . . . in its poorest form" (M657, S482).

The one who makes this accusation against the "acting consciousness" is the "judging consciousness." This second figure of the pair is an outside perspective on the action of the first self, and it sees in the actor's action a refusal to respect the standards and structures that situate people in relation to each other.[8] The judge condemns the actor in the name of what is universally right or good, accusing the other of being interested in itself and not the good and of having a one-sided and contingent perspective rather than an absolute commitment to an absolute good. The judge, then, would seem to have absolute moral authority on its side—would appear to be justified, that is, in condemning the selfish one-sidedness of the acting consciousness. But let us consider what is implicit in the practice of judgment: in making its judgment, the judge appeals "to its *own* law, just as the evil consciousness appeals to *its* law" (M663, S487), and "the content that it gives to that knowing is taken from its own self, as *this specific* self, is taken from itself as a natural individuality" (M659, S484–85). In order to criticize the acting consciousness, then, the judging consciousness must thus itself commit the same offence—that of arrogating to itself absolute authority—for which it criticizes the other.

The judge's condemnation of the actor is thus in fact a matter of hypocrisy. In its judgment, the judge cannot be said to speak on behalf of what is universally right or good, because it is selecting to notice only that aspect of the action—namely, its irreducible singularity—that seems important to it, and it is therefore no more "universal" in its perspective than is the acting consciousness. Furthermore, the judge's action of condemnation *itself* has more than one side, and, noticing an aspect different from the one the righteous judge notices in its self-interpretation, *we* can see the evil aspect of this action of condemnation. The judge's act of judgment is a condemnable act first because it assesses the actor unfairly, and thus immorally condemns another. It is condemnable, second, because it is in fact the taking of a stand *against action as such*, which is to say, *against the very possibility of realizing the good.* The judge does not *do* anything, even though the good *requires* agents. The judge "wants its judging to be taken for an *actual* deed, and instead of proving its rectitude by actions, does so by uttering fine sentiments" (M664, S487). The self-righteous judge is guilty of immorality, then, because in its judgment it appeals to its *own* law, and in its failure to act, it asserts that it values its own "moral purity" over the good—it is, as Hegel describes it, a "beautiful soul" that refuses to besmirch its purity by acting (M658, S484).

The relation between these two individuals is one of conflict: the acting consciousness seems to stand for transgressive, self-centered action, and the judging consciousness seems to stand for the harsh law that opposes that individual action. Yet each also brings something significant to this conflict. While the actor in a sense expresses disregard for the existent universal principles by which its social reality is organized, taking its own self-certainty to be "the essential being *opposed to the in-itself* or the *universal*, which counts only as a moment" (M660, S485), it also shows through its action that the good requires some version of this.[9] The *sole* agents of the good are individuals whose intentions cannot be proven to be morally pure, for they *always* rely on inward insight that cannot be made completely transparent (either to the agent herself or to others) or be neutrally analyzed by an unambiguous moral standard. Action will always be marked by the singular individuality from whence it ensues, and the good will always be more than an individual could possibly know or enact.[10] In order to be brought into being, what is right or good must be interpreted and done in a determinate way and by a singular self. And just as it is always possible that the actor is simply being selfish, so is it always possible that the actor is acting at the behest of the good, and at the behest of its conviction that it is called by the good to be its necessary medium. Similarly, while the judge refrains from itself doing anything to accomplish good in the world, pledging fidelity to the idea of goodness while not doing anything for it but self-assuredly presuming to judge in its name, the judge's stance is not simply bad, for the good *does* require judgment and discernment, however partial such judgment and discernment will be. Further, the judge's judgment is in a sense correct: the action of the acting consciousness is transgressive.[11]

Thus, while each consciousness is one-sided, and therefore criticizable, each is also essentially good.[12] Indeed, it is the recognition of just this point that defines the attitude of forgiveness.

It is the logical similarity between these two forms of consciousness—the acting consciousness and the judging consciousness—that provides the ground for the transformation of their relationship of conflict into a relationship of reconciliation. Because the judge's criticism of one-sidedness is in principle correct, the actor is capable of recognizing this real problem with its action on its own and is capable of confessing its selfishness. In Hegel's portrayal of this dynamism as an interaction of two consciousnesses, he imagines the actor turning to the judge, expecting confession to be met by the judge with understanding and identification: the acting consciousness expects sympathy from a judge who will recognize their shared plight of participating in the universal condition of one-sidedness and of inadequacy with regard to the universal ideal of goodness—from a judge, that is, who will similarly confess its own one-sidedness. In this act of confession, the acting consciousness introduces something new to the situation: the actor, in turning to the domain of communication, introduces the possibility of replacing the conflict of one-sided perspectives with the accomplishment of a shared perspective. In so doing, the actor implicitly recognizes that "the good" demands of the actor that it shape a context in which it and the other can come to a mutual understanding, a situation in which it may be able to make its perspective known in the perspective of the other and open itself to the same from the other. The actor thus in fact *supersedes* "its particularity, and in so doing posit[s] itself in continuity with the other as a universal" (M667, S490–91); it "declares their *identity* in its confession" (M666, S490). It understands itself to be a *moment* of a larger whole in separation from which it cannot make authoritative sense of its own action, being, and speech. Here this conscientious self finally realizes the reality of what it means to be self-conscious—to be self-conscious, that is, is to recognize, all at once, the significance of the larger social reality in which it participates and the fact that it can only take responsibility in and for that reality by acting individually and then by answering for that action through reconciling communication with others.

The confession of the acting consciousness, however, does not yet resolve everything, and here Hegel makes another significant point. Since communication is now recognized as the real site of moral action and interaction, and since communication is necessarily an action shared by two or more individuals, it is not sufficient for one individual to come to this recognition of the nature of its action and of what is actually significant *on its own*. The individual relies on others to help bring this situation about; the demands of reality and truth cannot simply be answered to by *one* being.[13] A single individual can have agency in making this shared situation come about by attempting to bring about a world in which others freely come to this recognition themselves and share themselves with it. To illustrate this point, Hegel shows what happens when the judge refuses to respond with a reciprocal and sympathetic confession of one-sidedness. Presuming itself to be fundamentally incapable of such a transgression and thus unconcerned with acknowledging solidarity in the unavoidable practice of transgression, the judge refuses to recognize the actor's confession and to forgive its transgression, let alone acknowledge its own. In response to the judge's refusal to act and to identify with the other, Hegel uses what might be the strongest language of condemnation in the *Phenomenology*: the judge, he says, "is forsaken by and . . . denies spirit" *and* hinders the "other's return from the deed into the spiritual existence of speech and into the identity of spirit" (M667, S491).[14] The actor can only make actual its recognition of the truth about individuality if the judge collaborates with it in coming to an understanding, but the judge has made this ultimate act of sharing impossible.

The lesson we should learn from all of this is that if singular insight and action are the necessary media by which the good is achieved in the world, then the reality of this inward perspective needs to be attested to and not merely judged by standards of universality or custom that are in some way inappropriate and alien to it. In other words, the reality of this inward perspective must be *understood*, which can only occur in the context of concrete, unique interaction. The actor has shown itself to be prepared for this, and thus the judge should see in the actor's confession the good it was trying to accomplish, the establishing of a context in which what is essentially human can be shared, for this can only happen if actual interaction occurs. Hegel in fact portrays the judging consciousness making the realization for which the situation calls in the act in which the "hard heart" of the judge is moved to forgiveness.[15] Forgiveness, as an act of accepting the transgressive action, is implicitly a recognition that transgressive singularity is shared, and that the significance of singularity to the good can be witnessed to in a way that itself enacts the good. The *real* good involves the actual relation of the two consciousnesses to each other and their identification with each other, the sharing and the understanding of singularity.[16] Each remains inevitably and irreversibly self-centred, incapable of being otherwise, but in confession and forgiveness what is added is a concern for the other that emerges from one's awareness of one's own inevitable self-centredness and a commitment to recognizing the singular insights of others upon which any actualization of the good relies. Concern for the other is manifest, on the one hand, in the fact that conscientious action is undertaken at all, in response to a situation in the world demanding action, but, since that response could be wrong-headed, concern for the other is also manifest, on the other hand, in recognition of the equal priority of the other, which is revealed in both confession and forgiveness.

This situation of confession and forgiveness is thus a mutual recognition of conscientiousness, which leads both the actor and the judge to displace themselves as the center of reality, recognizing that this center lies instead in their interaction and enacting a different kind of community than the communities of ethicality and universal right in that recognition. Inasmuch as our necessary condition is one of transgressing upon each other in our very efforts to act on principle, our mutual recognition amounts to the recognition that we are all, as Harris observes, "hypocrites *together*."[17] It is our concrete practice of accepting the necessarily finite (and thus hypocritical) perspectives of ourselves and our actual others that is "the reconciling *Yea*, in which the two 'I's let go their antithetical *existence*"; this "reconciling *Yea* . . . is the *existence* of the 'I' which has expanded into a duality" (M671, S494). It is only in thus establishing such a "we" that the hypocrisy of our self-defined singularity is overcome, and the coherent reality of the "I" is ultimately established. Thus, just as Hegel showed us the distinctive worlds developed around the principles of ethicality and right, so here we can imagine a world enacted around the practice of forgiveness, a particular kind of sharing and community that comes to be on the basis of the unique terms of each situation.

Forgiveness is offered if each recognizes what is in fact the case—that each must engage with the singularity of the other and enact its own singularity, in the context of a world that is shared, and that only this sharing, interaction, and co-dependence allow each one the opportunity for coherent self-expression. The very fact of action leads us conceptually to the necessity of forgiveness as a demand that is constantly upon us—actions can be made sense of if we accept the demand to interpret their significance, not solely in the terms of our singular perspectives, but according to the demands of sharing significance—that is, according the demands of having our perspectives and the perspectives of others be answerable to each other in the accomplishing of a shared interpretation, a shared discourse.

Recalling, now, our earlier discussions of ethical and posited law, we can also here recognize that this establishing of a shared interpretation, inasmuch as it demands of us that we be open to the singularity of the other's perspective, requires that we go beyond the terms of our established traditions and laws: the imperative of reconciliation is the imperative of establishing a *novel* communication with a singular perspective that does not automatically share the given, "external" terms for articulating sense. The singularity of conscientious action is, as we have seen, transgressive of the situations of others, and this transgression is equally the transgression of the established terms for doing things, a challenge to "the way things are" in which one asserts the *necessity* of making a singular intervention into a situation. Such transgression is inherently disruptive, but it is equally the very medium of our sharing. It is our "hypocritical" finitude that is the fundamental realization of our free humanity, and it is in recognizing and protecting this that we most fully act morally. Our moral concern for the world makes itself ultimately manifest in a concern for understanding this medium in its unique, singular, and historical manifestations, through our ongoing, unique, and singular interaction with others.

What is significant here is not simply the original action that was confessed and the original judgment that was revoked, but the communicative interaction that follows from confession and forgiveness, and this reveals yet another point that is important to note, concerning language. Conscientious selves perform determinate actions, but the significance of these selves cannot be reduced to the significance of these actions and the shape these actions take in the world. Indeed, through their capacity to use *language*, agents can transform, for both themselves and others, the significance of the things that they have done. On the one hand, the real, determinate things in the world are the results of action and testify to the presence of conscientiousness; they are not simply inert being, but signs of the exercise and accomplishments of conscientious action, the more-than-objective—or "spiritual," as Hegel might call it—presence of dynamic human beings. On the other hand, however, the real and determinate things that the conscientious self accomplishes and with which it interacts are not exactly adequate to or expressive of the nature of conscientiousness; it can come to learn or believe something new, for instance, that would transform its attitude toward its accomplishments. What is significant for an individual is not just any specific, determinate deed or product, but its insight, intention, and conviction, and it can conscientiously separate itself from any determinate thing it accomplishes, even though its very identity depends on its enactment of determinate things. Conscientious selves, says Hegel, know and declare this in the medium of language, through which they can share and understand each other's attestations as to their convictions, independently of the determinate things they accomplish. As Hegel writes, "the content of the language of conscience is the *self that knows itself as essence*. This alone is what it declares, and this declaration is the true actuality of the act and the validating of action. Consciousness declares its *conviction*" (M653, S479)—"*this alone*," and not the ultimate value of any determinate action. Language is the real world in which conscience lives, the genuine site of its achievement, because having language means having the power to communicate intention, to give an interpretation of the products of action, to share and be shared with.

Hence, the "word of reconciliation" *is*, Hegel claims, "*existent* spirit" (M670, S493); the language of reconciliation, the "reconciling *Yea*" (M671, S494), is an act and word that reconciles singularity and universality, a common sharing that is premised on the acknowledgment of singularity. Existent spirit intuits, as Hegel writes, "the pure knowledge of itself as *universal* essence in its opposite, in the pure knowledge of itself as the *singularity* that exists absolutely in itself [*der absolute in sich seienden* Einzelheit]—a reciprocal recognizing that is *absolute* spirit" (M670, S493). The experience of forgiveness is a central human experience: it is the experience of interaction and communication with actual selves, of coming to see oneself understood and acknowledged in another, of experiencing a unity with another that is *created* by our *interaction*, not simply already in being on the basis of our happening to exist in the same culture or tradition, or happening to be recognized by law as equal. Hegel states that "its actuality itself is only this, to be and to live in connection with others" (M645, S475); this is where human life really happens. The significance of Hegel's treatment of conscience is that it responds to this reality—to the fact that human life happens *here*, in the singularity of identity and the singularity of human interaction, beyond the (also real) systems of universality and particularity reflected in law and ethical life. The significance of Hegel's treatment of conscience is that it testifies to the significance of *created* unity, unity made real by *individuals together* in the context of their everyday attempts to make themselves in interaction with each other and the world around them.

CONSCIENCE, FORGIVENESS, AND THE SYSTEMS OF ETHICAL LIFE AND LAW

To understand more deeply what conscience and forgiveness are and what they entail, let us look more closely at how they implicitly resolve the shortcomings of ethical life and the condition of right. A system based on the universal rights of personhood, akin to that of the condition of right, is inadequate to the task of developing a sustainable relationship between human and world. The universal of the condition of right is one that shuts the person out of that system that defines her, inhibits the possibility of solidarity, and, by draining social life of its import, actually inhibits the possibility of self-determination. It founds an individual who, upon claiming her rights, is free to leave behind the terrain of human interaction. If the law operates solely on the basis of the formal identity of all, it does an injustice to the difference and dynamic becoming of the individuals that constitute it. Similarly, a system based on universal custom, akin to that of ethical life, is inadequate to the task of developing a sustainable relationship between human and world, for it does not recognize the singularity of each person and the singularity of their interaction, in a sense presuming that all truths about human identity and interaction have already been discovered and established. If custom operates solely on the basis of the familiar, it does an injustice to the possibility that something new or different could be introduced through singular insight and singular interaction. The model of conscience and its forgiveness provides a powerful alternative to the accounts of human agency and social interaction at work in the worlds of ethical life and the condition of right.

The sharedness and commonality that follow from the practice of forgiveness come not through the contingent fact of belonging to the same culture or community, nor through the fact, indifferent to individual singularity, of having equal rights, but through the experience and witnessing of singularity through communication.[18] *This* sharedness and commonality come from using universally available words, the universality of language, for the expression of a singular identity which without the universality of language would be inaccessible; they come from interacting in a universally available space to express a singularity that is inaccessible if it is not freely explained; they come from having an impact on people, and being impacted by them, through action that is accessible in principle and genuinely sharing that action in the sense of making it understood; they make possible the sharing of a universally available world by the sharing of orientations to it. Each person can in principle make herself somewhat understandable to others and can make her perspective speak to the terms of the other's perspective through language. The imperative facing the conscientious self is to learn—and not unreflectively embrace, as in ethical life—the fact of this solidarity through action, to recognize itself as implicated in the construction and sustenance of the good, even through its transgressive activity. The imperative is to learn the necessity and significance of conscientious self-assertion through and in response to interaction with others, and not—as in the condition of right—to immediately and independently assert self-certainty.

Action is always an interpretation and a reconfiguration of existing norms and practices; it always threatens to bring about a new understanding of the significance of laws and principles. Through this action and the forgiveness or understanding of it we keep these norms and practices, these laws and principles, accountable to the human beings in the name of whom they exist. In action, we implicitly express a concern not immediately for law and custom, but for other selves, and Hegel's discussion of confession and forgiveness seeks to reveal that priority to us and describe it for us, which is especially important insofar as it is often not taken to be a priority.[19]

Let us explore one final element that sets conscientious interaction apart from the interaction belonging to the familiarity of ethical life and that belonging to the formality of right: the infinite possibility of coming to understand. While ethical life always makes itself present as the irrefutable past out of which we emerge, and right or law protects the persons we are in the present, in abstraction from our pasts, the practice of singular interaction always presents the possibility of newness or lies ahead of us as something different that we have not yet captured or experienced. We can describe this point in at least two ways. First, the attitude of conscience is implicitly committed to the possibility of communication with anybody, and this means that the possibility of connection or interaction with innumerable, disparate others is always open to it. The conscientious self is in principle committed to the communication of its singular insight, in words that all, in principle, can hear and understand as expressions of such insight; what conscience says is open to being understood, beyond the confines of any particular form of identity and any particular action, by being more or less communicable in the universal community of language users. The conscientious self can extend beyond the confines of its customary world and engage in singular interaction with anybody, bringing to life the interaction made possible but not actual by the universality of personhood; the interaction that takes shape among conscientious selves is not interaction on the basis of familiarity, nor interaction on the basis of formality, but interaction that is constructed in response to the characteristics, qualities, and interests that singularly emerge in it. What this means, further, is that the "we" of actual conscientious selves—its communities of familiarity and solidarity—could also always take different shapes; the conscientious self could restructure itself around the introduction of new communicators and the introduction of new kinds of significance and value. Second, and similarly, the nature of the conscientious self is not exhaustively captured by the real and determinate things in the world, such as its actions, the products of action, its traditions, its communities, associations, and families. The conscientious self could always become something new, define itself differently, or find itself an obligated member of a different "world," and identifying its conscientious conviction as the site of its real identity emphasizes the centrality of this capacity for transformation, of the possibility that it could always describe itself anew. The conscientious self, in sum, is implicitly committed to the inherent plasticity of its meaning and identity.[20]

It is not the case, however, that the terms and conditions elaborated in the ways of life presented in "Ethical Life" and "The Condition of Right" become insignificant in the face of conscientious action, discernment, and interaction.[21] In action, in understanding, and in the practices of confession and forgiveness, these other mechanisms of sharing—customary and positive law—are also real and always mobilized. Our understanding of each other also involves understanding how our "ethical life" and our "universal personhood" have had an impact on our singular individuality and interaction. As we have already seen, our understanding of each other relies on our recognition of the ways in which our communities of cultivation and the universal community of abstract, universal personhood have an irreducible impact on our formation as individuals and on our interaction. While the individual can only participate in the ongoing life of the law and of the tradition by virtue of her singular difference, the state, laws, and other individuals are not merely external, and her relationship to them cannot be conceived as *consequent* to her individual singularity. Rather, they situate and enable that singularity, demanding her response and responsibility; they give her access to a particular form of identity and solidarity with others. The social framework and customs she inherits, conversely, are also not simply and immediately constitutive of who she is; she does not simply follow them as an *antecedent*.

In conscientiousness, we also run the risk of destroying or permanently altering for the worse the collective networks that sustain us, whether they take the form of ethicality or of legal order. The fact that the demand for conscientious action is an ever-present demand does not mean that it always has good consequences or that it only brings good things with it. The unconscious and conscious terms that structure shared social life are of enormous significance in their capacity to nourish human life and interaction. Both the power of ethical life and the universality of personhood assert their significance in our actions: what it is to be a conscientious self has developed in tandem with the development of the society that sustains this self, the world in which this self lives, the accomplishment of the freedom of a community reflected in ethical life and the accomplishment of the freedom of the individual reflected in the Roman Empire.[22] Conscientious action persistently runs the risk of destroying these, the very conditions of its possibility; the conscientious self they produce has the power to undermine them. "The wounds of the spirit heal and leave no scars behind" (M669, S492): at times this can involve an irretrievable loss—of meaning, of immediate attachment to a meaningful world, and so on, a loss for which conscientiousness always runs the risk of being responsible.[23]

CONCLUSION

With this discussion of the conscientious self, we have seen a reality not captured by the reality of living in a tradition or the reality of living as an abstract individual equal to all others. We have seen a stance that is in an important way beyond law and beyond the conditions in which we are shaped, that depends upon both but also enables a *meaningful* critical attitude toward both of them, akin to the attitude gestured toward at the end of the previous chapter—an attitude that does not deny their significance and their powerful effects. The conscientious self asserts that there is more to her than her external environments, conditions, and laws, that the life she wants to live may be different from the life that anyone else wants, that she reserves for herself the authority to decide about what is true and what is false and recognizes this to be a challenge and a responsibility, that she can respond to what she feels to be a calling and judge her sense of being called as legitimate, that she can enact identification with an other on the basis of the unique situation of their interaction. No matter what kind of conflicts the singularity of conscience may inspire, justice cannot be justice without including responsiveness to this ultimately authoritative singularity, which means that there is one dimension of justice for which a rulebook cannot be given, or the nature of which cannot be seen prior to actual, singular human judgment, action, and interaction.

This singular reality can always come into conflict with the realities presented by ethical life and positive law, but it does not do so *necessarily*. In singular acts of forgiveness, for which there can never be a rule, the reality of conscientiousness can be reconciled with the realities of ethical life and positive law. Indeed, because we have three elements here—ethical life, law, and forgiveness, all of which are associated with justice, with the just recognition of a significant and irreducible aspect of what it means to be human—we can say more than just that conscientiousness *can* be reconciled with the realities of ethical life and positive law. It may be, that is, that justice is, most generally speaking, the *imperative* to reconcile the realities of ethical life, positive law, and conscientiousness, to find oneself answerable to all of them in any given action.[24] While the principle of law is universality, and the principle of custom is particularity, the self is always singular, even in its attempts to enact and do justice to that universality and particularity. The self is, in a sense, the very traversal of the distance between singularity and universality, between singularity and particularity. This traversal must be *recognized*, or rights, laws, and custom must be made answerable to the unique instances of solidarity that inspire and guide individual action and to the diversity that makes human action significant and productive of value. They are *in fact* answerable, because of their reliance on individual action; they are dependent on the transgressive action of the conscientious self who acts against the community and its universals, and they are the products of the collective that enacts them, not the abstract and independent dictates of a judge who stands above the fray. The conflict between acting and judging consciousness shows the inevitability of human solidarity in individual action and the hypocrisy of the perspective that grants a life to universal principles of social organization that is other than the life of collective action and transgression.[25]

Spirit is the forgiving community of forgiving individuals that, in its acknowledgment of the centrality of individual activity to its body, but also of the inevitability of individual transgression of the universal that is invoked to sustain individual being, worth, and dignity, must continuously restructure itself to accommodate this activity. It is the role of legal and institutional forms to reflect our prior and more fundamental sociality and to leave room for solidaristic action against the injustices they sometimes perpetrate. The tragic fate of both ethical life and the condition of right is transformed with the influx of forgiveness, and so also can the fate of contemporary law-based societies and the complicity of legal and traditional principles in exploitation and injustice be transformed by the demand of forgiveness: that is, the demand that we acknowledge the relativity of our social positions and the shared nature of conscience, and the demand that we invest ourselves anew in the social realm that exists only through our action and solidarity, oriented toward the possibility of understanding and being understood.

CONCLUSION TO PART 1

For each of us, our existence as beings who bear responsibility and to whom others are in turn obligated is characterized by a variety of differing, and not automatically compatible, aspects. It has been the project of these first five chapters to identify these aspects systematically and to articulate the fault lines, so to speak, that define the problematic, overlapping boundaries between them. To conclude part 1, let us review the nature of and the relationships between the three aspects, setting the stage for an exploration of further political issues in their light.

The first aspect is that of ethicality. It is an *essential* aspect of our being that it is cultivated or cultured in a particular context, one that is organized in terms of very particular—*not* universally shared—historical, social, cultural, economic, political, and familial characteristics, and in Hegel's discussion of ethical life we witness the elaboration of this key point. We have particular identities; we belong to various groups, communities, and cultures that leave an indelible mark on us. Because these contexts create in us the capacity for judgment, our judgment is necessarily oriented and disoriented by them. They make us who we are in ways that we cannot see clearly and that we could never completely understand. They instill in us an immediate sense of the way things are and the way things should be, inspiring in us an immediate kind of responsiveness to the world around us and cultivating in us habits of perception, understanding, and action. They cause us to be distinguished from others of different groups, communities, and cultures in a way that makes understanding and identification with these others challenging. We are defined by these contexts, by their "rules" and our "habits" in relation to those "rules," in a way that is fundamentally overlooked by modern conceptions of human beings as primarily self-making and individual.

As a real piece of human reality that is of profound significance for human beings, the force of ethicality must be recognized and addressed by the theory and practice of justice, but the reality of ethicality has both negative and positive significance. Because of it we are recipients of a cultural wealth and a set of capacities we would lack if we were left solely to our own devices, but we are also inducted by it into bad habits, practices, and values, as well as into a certain blindness with regard to our own significance and the significance of others. We can come to think of ourselves and those around us, that is, as uniquely embodying what it means to be human, and we can thus devalue practices, groups, and cultures that are alien to us. Further, we may want *not* to be reduced or held to a certain way of life, if it has had a negative impact on us, but our desire to wrench ourselves away from it can be frustrated; its influence on us and the commitment of others to it can make departure difficult.

The second aspect, that of universal right, responds to the negative aspects of the operation of ethicality—that ethicality can make us blind to the significance of people and practices that lie outside of our terrain of familiarity and can make it difficult for us to exercise our freedom in defining ourselves differently. If we are honest about what it is like to be human, we will recognize the need to posit self-consciously formulated, rather than inherited and automatic, rules about how to live together that fairly and honestly recognize people as people, rules that are detachable from our particular arenas of familiarity. The invocation of universal right is the most significant mechanism by which this blindness that tends to favor as well as restrict us to our own arena of familiarity is corrected. Universal rights assert the reality of universal validity, the idea that everyone counts, not simply by virtue of the place from which he or she happens to come, or the community to which he or she happens to belong, but simply by virtue of being human. Because of the power of ethicality, we may not see the reality and equal validity of others, so we have learned, historically, the necessity of positing universal human rights, and we have learned the need to keep ourselves accountable to these rights and the principle of universal validity they express. Also, while we inevitably feel the draw of ethicality, we may also be inclined to set our own terms for our own lives, and we may feel the desire to assert our irreducibility to the terms of the life that brought us into being and to separate ourselves from them. Modern law grants us a certain measure of distance from the contexts that have formed us and from the characteristics that are associated with us and taken to define us, upholding our possible involvement in the production, creation, and revision of these contexts. With the protection of law, we can be *actively*, not simply passively, oriented toward our way of life. We can be who we *decide* we want to be, and we can be assured that we are worthy of recognition no matter what we choose in that regard.

We have seen that the principle of universal right is of great import in the formulation of justice and the structuring of human communities, but it, just like the principle of ethicality, also has limitations. The idea of universality is also not exhaustively responsive to the nature of human identity and human life, as it cannot adequately recognize our particularity. Its insufficiency leads to the illumination of the significance of yet a third principle—that of a commitment to conscience. Fundamental to this principle is the idea that I am more than the identity that is in a sense enacted on my behalf by the communities to which I belong and also that I am more than just one abstract human individual among many. Hence Hegel's third point about the nature of human beings: we are also beings of "conscience," or oriented toward the world and others in a way that is driven by our singular perspectives, such that one may be led to say, "*This* is what I feel called to do; *this* is what I know to be most significant, independent of the dictates of any authority external to me." The commitment to conscience extends beyond ethicality because it is I who decide what is right, and it extends beyond right because what I decide and who I am are not transferrable to another person or context. We are ultimately answerable to ourselves and to each other in our singularity, and hence answerable to the singular, unpredictable demands that emerge in our interaction. What this means, in fact, is that we are required to be in principle committed to the possibility of *forgiving* what may seem to be transgressive action on the part of other conscientious beings. This forgiveness is the occasion for a specific kind of interaction that accompanies the exercise of conscience, a kind of interaction that is similarly singular and that takes its lead not from the familiarity of ethicality or the formality of law but from the singularity of the beings interacting. Laws and rules, social practices and cultural expectations, must not be invoked in such a way as to conceal, subvert, or deny the reality of conscientiousness and conscientious interaction; the existent—customary and posited—rules structuring any human society will never be adequate to characterizing the terms of our obligations in the face of singular situations and interactions.

While this third aspect—conscientious insight, action, and interaction—need not be opposed to the other two—ethicality and universality—it *may* be thus opposed, and, further, its possible reconciliation with ethicality and universality is itself not something that can be regulated by rules. Further, recognizing the value of conscience is one way of allowing for identification and transformation of the possible injustice that can come to characterize formal law, when it structures and stabilizes social arrangements that are unjust and in its stability prevents a more just framework from developing. What the principle of conscience and its forgiveness requires is that we must rest to a certain extent unsatisfied with any *determinate* mechanisms of justice, such as law and the communities by which we are cultivated; we must make the present hospitable to the possibility of future transformation; we must be open to being influenced by others and not allow our institutions and laws to accomplish such transformative interaction for us.

The principle of conscience and its forgiveness captures the dynamic and responsive character of the relationship between human and world, a relationship that Hegel tracks throughout the *Phenomenology*. The *Phenomenology*, that is, follows and analyzes the development of a relationship between the self and others, the individual and the universal, the human being and law; it explores the kinds of worlds made possible by different conceptions of what it means to be human and the kinds of persons made possible by different kinds of worlds. Just as Hegel shows us the distinctive worlds of ethicality and right, so we can imagine a distinctive world, a distinctive community, enacted around the notion of forgiveness. The forgiving community would be one that allows the life of the community to be lived through singular individuals; it supports the development, diversification, and ever-increasing mediation of that relationship; it refuses to assert its customs or laws in such a way that represses the operation of conscience absolutely.

In this first part of the book, we have seen that law and the relations of universality it inaugurates, ethicality and the particular communities of belonging, and forgiveness and the irreducible singularity of human action and identity are all differently necessary dimensions of human life and fulfillment and thus must all be included in a robust account of justice and the nature of human life.[1] As we have seen, they supplement each other: while relations of ethical life are primary as the conditions under which it is possible to have something like laws, law in turn enables the healthy development of those relations and that life, providing resources when it is obstructed, and the principle of forgiveness introduces the significance, beyond law and custom, of what life is mostly like, lived as it is by singular beings in the context of singular interactions. Ethical life is real, as the ground out of which individuals are cultivated, but it cannot be relied on to sustain on its own a healthy social reality in which individuals become habituated to sophisticated and orderly interactions and become empowered to challenge and exit poorly functioning social and interpersonal relations. "Love 'requires the *Aufhebung* of right,'" writes Harris, "but when love fails, there is necessarily a return to the level of right."[2] Law enables those protected by it to step outside the terms of the determinate contexts of their particular ethical development, giving them new resources in those cases in which their ethical and social relations inhibit the development of healthy individuality, and it can also *aid* in the development of healthy ethical relations, since it can be invoked as a mechanism by which to establish the possibility of future and better ones. Whereas the purpose of law is to provide an authoritative and predictable framework that allows us to engage comfortably with a world and in so doing enact a shared social reality, as stable and determinate it also risks entrenching and perpetuating a particular vision of human nature, difference, and interaction, and giving form to situations and interactions, the significance of which cannot be conclusively formulated. Laws are beholden to the ethical relationality that inspires them and that sustains individual identities, and they must not be asserted as absolute and opposed to important social transformation. The risk of law is that it can be used to stifle the reality of ethicality and prevent the appearance of a new kind of reality and new forms of difference and interaction. This risk can be responsibly negotiated, however, if law is not upheld as the ultimate authority but is held accountable to the dynamic nature of the human reality whose protection is its motivating ground. It is responsibly negotiated if we recognize the significance of the singularity of identity and interaction and hold ourselves responsive to it, comporting ourselves to ourselves and to others with an attitude of forgiveness.

In this discussion of the relationship and tensions between ethicality, law, and conscience, what we should note is that we have developed a broader perspective than each of them asserts on its own that reconciles them to each other, or that we have come to make sense of the tensions between them by understanding the ways in which they work toward the same thing—namely, justice.[3] We can make a further observation in this context about the general nature of Hegel's philosophy: it is generally oriented toward the goal of the production of such a broader perspective. It involves both a training of human perception and understanding, on the one hand, and an accurate account of the reality that is perceived and understood, on the other, and these two—our perspective and reality—are connected. When we are faced with a tension in that reality, with what seems to be a conflict between irreconcilable elements in it, the tension is often one contributed by our own limited perspective and requires the elaboration of a better conceptual apparatus. Through a transformation in our own thinking we can give ourselves the resources with which to imagine a new perspective through which the elements in tension with each other are in fact reconciled.

The broader understanding that we have developed here is broad in various ways. First, it sees that the properly responsible attitude is the one that recognizes that ethicality, law, and forgiveness are all operative in pursuit of the same purpose and hence are not fundamentally at odds with each other but equally necessary for the project of developing and enacting concern for human reality—that project by which each one is in fact motivated. They are reliant on each other in their complementarity: each fulfills a unique task, one that the others cannot fulfill, but through their commitment to justice in principle they are indirectly committed to the tasks that the others perform *and* committed to the idea of their own inadequacy to justice. Second, if the tension between these three elements of justice is the site of responsibility or responsiveness, then it is not exactly right to understand these three elements to be ultimately at odds with each other. The tension between them has the capacity to enliven responsibility—or, the truly responsible attitude is one that recognizes and struggles with the undecidability between law, forgiveness, and ethicality, that lives with and enacts responsibility only in the context of their tension. Neither law, forgiveness, nor ethicality can be taken to be fully authoritative for any particular case; there are no exhaustive, incontrovertible rules or guidelines by which complex human situations can be negotiated free of risk. Questioning the "fit" of universal principles and particular situations, re-evaluating the way in which our customary relationships and sense of belonging leads to our development as ethical individuals and communities, and recognizing that a final answer to how to deal with singularity cannot be given—all of these tasks should aid in the renewal of moral and political attentiveness and transformation and in the perpetual assessment of laws.

We can see, finally, how the tension between law, forgiveness, and ethicality is significant for a divisive disagreement in critical political attempts to locate and define the possibility of resistance and critique, one that is addressed to some extent in part 2 of this book and to a greater extent in part 3. One set of political views, aligned mostly with liberal commitments, identifies the powerful effects of the invocation of rights in practices of resistance, and another set, in which we can see the influence of Foucault, identifies the homogenizing and conservative (insofar as they serve the *status quo*) values perpetuated by and reflected in a discourse of rights. Hegel's location of responsibility in the irreducible tension between law, ethicality, and forgiveness shows the import of capturing the force of each side in a dispute that is ultimately irresolvable, but *the very irresolvability of which is a kind of resolution.* The ultimate values expressed by Hegel in the principles of ethicality and forgiveness call attention to the singularities to which law cannot do justice, to the situations that cultivate us as moral agents, and to those to which we need to be attentive in order to practice ethical concern. These values illuminate the fact that there will always exist new identifications that are unrecognized and unrecognizable according to the particular vision of human life implicit in law's operation, as well as the fact that it is vital to figure out ways in which to allow these identifications to appear. These values can inspire attention to the ways in which law irrationally restricts and excludes, or the interests operating behind it that serve to render its force partial. The ultimate value of law, on the other hand, allows common practices of interaction to sediment, gives us recourse to something beyond the sometimes destructive determinacies of our singular lives, and opens up the space we might need in order to interact and develop in singular and unpredictable ways. Each value is irreducible to the other and necessary to the other; each is at once problematic and necessary. Law structures and abets social interaction and enables individual identification with a rational space not determined by particularity, but the idea that there is a determinate answer to every situation and individual is a hindrance to the exercise of responsibility.[4] To rely merely on the moral force and value of ethical relations is to deny law's role in ordering them and to leave individuals stranded when these relations deteriorate. Posing forgiveness as an ultimate answer to how to live together is similarly problematic, in that its very nature is to keep the question alive for us of how to respond responsibly, a question only answerable by means of our singular perspective. Our various philosophical, political, and ethical struggles can and should be understood in the context of this tension, as striving to answer to the integrity of the three poles, that of singular identities and situations, that of ethical relations and contexts, and that of law. Closure on their tension will only deny the force of their opposition, diminish the effect of political responsibility and responsiveness, and deny a future to imagination.

In part 1, we have examined independently these three points about the nature of human life and the forms that responsibility or responsiveness to it should take. In so doing, we have developed a set of principles or fundamental points about the nature of human life and human responsibility. Part 2 turns now to the issue of the *actuality* and *practice* of law, to treatment of the mechanisms by which law is shaped and enacted and by which its transgression is dealt with. It turns from the individual as the bearer of right to the determinate structures by which that right is formulated, shaped, and upheld—the mechanisms of authority involved in both governance and punishment, the political bodies involved in the enactment of law and the protection against and punishment of its violation. But the aspects of ethicality and forgiveness show themselves to be continually called upon as supplements to the embodiment, exercise, and maintenance of law, and hence we will again be called to address the issue of how these three principles—ethicality, law, and forgiveness—can be reconciled in *practice*, or in the context of the real political contexts and mechanisms designed for the enactment and sustenance of law.

Law must be made, promulgated, executed, interpreted, and sustained; hence its very being or nature involves determinate legislative, executive, and interpretive powers and structures of punishment. In chapter 6, we discuss the nature of the body or bodies that legislate, execute, and interpret law, and we do so by examining Hegel's critical analysis of the French Revolution, since it shows the problems with a political reliance on law to the exclusion of answerability to the realities of specific human communities and exclusive human singularity. In chapter 7, we discuss the transgression of law by crime and the suitability and shortcomings of the response to crime that is demanded by the logic of law, identifying again in Hegel's discussion thereof a turn to and reliance on the principles of ethicality and forgiveness. For this theme, we move from the *Phenomenology* to the *Philosophy of Right*, since the issue of crime and its treatment is of such decisive import in that later text.

PART 2

THE ACTUALITY AND PRACTICE OF LAW

6

THE IDEAL NATION AND THE REAL NATION

We saw in chapter 5 the importance of the conscientious stance that is prepared to act in the world, here and now, to bring about change. The revolutionary consciousness seems especially to exemplify this attitude. In considering Hegel's analysis of the French Revolution in this chapter, we will be considering the significance of the revolutionary demand for a new world, a world unchained to any determinate past, traditions, time-honored hierarchies, and modes of organization. The world of the French Revolution is also a world constructed around the ideal of universal law and on the basis of ideally rational individuals capable of identifying with it, so the revolutionary world also exemplifies the power and significance of law. In this analysis, however, the need for a structured world with determinate content becomes powerfully evident. Hegel shows that the new world of the Revolution is a merely ideal world, ill suited to reality and capable of operating only in principle, through ideal individuals who are linked and committed to each other only indirectly, by virtue of their identical attachment to a pure reason, a universal law, and an ideal nation.

In this chapter I explore the ideal revolutionary nation that can never be enacted in order to illuminate the significant nature of its opposite—that is, of real nations enacted by real individuals, linked to each other in response to the determinate, local demands that arise in the context of a shared spatial and temporal life, a shared, modern ethical life. Hegel's treatment of the "Absolute Freedom and Terror" of the French Revolution reveals the reliance of law on singular political judgment and a specific political terrain, the reliance of justice and democracy on particular and exclusive contexts, or nation-states, and the reliance of revolutionary consciousness on meaningfully differentiated social structures that pre-exist its pseudoconscientious stance.[1] In it we can see how theories of justice and democracy must be responsive and appropriate to the qualities of the *real* nation—its trouble with principle, its determinate inheritance from the past, and its democratic openness to the future. In the first section I discuss the French Revolution's ideal nation and ideal citizen. The second section treats the local and determinate *space* of the real nation and the issue of justice, and the third treats the *time* of real nations and the issue of democracy.[2]

"ALL REALITY IS SOLELY SPIRITUAL": UNIVERSAL REASON IN THE FORM OF A NATION

A family, a soccer team, a school board, a labor union, a group of friends, a municipal government, a couple, a church, a hair salon, and any other collective in which more than one person participates has an identity that is irreducible to and greater than the single identities of its members. When we participate in such collectives or groups, we in some sense take on the identity of the group as such and live in and through it, even if we do not recognize ourselves as doing so; the identity of the group is not merely an addition to our identities as individuals, but transforms them. We do not participate in these groups only to further and satisfy the demands of our own identities, even if we think we do; the group has a meaningful identity of its own and on its own terms, and because of that we have reason to participate in it. Indeed, in an important way, who we really *are* is elaborated by such collective forms of identification to the extent that we find the grounds for our own identity in that larger identity, and thus to be ourselves is to be a part of it. Who we are is not reducible to our personally circumscribed identities, but it is elaborated in collective projects and identifications, beyond what might appear to be the boundaries of individual selfhood.

A significant aspect of such collective forms of identification, however, is that they are to a certain extent *exclusive*: they can function only if they have, so to speak, a restrictive admissions policy. A family, a soccer team, a group of friends, a church, and other such forms of identification cannot be fully inclusive, for in order to be what they are, they must, for example, be limited to a certain *number* of participants and limited to a certain *kind* of participant. A soccer game, for instance, ordinarily involves two teams of eleven players each, with the addition of several substitute players. A single team cannot accomplish its collective project of playing soccer well if it has fewer than eleven players and more than, say, twenty—too few will require more work of its members than they can reasonably be expected to do, and too many will mean that its members will not have sufficient opportunities to meaningfully participate in the game. This is a quantitative restriction, but there are also qualitative restrictions; team members cannot play effectively if they do not have a sufficient number of teammates who play at approximately the same level as they do. Hence, various kinds of limitations on membership are required in order for collective units to accomplish their respective goods or goals. We exist in exclusive communities, and in that existence we are often challenged to establish a balance between the expansive desire to include and to be with people and the restrictive fact that we can only "be with" people well if their number is limited. This is a tension that animates human life: the tension between the desire to know people—to experience them, talk with them, and learn from them—and the fact that we can only do this in a meaningful way if we are selective about the kind and number of people with whom and situations in which we do this. That is, we can only be open by being closed or be affected by and engaged with people by closing off other possibilities of being affected and engaged.[3]

I begin with this discussion in order to bring into relief the particular kind of collective identity accomplished by the society of the French Revolution. Its force and revolutionary significance, as opposed to that of the exclusive groups described above, lie in its explicit adoption of the policy of *universal inclusiveness* governed by universal law. According to Hegel's account, the collective form of identification intended by the Revolution is one that in principle includes everyone; it is the "universal brotherhood of man." The Revolution asserts about the *human as such*—beyond any given human being's particular interests, activities, and specificities—that all are to be included in a "universal humanity"; this is the form of collective identity that the French Revolution articulates. As such, this group is logically distinct from any particular community or collective form of identification, and it rejects the particularism of other forms of identification, or the significance of what we have analyzed under the term "ethical life."[4] While these other forms of identification are also general, in that they are shared by and common to their members and transcendent of their particular differences, their generality, unlike the abstract universality of the group "universal humanity," is only partial.

The assertion the Revolution makes about the "human as such," and the ground by which this collective identity is construed, concerns the capacity to reason. The capacity to reason links us as individuals to what might be called a "universal point of view"—a point of view that is available to anyone who can reason—that makes demands on all of us to recognize a self-same universal truth. In linking us to a "universal point of view," reason brings us out of the particularities of our day-to-day lives and perspectives and draws us toward unity and identification with others, since through it we are in principle capable of recognizing to be true the same things that they do.

This implies, further, that we are also thereby unsuited to a system of social hierarchy. If all are capable of reason, and that capacity to reason leads us to the capacity to identify the same truths and recognize the same reality, then all should also be construed as equal. To allow relations of superiority and inferiority between us would be to deny this capacity for universal identification through reason. The social significance of all contingent, particular difference, according to the terms of the Revolution, must be eradicated, and along with it all social hierarchy based on such difference, so that this "ultimate thing" might be respected and revered in everyone. In knowing and willing, the revolutionary individual manifests that universal aspect of himself: his knowledge and freedom are the exercising of universality, and his value is located in that exercise.

The revolutionary nation, the nation of equals, asserts, upholds, and defends the rights that are essential and due to every individual as rational. In so doing the nation is identified as their essence, their relation with which is the most central and powerful factor in their identity. They identify with it by virtue of their rationality and leave other determinations behind, so their privileges and fates no longer depend on aspects of their identities over which they have no rational control, on aspects of their identities that others do not share with them, or on things that they do not make and choose themselves. The political relevance of all contingent individual and social differences is eradicated, and all citizens are one in their identification with the nation; all share, through their sharing in reason, the rights it grants; all contribute to *making* the arena of their interaction, which is undefinable in advance of their creation of it.[5] Their agency is empowered by its agency; their wills are its will, and vice versa. Each citizen is identified and identifies himself immediately with the nation, with the "universal" or "general will," transcending any mediation by particular characteristics and exclusive forms of collective identification; each is a direct representative of the nation as such.[6]

The identification with universality here achieved is the bulwark against the political influence of contingent, private particularity. What Hegel calls "masses" and "spheres," or particular domains of action, of labor, and of power that are distinguished from each other, cannot be considered the essential units of society and no longer play a mediating role in the relationship between individuals and their nation. Rather, individuals are marked as the essential units, and they relate not to masses or spheres but to the whole, to the *universal* work (M588, S435). As the third article of the 1789 Declaration of the Rights of Man declares, the principle of sovereignty resides in the nation, and all authority emanates therefrom. The nation has authority, as the ground of all rights-bearing subjects, by virtue of recognizing and upholding their essential singularity as rational persons; it has authority because it is the universal embodiment of their reason. Reason is the supreme equalizer, rendering all individuals identical representatives of this authoritative nation and preventing the particularities of privilege from determining the operation of power.

To understand the constitution and the shortcomings of this nation and its citizens more clearly requires that we highlight two issues. The first issue concerns what this nation, its citizens, and their relationship to each other *are* or what kind of characteristics are taken to be defining for them. The second issue concerns the question of what can be *done* in this context or what kind of agency is supported by this conception of nationhood, of citizenship, and of the relation between nations and citizens.

First, with regard to what *is*: the defining characteristic of the nation is that it is nothing but the general will—the will of the community of rational individuals committed to upholding itself as such. It is thus also in a sense *each* individual who, by setting aside its particularity, is immediately identified with this general will. The nation is an ideal form to which all revolutionary citizens belong in principle, as ideal forms themselves; as Hegel says, "all reality is solely spiritual" (M584, S432). Not to be confused with any *actual* nation, the nation is the universal will, which is the essence of law, an essence to which all other laws refer as their source and origin.[7] It is itself the foremost or primary law, requiring that in all things the ideal nation be sovereign. Each rational individual, by identifying with the general will, commits itself to the maintenance and execution of that one law.

Further, the *individual*, identified immediately with this ideal nation, is also an ideal form and also not to be confused with any of its particularities, or, indeed, with any particular individual. In the revolutionary context the *rationality* of each (male) French citizen is the key to his identification with the general will: reason renders all identically capable and deserving of representing that will and prevents the particularities of privilege from determining the ownership and exercise of power. Thus it is only in their ideal forms that individuals identify with the nation and with each other, or that the relationship of belonging to the nation and the relationship of identification with each other is articulated.

Finally, the *unity* of rational beings in the nation is ideal as well: the rationality they hold in common, and not their particularities, is the ground for their identification with each other. While individual rationality is the ground for individual inclusion and legislation in the ideal nation, the rationality of *all* such individuals is the ground for their unity and cooperative participation in it. The nation is the unity of rational wills *in principle*, in the universal exercise of reason and in abstraction from particularity.

Before we move on to what can be *done* in this context, let us compare this last point, concerning ideal unity in the nation, with models of a certain kind of intersubjective identification described by Kant and Rousseau. Like the nation described here, what Kant calls the "kingdom of ends" is an ideal community to which all rational individuals belong in principle, on the basis of the exercise of their capacity for rationality.[8] Individual rationality is the ground for inclusion and legislation in this kingdom, and the shared characteristic of rationality is the ground for the unity *in principle* of all rational individuals. This rational identity grants each the position of legislator in this kingdom, and this identity is the ultimate law to which all particular actions and laws must conform. What Rousseau calls the "general will," similarly, stands for the ideal identification of the individual with the universal, the mobilization of the individual rational will by the principle of the good of the whole or the universal. The body politic is "a moral being that has a will; and this general will . . . always tends to the preservation and the well-being of the whole and of each part, and . . . is the source of laws."[9] As Rousseau writes, "each of us puts his person and his full power in common under the supreme direction of the general will; and in a body we receive each member as an indivisible part of the whole."[10] The general will and the kingdom of ends are like the nation as ideal political reality, to which ideal rational beings belong by virtue of their rationality and their capacity to identify with the universal or the demands of reason. The unity they achieve is a unity in principle; it is indirect and contingent upon the identification of each with the universal. In analyzing the ideal unity of the revolutionary nation, it is ultimately the interpretation and evaluation of these basic and highly influential approaches to interpreting our moral and political life that are at stake.

Hegel's response to these various ideal forms—that of the individual, the nation, and the unity of citizens—is quite critical. The ideal nation, the ideal citizen, and the ideal construal of relationships among citizens are all ultimately distinct from any actual nation, citizen, or relationships, and thus any *actual* nation, citizen, or relationship among citizens is open in principle to being construed as a departure from pure universality, since it has a determinate, one-sided, and fixed character that is incompatible with the universality that justifies its existence and operation. The problem with the ideal nation, therefore, is that it cannot actually exist.

It is here that the question of what can be *done* in this context becomes significant. The foremost agent here is the ideal nation with which all citizens are identified in principle. In order to be existent, effective, and authoritative, however, a nation must accomplish actual things; it must make and promulgate specific laws, it must bring its authority to bear on particular situations, and it must create determinate opportunities for its citizens' exercise of their rights and freedoms. Doing such things relies on a couple of conditions: it requires, first, a particular decision, and second, a particular action—the decision demanding the *subjective initiative* of an individual and the action entailing a *determinate change* in objective actuality. That is, decisions require single individuals, and accomplishments must be determinate.

But here the ideal nation and the abstract identification of all with it seem problematic; they seem to be potential *obstacles* to the possibility of doing a determinate thing for a determinate person or population. With regard to the aspect of subjective initiative, that is, decision will always be "factional" and not the expression of the "general will," because a decision cannot be made by everyone. Hegel writes that "all other individuals [*Einzelnen*] are excluded from the entirety of this deed and have only a limited share in it, so that the deed would not be a deed of the *actual universal* consciousness" (M589, S435). One person must make a decision and carry out a deed in reality, but what is entailed thereby is an authoritative self-assertion of that person above the others, an appropriation of decision-making power and the deed that prevents others from having it as their own. In the case of the actions of a nation, the one person who performs them interrupts the identification of others with the nation, or the identification of others as its agents, which was in fact the operating principle of this nation.[11]

Further, for the nation to operate, determinate changes must be made in objective actuality. With regard to this, Hegel writes about individual consciousness that it

> can achieve no positive work, neither universal works of language nor of actuality, neither laws and universal institutions

> of a *conscious* freedom nor deeds and works of a *willing* freedom . . . Universal freedom, which would have differentiated itself in this way into its constituent parts and in that very way would have made itself into an *existent* substance, would thereby be free from single individuality [*einzelne Individualität*], and would apportion the *plurality* of *individuals* to its various constituent parts. (M588, S434–5)

The accomplishment of a single thing in actuality is inadequate to the ideal identification of the individual and the nation, for a single thing will always take shape in a particular part of the world and be for some and not all, excluding individuals from the piece of reality allotted to others. As an *existent* substance, such a thing will become relevant for a particular individual or group of individuals; the many individuals will each be assigned to a part, not to the whole, and hence there will be some parts with which they have no connection. Actual reality is one-sided, contingent, determinate; it belongs to the domain of necessity and not freedom; it is subject to forces other than the universal rational will and is prone to being partitioned; it is not equally and homogeneously available to all. If the revolutionary individual acts, he jeopardizes the project of absolute freedom: his action is that of a singular self, not an action belonging to everyone, and is thus inherently factional. Implicit in the revolutionary context is the fact that, if absolute freedom is the ultimate value, then singular selfhood and action are essentially factional and must be eliminated.[12]

From the point of view of initiative, *nothing can be done*, since initiative can only be singular; and from the point of view of actuality, *nothing can be done*, since any accomplished thing can only be particular. If nothing can be done, then this ideal polity cannot in principle be enacted and made real, and neither can the ideal citizen be actualized; the freedom it is supposed to have cannot actually be exercised in a determinate way, and the nation cannot be a determinate home for it. The establishment of an actual order of real individuals would constrain and particularize the operation of principle. Neither of the extremes that Hegel describes in section 590—the "simple, inflexible cold universality" and the "discrete, absolute hard rigidity and self-willed atomism of actual self-consciousness," or the absolute law in the form of nation and the single, abstract self—can exist in reality. They constitute the world of pure will and pure universality that has "no content, possession, existence, or outer extension" (M590, S436). As unreal and abstract, this universality and this selfhood exist in principle but are impossible in actuality. Purely rational, legislating individuals could neither make a world nor inhabit one already made, since all actuality is an offence against ideality and all particularity an offence against universality.[13] The pure identification of singularity with universality makes the elaboration, whether original or inherited, of a concrete, particular, and differentiated world impossible.

Since the revolutionary individual cannot in fact make a decision, perform an action, or accomplish an object, he does not essentially exist at all in this world; thus is it fitting for his death as well to be meaningless. With no platform upon which life might be meaningfully lived, even death loses its significance; if there are no actual selves, erasure under the guillotine has no significance. As the supreme being goes out with a whiff of "stale gas," as Hegel writes, so do abstract individuals (M586, S434). Their deaths, because of the eradication of any moment of significance beyond individual self-consciousness that could meaningfully situate or encompass its demise, have no meaning.

For something to be done, for a living world to be a home for actually existing and determinate individuals, this world would have to come to terms with the singularity of decision and the determinacy of actuality, with the phenomena previously studied as "conscience" and "ethical life."[14] For the freedom that is *purported* to become freedom that is *practiced*, the general will must be elaborated in relation to the particular, practical constraints facing effective agency in an actual world, in relation to the differences that put singular persons in positions of decision-making in various spheres, and in relation to the specific characteristics and demands of objective reality. Freedom can only come to be in the context of constraint and specificity, or in the context of an actual establishment with actual, particular qualities.[15]

Let us address now the issue of what kind of *relationships* among or *unity* of individuals is possible in this revolutionary context. In it, a straight line extends from the individual to the universal, with nothing to mediate that identification. On its own, and by virtue of its own rational will, each individual is identified with the universal, in what, following Bernstein, we might call a vertical relationship.[16] The individual's relationship with other such individuals is in this context only indirect; it arises only by virtue of their common possession of the same identical attribute of reason. In Kant, similarly, we see a departure from the purely personal, private, or subjective in the direction of the universal—what is accomplished by the revolutionary consciousness—such that each individual is more than merely a private self limited by its particular circumstances, and thus oriented somehow to others. This leap, however—for Kant and for the revolutionary consciousness—is not accomplished by means of *actual* intersubjective sharing and communication, which we have analyzed in the previous chapter as "forgiving communication." Beyond each human being understood in its particularity—that is, as female or as French or as working class or, in general, as possessing determinate qualities that radically influence the way in which life is lived and the others with whom it is lived—is the universality of reason, and we are its instantiations or examples, eternally unified with each other by virtue of its power. This emphasis on reason does not support the attempt to achieve society directly, by supporting the idea of entrance into and participation in the actual domain that is uniquely accomplished through interaction, and for which our particularity and singularity are the overwhelmingly relevant phenomena. Through emphasis on this aspect of human identity, Kant and the French Revolution would aim to articulate and achieve society indirectly, by aiming at something that each of us has on our own and that others have too.[17]

What falls out of the ideal equation of the individual and the nation, out of the relationship between abstract singularity and abstract universality, is the determinacy or particularity of human agency and of human interaction. In identifying with each other indirectly by virtue of what they hold in common, revolutionary individuals engage not with the particularity and distinctiveness of others that they would only access through actual communication and sharing, but with their universalizable aspect—that which renders them identical. In fact, *that* they are considered identical would render useless and superfluous any actual interaction; they would already know how others are significant merely by knowing how they themselves are.[18] To reason, in the revolutionary context, is to be able to engage in an activity that is irreducible to or undefinable by one's particularity. Similarly, to be construed as a universal legislator, as individuals are in the revolutionary context, means to be able to occupy a position in the world that is irreducible to or inexhaustible by one's particularity, an abstract position that is the same as that of others, from which one exercises the same rights, privileges, and freedoms. Such formulations leave behind the determinate, actual world and interaction on its terrain.[19]

With his analysis of the French Revolution Hegel challenges each of these elements: the ideal nation, the ideal citizen, and the ideal character of relations among citizens. The positive claim that we can derive from his account here is that actuality, as the realm of determinacy, can be rational, but only in the terms of a rationality understood differently. Singular decision, determinate actuality, and particular interaction, in the context of a different social framework, do not have to be the enemy of principle, the failure of universality, or the transgression of rationality; on the contrary, a universality based on the presumption that its determinate embodiment signifies its demise is an empty universality, one that cannot tolerate any deeds because it cannot "concentrate itself into the One of individuality and put at the head a single self-consciousness" (M589, S435) and it "can achieve no positive work, neither universal works of language nor of actuality, neither laws and universal institutions of a *conscious* freedom nor deeds and works of a *willing* freedom" (M588, S434). Having now considered Hegel's critique of revolutionary society, I want to explore the different picture of nationhood, individuality, law, reason, interaction, and, finally, belonging that Hegel's account implies—a picture that would allow for the building and sustaining of an actual world.

THE SPACE OF REASON AND THE DETERMINACY OF JUSTICE

Given the fact that decision and action involve singular beings and determinate objects and realities, the relevant phenomenon of analysis here is a specific human context with determinate characteristics, not the in-principle universal context happening beyond space and time, beyond the determinacies of human interaction. The fact that decision, action, and interaction involve a specific context has a significance that is ambivalent. On the one hand, any such contexts can be made to be responsive to real individuals, but on the other hand, because it is for these individuals, it is not for others; in being open to some it must be closed to others. In this section we will explore this ambivalent space, identifying how justice implies injustice and inclusiveness, exclusiveness. And we will approach discussion of all three elements—the nation, the individual, and intersubjectivity—from the perspective of this last element, the intersubjective relations among citizens.

It is relatively straightforward to describe the kind of unity and community that Hegel implicitly opposes to the revolutionary model here, since we have explored in detail the various problems with the revolutionary model. This alternative unity and community, most significantly, is established internally—not externally—via the actual exercise of communication and sharing or through what Bernstein calls *horizontal* relations.[20] They are a unity and community not accomplished merely in principle, but also through determinate interaction, in and through which approximations of universality such as laws and institutional principles are developed and revised. While immediate, vertical belonging to an ideal nation is belonging to and being called by a larger whole to which the person beside me only incidentally belongs, involving an indirect relation to others by means of our individual relationship to the whole or to the universal, mediated, horizontal belonging, by contrast, involves belonging to and being called by those others; it is an indirect relation to the whole or the universal by means of one's relation to others. This mediated kind of belonging is richer and more determinate than the holding-in-common of reason and the legislating-in-common of law, and it enables the building of an actual, determinate world in the spirit of creativity and responsiveness. In the context of mediated belonging, the actual individual belongs to a *real* nation, a "we," which means that she relates, as an "I" in that "we," not merely to a principled unity transcending all individuals in their particularity, but also to actual, specific, and embodied others mired in the dynamics of their local interaction in a determinate nation. These individuals are always engaged in the process of achieving or producing a unity sufficient to enable the exercise of singularity and particularity in relation. This is *produced* universality and *cultivated* unity—not the principled universality and abstract unity of the revolutionary framework, and the process of its production and cultivation is of the utmost significance, demanding careful attention and acute sensitivity. Answerable to determinacy and its unpredictable demands, this universality and this unity are in principle never conclusively accomplished; they always remain yet to be done.

The individuals involved in this interaction are not "universal humanity," like the revolutionaries. All individuals have particular qualities and determinate identities that are not captured by the idea of a universal humanity but that are significant for the way in which they live their lives and thus something for which they could demand a certain kind of recognition and hence justice. They belong to groups and communities that are exclusive and not infinitely universal; they engage in activities that are local and limited by space and time; they have specific visions about who they are and what they want that are distinct from and sometimes opposed to the visions of others. The political framework of the Revolution, in advancing a general human in abstraction from all actual, particular qualities, is in a sense *opposed* to all of these human beings, whose lives could never be lived universally and whose particular characteristics and visions of life call for recognition; it is opposed to all of the elements that might mediate their relationships with the nation, with others, and with themselves and hence opposed to real things with value and the real people for whom they are valuable.[21] Justice is never justice for the universal individual, but justice for a son, a Kenyan, a Muslim, a university professor, a woman, and it involves houses, space, food, farms, municipal boundaries, grocery stores, health, bicycles, lawyers, and so on. Any political framework has to respond to the claims, needs, and demands of *these* individuals in relation to *these* things—even while providing them with universally identical and available legal mechanisms with with which to depart from or change their particular roles, responsibilities, and communities when necessary.

If the determinate interaction of singular human beings is shown to be of political and social significance, then the reason and law of the Revolution are inadequate. Abstract universal reason as the basis of identification between the nation and the individual, and the abstract law this universal individual posits, are similar to the formal reason and the law made and tested by the tyrannical agents Hegel studies and ultimately criticizes in his chapter on reason in the *Phenomenology*, which we considered briefly in chapter 5.[22] But reason as the basis of a mediated identification between nation and individual, for Hegel, is reason as *spirit*, as the historically determinate operation of communication and recognition achieved only in the realm of determinacy, among determinate beings. It is not merely the universal point of view described above, the occasion for an abstract, universal identification with others, but a reason that operates in real situations, through interaction with an actual, determinate world and actual, determinate others. This is reason as the occasion through which we can be made answerable to determinate others, but also as reason historically formed in response to communicative interaction with them. This reason emerges from and elaborates the shared communicative substance through which we are placed in proximity, and that our proximity in turn forms. It does attach to human beings apart from their particularity, but it becomes relevant only in relation to particular situations, objects, and questions, waiting upon how, when, and where this world gives itself, dynamically engaged with its wealth of determinacy. Reason is shaped by and becomes operative through the unique event that calls it into action and spurs its response. What has priority in this account of reason as spirit is the determinate realm of interaction, the space or site in which we witness to singularity and work toward universality only by withholding from an exhaustive definition of such universality and what it requires.

Law, reconstrued in a manner analogous to this reinterpretation of reason as spirit, must also be understood as a legal *substance* that enables and reflects proximity, interaction, and communication and that is formed in response to the determinacy that characterizes that interaction and communication. The shared communication structured by reason and the shared space structured by law are accomplished by responsiveness to the particular demands of others and exist for that reason as the media by which needs and demands are in turn communicated and our responsiveness to them articulated. The *real* nation, as the shared substance in which reason and laws operate and which they structure, is far from a principled unity transcending all individuals in their particularity. On the contrary, it is a historically and culturally determinate phenomenon, demanding local attention and enabling our engagement with each other, instead of our mutual exclusion and isolation.[23]

If universality, reason, and law are exercised and enacted only in determinate contexts and in response to specific demands and needs, then they are not exercised and enacted in a way that is available everywhere for everyone; they take a specific shape in response to the nature and demands of their context and are made to speak to those present. Thus, the determinate nation, simply by virtue of being determinate, has boundaries, which means that it is inherently exclusionary. Responding to the demands and needs of some, the real nation neglects the demands and needs of others. Establishing a limited, structured, and organized terrain through which justice can operate, the real nation at the same time establishes limits beyond which its concern for justice is no longer operative, thus marking itself as partial and unconcerned. Its boundaries articulate the limits of its responsibility, but its commitment to responsibility is in tension with such limits.[24] The determinacy of the nation overcomes the problems of the ideal nation—which, because it can be actualized only as the refusal of all particularity, *cannot* be actualized—but in doing so the determinate nation also loses the universality that was the ideal nation's "guarantee" of justice.

This is the problem for the determinate nation or legal framework: it is emphatically not universal, but one-sided and exclusionary. Law exists as an attempt to protect the worth of single selves, by declaring their inherently universal worth, but because it must be determinate it must evade responsibility for supporting the absolute worth of other single selves. Law's determinacy is two-fold: on the one hand, it speaks only to the human beings who are present to it, who are counted as under its umbrella, and on the other hand it must state determinate things and establish real, determinate means of protection and respect for determinate human beings, which is to overlook or transgress other instantiations of that value. To take a determinate step, to institutionalize a legal order for the protection of particular human beings engaged in particular activities and interactions, is hence a risk, a problem for justice. But no principle, code, or rule can be invoked as a solution to this problem, since *all* such universals are contingent upon the contexts that enliven them.

Law is a particularly ambiguous phenomenon, pilloried as it is between the conflicting poles of universality, singularity, and particularity: it is invoked to protect unique or *singular* individuals, whose value is irreducible to their particular characteristics, and it does so on a *universal* basis, but only by taking a *particular* form. First, in liberal democratic contexts law is powerful because of its insistent universality, adhering to people by virtue of what they have in common beyond their empirically qualified characteristics and desires. That is, this kind of law signifies, in principle, a rejection of the determining power of any particular authority, tradition, or custom that would override or overrule the inherent value of law-governed individuals. Second, however, laws have to announce and accomplish particular things or values in the actual, already existent world; no law can immediately articulate a universal will but is embedded in the determinate constraints of determinate worlds. And third, the universal cannot in fact be articulated independently of singular selves; it is wedded to thinkers and legislators, contingent on the decisions and protection of living, singular beings. In order to protect and uphold human value, laws must be decisive with regard to the nature, characteristics, and activities of the human in the context of a particular world. The right to vote, the right to free assembly, and laws governing taxation and representation, snow-shoveling and jaywalking, for instance, are the results of decisions about the nature of human beings, their interaction, and the world they inhabit together. Institutions constructed to uphold these laws and foster human beings inclined to support them also involve very particular and concrete interpretations and decisions about the nature of human agency and interaction. Any determinate law or institution is *ambivalent*, since it is an attempt to respond to universal demand in a particular way, an attempt to support singular, free human individuals in a restricted and potentially restrictive way.

This situation of ambiguity, however, is the context in which issues of justice and responsibility are actually at play. Justice and responsibility themselves matter only in the context of *necessary one-sidedness*: it is only in this context, faced with real people and real situations, that we face the pressing demand for just response, that we become alive to the issue of justice. And without an exhaustive blueprint, a presupposed and principled universality that would reliably order and organize all determinate particularity prior even to its appearance, and that would guide attempts to exercise responsibility and achieve justice, the question of how this justice and this responsibility might be achieved and exercised becomes pressing. To refuse the task of judgment by falling back on the formality of law and procedure is to set up obstacles against responsiveness to human demand, which always comes in singular form. The citizens of the ideal nation believed they had, in their ideal of abstract reason, a principle that would guarantee justice. Without the existence of a fixed, principled, and abstract universality that might exhaustively guide us in the details of our interaction, we are opened to the need to discover the needs and demands, the capacities and limitations, of particular situations and singular selves. In this context, continuous attention is necessary and continuous failure is likely—failure to adequately respond and enable the distinct flourishing and unique, creative identities of singular selves.

The priority of horizontal interaction out of which and in response to which any universal arises, as opposed to the priority of universal principle and the vertical and indirect relationship it engenders, renders justice and responsibility to a certain extent unspecifiable before the context in which the demand for them arises. Justice is always done *to*, and responsibility is always taken *for*, a singular person or particular situation. Justice and responsibility are demanded by determinate human beings and called to effect determinate things for these beings: justice cannot be justice, nor responsibility, without taking shape in a determinate world in response to a specific demand. Justice and responsibility only exist in this context of responsiveness, with recognition of the fact that a decisive thing must be done. The operation of justice and responsibility solely through universal principle would be a mechanized fabrication according to plan that disregards the singularity of the selves who demand justice and that decides what justice looks like prior to the emergence of specific requests for it. It is, in other words, only *without* the infallible guidance of universal principle that human attention and careful concern are mobilized.[25] The emergence and exercise of justice and responsibility are only possible in the absence of an ultimate answer with regard to this duality between determinacy and universality—in the absence of a law one would merely have to follow—and in the attentiveness that such an absence would have to inspire.

It is also true, however, that justice requires us to *enable* responsiveness by establishing laws and institutions that express it or that express a commitment to the value and worth of all and that empower a universal recognition and communication. This is indeed one aspect of justice, one way in which it is made concrete. But justice also requires that we respond in determinate ways to determinate situations *and* that we make room for the singular and unpredictable appearance of *new* situations of communication and sharing. Justice requires a closed determinacy that is articulated in laws, practices, and institutions *and* an openness to responding in the here and now to singular requests for justice. Even further, it requires an openness to future articulations, a structured space of actuality—legal and communicative—designed for the pursuit of a responsive, unstructured, and open possibility and for engagement with a determinate inheritance in a resolute openness to the present situation and the possible appearance of the new. Justice requires that we do something determinate, in the realm of particularity and in response to determinate demands and situations, but also that we recognize the possibility that determinate action might prevent the appearance of a new demand, a new human, a new singularity that remains to be understood and hence "forgiven." It is not exhaustively oriented by a principled universality or by a specific form of responsiveness in the here and now, but it is also oriented by the aim of the production of a "universality to come." What is learned in interaction on the terrain of real, inherited nations is both the determinate, identifiable particularity of given human beings and also the ultimate singularity—and therefore ungraspability in principle—of how they call, and how they *will* call, for justice.

THE TIME OF REASON AND THE CULTIVATION OF DEMOCRACY

In this final section I want to move from a discussion of the specific *space* of justice to its *time*, and to explore the *temporal* aspect of determinate world-building and the idea that the revolutionary consciousness can neither make a world anew nor inherit one already made. Here I want to oppose to the instantaneous time and the meaningless death of the revolution a conception of time and an account of passage and death that is characterized by an answerability to past and future or characterized by the notion that the present is mediated by past and future and is therefore neither merely beginning nor merely end. In this conception of time as passage, death can be construed as meaningful as the symbol of the inherently temporal character of experience. It is, that is, not merely reducible to "cutting off a head of cabbage or swallowing a mouthful of water," which is the shape it takes in the French Revolution (M590, S436).

According to the horizontal model of belonging discussed above, the individual finds herself involved with actual, specific, and embodied others always engaged in the interactive process of producing and achieving unity and community. Here we must introduce a temporal element into this scene of interaction: the basis of this engagement and communication is more than simply the material of the present. This engagement extends beyond spatially determined relationships with the particular others with whom we come into contact here and now and beyond existing political shapes. The rationality of the individual, understood in the broader "spiritual" sense that I have been discussing, is the occasion for an expansive communication also with those before and beyond it, through the mediation of determinate institutions, practices, and other networks of communication in which reason is embedded. Reason, that is, in the form of meaning and its communicability, pre-exists and survives the demise of the singular self, enabling its communication with past and future generations. Similarly, laws must precede and outlast past and future legislators and citizens in order to accomplish the protection of those in the present; laws cannot simply be tied to the rational, present self. In fact, the singular individual's autonomy and identity, as exercised through law, depends on the *impossibility* of its full ownership of and authority over law. The individual cannot but live, as an active and creative I, *from* this temporally differentiated "we," and out of its actions and their sedimentation over time—all that which constitutes the actuality in relation to which she forms her own sense of possibility.

Temporally speaking, real, determinate nations are situated in an orientation to past and future, to inheritance and to production, to ethical life and to the stance of conscience. The identities of real individuals and real nations take shape in reliance upon particular, determinate inheritances from the past and a mobilized responsiveness to the singularity that the future may hold in store. This present is not fully transparent or the product and playground of a fully conscious self that can make its terrain a mirror, reflective purely of its fully present and rational will. It is the arena in which the individual is cultivated as a participant, with the help of the accomplishments of the past, as responsive to what may come in the future, and as mostly blind to the temporal roots of its feeling of presence to itself.

The revolutionary consciousness, by contrast, has no sense of the notion of time and passage upon which law, reason, and its own identity in fact depend; it conceives of revolution and the abolition of the past as an absolute beginning and end, which, once achieved, retains nothing from the past and leaves nothing to be done in the future.[26] Indeed, we can see in the invention of the French Republican calendar in 1793 this break with the past and an attempt to create a new time, one that would reflect this society's conception of its self-creation and self-reliance and its separability in time from any other society.

Regardless of its shortcomings and incoherence, however, the Revolution was a significant human accomplishment, according to Hegel—one that continues to contribute something important to thinking about political life. In the context of this treatment of time, for instance, we should observe that, for the sake of a transformed and transformative understanding of the present, *any* political framework must in a sense be conceived of as a beginning, or it must retain some sense of the significance of revolution. No fixed, determinate way of life, that is, can ever be conceived as *the* answer to the question of how to live together; if it operates as such it will preclude the appearance of new values and new insight. A political framework must be able to allow the emergence of something new and unpredictable according to past patterns, of a determinacy to which individuals will become newly and unpredictably answerable, or in relation to which they will be called to develop new ways of acting and thinking. The risk in this case is that only the future contains the terms to which what is constructed in the present will have to respond, and that in creating something new we invite those unpredictable terms into existence and become answerable to this future in a way that unsettles our agency in the present.

But no revolution, and no revolutionary instinct, can *merely* be conceived of as a simple beginning. Determinate history and traditions are drawn always along in it, as the indispensable conditions from which we orient ourselves to the future; they constitute the language that enables the interaction through which unity and community are produced. They are the sedimentation of free activity, on the basis of which we can act freely, resourcefully, and creatively.[27] To learn to see the freedom embedded in determinate things, in the world, and in social institutions and practices is to learn to see democratically, to see in a way that is hospitable to the free nature of the beings that have bequeathed a world to us.

This account of a temporality distinct from the atemporality of the French Revolution explains partly why death is treated the way it is in the revolutionary context. A society that considers itself persistently new, and that operates on the basis of principles that are atemporal and unchanging, cannot adequately, in a genuinely human way, recognize death, linked as death is to the passage of time; death is compared to the end of the life of a vegetable—"cutting off a head of cabbage" (M590, S436). In Hegel's alternative version of the present, however, death reflects the nature of spirit as history and as cultural transmission. For this insight we can turn to Hegel's discussion of "ethical life" again, which is centered around the issue of the sanctification of death. In it a natural passing-away is transformed into a meaningful, spiritual event embedded in the production of a human society.[28] With the idea that the present is inherited and produced, death becomes meaningful: our lives are meaningful not merely in relation to us but in relation to the way they are lived through and on the basis of others, in relation to the way in which others live through and on the basis of us. The sanctification or remembrance of death represents recognition of the fact that human meaning is oriented to more than just the necessity and facticity of the present.

However, just as the earlier characteristic of *spatial* determinacy instigated a concern in the name of justice, so this *temporal* determinacy raises a concern about justice as well, one linked with the concept of democracy. The revolutionary consciousness points in fact to the antidemocratic nature of inert and sedimented actuality. That is, this actuality is in a particular sense antidemocratic insofar as it fails to express recognition of the initiative of this present, free, and creative self, and it denies the free, rational insight of this self by privileging the authority of the world as it is inherited, in its historical sedimentation and particularity. This is, indeed, a legitimate challenge: how can democratic culture, if it is sedimented, inherited, and transmitted, reflect the existence and contributions of the present, creative, and free self in the name of whom it is invoked? One answer here is that the instantaneous time of the Revolution cannot account for the formation and cultivation of potentially democratic beings; they in fact have to *learn* the capacity for subjective insight and freedom. Democracy must already exist, as an inherited artefact *not* of our own making, in order for the practice of democracy to be possible, precisely because it needs to be learned. Democracy is only fostered and enabled by determinate practices of education and culture, by the determinate structures and inherited practices of an "ethical life." Individual rationality and democratic participation are not immediately achieved but an accomplishment of the passage of time and the transmission of cultural knowledge, and death and its counterpart, birth, underline the coming into being and passing away of those who would participate in this democratic form.[29] A society that scorns death is one that scorns the passage of social forms and scorns education into the transmission of culture—a sedimented determinacy, again, that enables openness to a new future.

CONCLUSION

The real nation involves the production of a society engaged in trying to actualize the possibility that the people in it could live together well; it is organized around a responsiveness to internally generated and intersubjectively communicated needs and demands. It involves people who live in proximity to each other and who enact their freedom in particular ways; it involves the particular just and democratic practices that each of us has learned and adopted or rejected, and in relation to which we have developed our own visions of justice and democracy; it operates on the basis of an unconscious inheritance and a continuous projection beyond its current shape. This is a world that is more than one's own will, a world in which there is in fact a before and a beyond, one that makes the localized present meaningful and that exists to be discovered, through the determinacy of interaction, by each determinately situated and circumscribed self.

Studying Hegel's analysis of the world of the French Revolution has given us the opportunity to see the three different dynamics of justice at work in a particular political context, a context that has been very significant historically in its agency in the establishment of a modern political world. This study has shown, I hope, the problems invited by identification between individual and universal that is unmediated by the particularity of ethical life, the problems facing a pseudoconscientious stance detached from particularity. It has shown the ways in which real nations must negotiate these different aspects of justice if they are to foster life and action. It has shown that justice and democracy always take a determinate *shape* in the practices, laws, and institutions through which they speak and in response to the demands they must determinately meet, but that they also always have a shape yet to take, in response to the singularity that will always make new demands of them. They both arise in and enable a particular temporal and spatial interaction; they must be both closed and open, actual and possible, and oriented to the production of a universality that will do justice to both particularity and singularity. They must, that is, be the material and the imperatives of a *real* nation, one not achieved in principle but produced in practice—one that wrestles with the necessity of determinacy and exclusion and the possibility of universality and inclusion.

7

CRIMINAL ACTION

A further important aspect of law, beyond the determinate sites and agents of its enactment, is the way in which it is mobilized to deal with transgression of it. Developing a conception of the nature and operation of law also requires developing an account of what it entails with regard to its transgression in the form of crime—how it takes the shape it does so as to prevent such transgression and how it is restored, renewed, and shaped following such transgression. The *Philosophy of Right* offers a complex account of the intricate ethical ground of individual right and the intricate ethical context that crime against such individual right transgresses. Hegel's purpose in it is to describe the many layers of reality that are invoked by crime and by the response to it, including what the criminal does in committing a crime, whom the crime offends, what shape responses to it should take, and what kind of consequences these responses have. This chapter discerns and describes these aspects for the sake of both illuminating the power and significance of Hegel's account of crime and exploring once again the nature and limitations of law as manifest in its capacity to respond to crime and its necessary relation to the reality represented by the notions of ethicality and forgiveness.

We will turn here, again, to a familiar starting-point—to a consideration of the nature of "ordinary" action—so as to be able to discern what specifically makes action "criminal." In the first section I discuss the ordinary context of agency out of which crime erupts as a transgression. I give an account of the nature and conditions of agency so as to be able to see the way in which criminal action prevents—for the criminal, the victim, and others—its successful exercise. This analysis of the conditions of agency also allows us to see, in the second section, the sense in which law is rational and authoritative and punishment is just. In the third section, however, I consider the limitations of law—how it can in fact be like criminal action in that it can lead to a violation of the conditions of agency. With this critique of law in hand, we can address, fourth, Hegel's theory of punishment through the lens of pardon or forgiveness, a power allotted to the monarch as the highest representative of the authority of the law. This will return us in the fifth section to the priority and authority of the conditions of agency over law and hence to the nonretributive aspects of Hegel's view of punishment—in other words, the authority of modern ethical life or of the set of conditions that create in us the capacity for agency and authority in the first place and through which law acquires its significance and prerogative. This authority, however, is not one that can be systematically justified; nevertheless, the possibility of genuine ethical and political responsibility on the part of the human beings it authorizes can be located in its very unjustifiability.

"ORDINARY" ACTION AND CRIMINAL ACTION

To see clearly the nature and consequences of crime, we must first see what it is that it disrupts, and to do so we will turn again to an exploration of the nature of ordinary agency, of noncriminal action and interaction, supplementing further the fourth and fifth chapters' considerations of the nature of action. With an account of the defining characteristics of action in general, we will be able to identify what makes action criminal and transgressive, as well as what constitutes a right response to such criminal action.

To establish the grounds for a comparison of action as such and distinctly criminal action, we can identify two specific characteristics of action in general. First, action is the action of a free, indeterminate, and inwardly infinite universality; that is, it is performed by an individual who can resolve to act in multiple, unpredictable ways and who can separate itself from any given content; but, second, this free universality must be resolved to enact a particular content in a particular place and in inevitable contact with particular others—or, in the actual performance of its freedom, the individual does a particular thing in a circumscribed and particular context. Hegel distinguishes and describes these two factors in the introduction to the *Philosophy of Right*:

> the will contains (α) the element of *pure indeterminacy* or of the "I"'s pure reflection into itself, in which every limitation . . . is dissolved; this is the limitless infinity of *absolute*

> *abstraction* or *universality*, the pure thinking of oneself [and] (β) . . . the transition from undifferentiated indeterminacy to *differentiation, determination*, and the *positing* of a determinacy as a content and object . . . the absolute moment of the *finitude* or *particularization* of the "I." (*PhR* 5 and 6)

Let us look more closely at these two aspects of action, exploring what Hegel means by these technical terms.

In describing the first aspect of action as "the limitless infinity of absolute abstraction or universality," which we could call the "subjective" aspect, Hegel is identifying the fact that action is performed by a being who can put aside or take up any particular determination in a way in which she decides, who can decide on her own the principles according to which to act, and who can decide on what determinate content will be invoked to fulfill that principle. Such "limitless infinity" is integral to having a free will, to being an "I": "*one aspect* of the will is . . . this *absolute possibility* of *abstracting* from every determination in which I find myself or which I have posited in myself" (*PhR* 5R). In this sense, then, an agent is always an *authority*, determining her own stance with respect to the determinacies of her world.

The second aspect of action that Hegel identifies, which we could call the "objective" aspect, stands in tension with the first: free activity is not free or real unless it accomplishes some actual thing in the world and unless it subordinates itself to the demands implicitly posited by that externality. This is what Hegel means when he says that in action there is a transition "from undifferentiated indeterminacy to *differentiation, determination*, and the *positing* of a determinacy as a content and object" (*PhR* 6). Action has an irreducibly finite and determinate character, in addition to its infinite character; any given action is only ever specific and places its agent squarely in a position in which she will be affected—indeed, determined and limited—by the framework in which it is done. I have to engage in a particular project or purpose in order for my freedom to actually have an existence; the principle of my action, though universal, is only actualized in relation to a particular content. Further, that content comes to matter to me in a very specific way and for specific reasons; the context in which I enact such a content is not simply an abstract platform in which all agents, entities, and opportunities look the same. This world, with its own demands and conditions, is a concrete, external arena that now makes a difference to me, that constrains the infinite determinability of my will, because of the way in which I choose to commit to it.[1] This external arena thus exercises authority over me, insofar as I now have to meet the standards internal to it so as to do *my* thing. Thus is my own subjective authority with regard to self-authorship—my own self-creation and self-determination—internally dependent upon the objective authority of my environment.

The subjective and the objective, the universal and the particular, are the paired elements that Hegel construes, not as independent realities, but as two *moments* of a larger reality. "The activity of the will" consists in enacting their unity or consists "in sublating the contradiction [*den Widerspruch aufzuheben*] between subjectivity and objectivity and in translating its ends from their subjective determination into an objective one, while at the same time remaining *with itself* in this objectivity" (*PhR* 28). Hegel describes this reality in various ways: "The will is the unity of both these moments—*particularity* [*Besonderheit*] reflected *into itself* and thereby restored to its *universality* [*Allgemeinheit*]. It is *singularity* [*Einzelheit*], the *self-determination* of the 'I,' in that it posits itself as the negative of itself, that is, as *determinate* and *limited*, and at the same time remains with itself [*bei sich*], that is, in its *identity with itself* and universality; and in this determination, it joins together with itself alone" (*PhR* 7). In the Remark to section 7 Hegel writes that "every self-consciousness knows itself as universal [*als Allgemeines*], as the possibility of abstracting from everything determinate, and as particular [*als Besonderes*], with a determinate object [*Gegenstand*], content, and end." He adds, however, that "these moments [of universality and particularity] are only abstractions; what is concrete and true (and everything true is concrete) is the universality which has the particular as its opposite, but this particular, through its reflection into itself, has been reconciled [*ausgeglichen*] with the universal" (*PhR* 7R).What this reflection on the two aspects of agency and their unity show is that *the "I" only exists as already having reconciled this tension*. Strictly speaking, an agent never occupies the position of "limitless infinity" but exists instead always "after the fact," so to speak, of the particularizing of that will, and, conversely, the particularizing of that will is always a trace of the power of that limitless infinity, a real thing that only exists as something that could be or could have been different. There only are agents who are *essentially* determined by their environments, and we possess our freedom as already formed, already conditioned.[2] I belong to all the contexts that inform my experience, and through that belonging my capacity for self-determination—indeed, my very self—grows. But I belong to these contexts in a way that makes them *belong to me*, since I am the kind of being who makes the world its own, who takes up the world to which it belongs as the occasion for its self-determination.

We can see here why this preliminary analysis of the reality of freedom is an analysis of *property*. In property, in its most immediate form as *my living body* and in its more extended and mediated forms, both aspects of the will—its infinite determinability and its finite determinacy—are at work. My agency is enacted in and as a body, in and as property, in and as worldly actions, through all of which I am—or my free will is—necessarily defined and determined by externality. While this externality in a certain sense constrains my free activity, it in another sense increases the effects and the opportunities of free activity—indeed, freedom becomes *actually something*, rather than the empty nothingness of "limitless universality." In interaction with "property" my capacities as an infinitely self-determining being are developed and increased; it exists for me as a kind of support for my "limitless infinity."

The determinate enactment of freedom in property and in a determinate, worldly sphere of activity brings with it involvement with other agents.[3] We have already explored in chapter 5, especially in our treatment of the "spiritual animal kingdom," this notion that action is the extension of the actor's being and freedom into the world, an extension through which the actor becomes dependent on others and on the institutions that structure their relationship with the world. Similarly, we saw in chapter 4 that, by making things into one's property and by entering into contracts with others, free action makes reference to the wills of others and presupposes recognition by them.[4] Here in the *Philosophy of Right*, in his discussion of "Abstract Right," Hegel writes, "This mediation whereby I no longer own property merely by means of a thing and my subjective will, but also by means of another will, and hence within the context of a common will, constitutes the sphere of *contract*" (*PhR* 71). He continues: "Contract presupposes that the contracting parties *recognize* each other as persons and owners of property" (*PhR* 71R). "The implementation of my end therefore has this identity of my will and the will of others within it—it has a *positive* reference to the will of others" (*PhR* 112).[5] For action to work—for the realization of its defining end to be accomplished—action must *already* take into account these others, whose wills have the structure of will we have just been analyzing; negotiation with others is not something optional but is presupposed within all action as its facilitating condition.

Furthermore, this negotiation is not primarily something done explicitly nor something one does "on one's own," in any given moment.

It is precisely law and the institutions of social life that provide some of the key terms and parameters within which the successful negotiation between different wills is accomplished. Indeed, social structures arise and take shape as a response to the demand for this negotiation; they are the shared form that human beings give to this negotiation such that it can happen smoothly and, indeed, automatically.

Negotiating and contracting agents, however, have a very particular kind of relationship with the laws and institutions of social life: these agents already exist inside a specific legal and institutional order that always presents to them a specific content for their free activity. In acting, such agents are always implicitly, even if unconsciously, relying on an "ethical life," on the fact that they share in an organized social world whose terms and conditions they have to a large extent internalized.[6] It is only in this *belonging* to a shared social world that one is an agent. As an agent, one has actions "of one's own" and has property that "belongs" to one only on condition that one belongs to a shared human community, and hence the *Philosophy of Right* culminates, and its various themes find their conclusions, in an analysis of the form that that shared community takes.

With the help of this analysis of noncriminal action, we can diagnose what is wrong with criminal action. The criminal acts, it is true, and in so doing enacts herself as a being characterized by the first moment of action, that of "limitless infinity"; in fact, she represents herself in her action as unlimited by determinacy, "abstract" from it, and capable of "dissolving" it. In other words, she enacts or expresses the first characteristic of action by treating the limits that determinacy puts in her way as though they were nothing. In her action, however, she is dishonest about the *essential* relation between the two aspects of action—its "limitless infinity" and its "specific determinacy." She denies the essential dependence of that infinite capacity on the established specificities of the domain of action, of the concrete world; she fails to acknowledge her dependence on the many layers of mediation at work in determinate particularity. The *Philosophy of Right* shows that action, its products, and the standards it involves are not unambiguously one's own in any straightforward sense, since they are shaped and determined by the world and by others in that world. Crime is a way of unjustly appropriating to oneself what should be recognized as belonging also to others. This appropriation is a denial of the authority of the shared, external world to define and constrain the will of the criminal—a denial of her need for this realm and for recognition in it. The criminal, however, nonetheless depends on the world, whose coherent functioning offers her a functional environment in which to reap the rewards of her criminal action. The ability of the criminal to be an agent implicitly depends on the recognition of the wills of others and their acknowledgement of the world as shared, but her action is explicitly a denial of those wills. Thus at the level of the finite realization of the will, criminal action, *qua* action, contradicts itself. Crime navigates intersubjective space through force, and, Hegel writes, "force or coercion immediately destroys itself in its concept, since it is the expression of a will which sublates [*aufhebt*] the expression or existence of a will" (*PhR* 92).

Criminal action, therefore, simply by virtue of its being action, implicitly asserts and relies on something that it explicitly denies. In acting, the criminal externalizes her will in the world, but she negates the authority of this realm that provides her the opportunity to act, to express her will, and to be determinate—to give her freedom being. The criminal asserts a principle behind her action that others cannot affirm and asserts her own authority in abstraction from the conditions that make action and authority possible. She rejects the vast historical and social accomplishments by which her action is inspired and becomes meaningful. She asserts in crime that the conditions of her action lie within herself, that she is her own author, that she is fundamentally separable from that network of norms, standards, practices, and expectations to which action must be responsive and by which it is made possible. Crime is a self-authorization that ignores the co-constitution of self-authorship by social, legal, and political structures of recognition and interaction. It thus shows on its own terms why and how it is unsuccessful; no alien, external standards need to be invoked in order for it to be judged as incoherent.

LAW AND PUNISHMENT

In light of this account of noncriminal and criminal action, Hegel's justification of punishment is clear. Crime is, as Bernstein puts it, "the criminal's illegitimate claim to legislative authority,"[7] and punishment is a response made in the name of legitimate authority. First, punishment negates this false authority; second, it restores the victim's authority; and third, it asserts and restores the authority of all of those who participate in and construct the world that enables individual action, whose authority was undermined by the criminal's audacious assertion of a principle that could not admit of general assent. If the assertion of authority in crime is the denial of authority in general, then crime demands its own transcendence. The human beings who together develop and constitute the social and material conditions under which agency is undertaken, whose agency both contributes to and derives from these conditions, demand a response to that action that denies their agency and right.

First, punishment negates the false authority asserted by the criminal, but in so doing it restores for her the possibility of genuine agency and authority. According to Hegel, the criminal is the author of her own punishment as much as is the society that carries it out; in fact, their shared agency in this regard is a microcosmic picture of the shared conditions of agency in general. Punishment is authored by the criminal to the extent that in committing the crime the criminal has undermined the conditions of her own action, and punishment, in asserting the reality of these conditions, is in principle aimed at restoring to the criminal her capacity to act. By negating her false authority, punishment verifies and replenishes her authority and agency, which she herself posited as valuable in acting. The conditions of action are restored to their rightful place, in which they can again promote her agency and authorship. Punishment is thereby an expression of the criminal's own freedom and must be included as an institution of freedom in ethical life because it extends from, honors, and replenishes the conditions of the criminal's own free agency.[8]

The second aspect of Hegel's justification of punishment concerns the victim. To deny the right of the victim is to deny right as such, in its universality, and therefore *to deny the very right by which the criminal's own free action is authorized.* The punishment is the assertion, on behalf of the victim, that his authority is actual and that the crime was essentially null, nothing, or that the assertion made by the criminal concerning the nullity of the victim's authority was not true.[9] Freedom requires self-externalization, taking up a relation to a world, through the subjects, objects, and institutions of that world, in such a way that the self in self-ownership and self-authorship is propelled outside of himself. The punishment of the criminal is a reaffirmation and restitution of the self-externalizing agency of the victim, the reproduction of a situation in which such agency can occur. Punishment is an assertion of authoritative agency as such, a clearing of the way for it, in the face of the criminal's attempt to efface it.

There is also a third justification for punishment in Hegel's description of noncriminal and criminal action. Crime is committed not only against its immediate victims, but against the community as a whole; or, in other words, the victim is not simply a discrete individual, not solely self-contained. In section 218, Hegel writes that crime "is no longer an injury merely to a *subjective infinite*, but to the *universal* cause [*Sache*] whose existence [*Existenz*] is inherently [*in sich*] stable and strong," and law is thus a formal representative of the authority of the "universal cause," in punishment (*PhR* 218). Agency is a function of the enabling power of relationships, social practices, and institutions of collective life, and crime damages that enabling power. It hinders the entrance of *all* individuals into the realms in which they exercise their agency in relation to others and build lives. The fact that crime is an injury to the universal cause actually "increases the magnitude of the crime" (*PhR* 218). If identity is mediated, then crime against that identity has an effect on mediating institutions and relationships of all kinds.[10] If punishment were not the response, the crime and its accompanying claims "*would otherwise be regarded as valid*" (*PhR* 99) and would undermine the effectiveness and meaningfulness of such mediating institutions and relationships.[11] Ultimately, then, punishment must be understood as the action of the substantial community as such.[12]

In the *Philosophy of Right*, law is characterized as that which mediates the pluralistic realm of universal individuals; it exists in service of the negotiation of free individuals with each other. To break the law is to fail to recognize one's dependence on others and on their lawful behavior; it is to deny that their "graceful" acquiescence to law and their co-construction of a unified life are conditions of one's own selfhood. That which allows for the possibility of authorship—sociopolitical structures of recognition and interaction, affective ties and obligations, education, and so on—constitutes the context in relation to which law has its authority and by which it is guided. Law and punishment have an essential and nonarbitrary connection with this shared life; they emerge and gain legitimacy from it and from its necessity to individual life and agency. In the next section we turn to consideration of the consequences that this necessary contextualization of law has for its very operation, exploring Hegel's various challenges to law in the *Philosophy of Right*, which emerge from its necessary immersion in a living, dynamic, and substantial political life, and addressing the possibility of a source of authority that is irreducible to law, to which law is indeed accountable and by reference to which it can be challenged and transformed. Further, in the following section we will identify the consequences of this critique or circumscription of law for Hegel's theory of punishment.

THE INADEQUATE AUTHORITY OF LAW

Up to this point, I have shown how criminal action is a deficient form of action because it hinders the agency and authority of the criminal, the victim, and the "universal cause" or "united life" (*PhR* 218). I have shown how punishment is authorized by the criminal in that her agency in fact relies on the existence of external conditions of agency, which crime damages, and punishment in some sense reasserts these conditions of agency. Further, I have discussed how the authority of law is revealed in punishment and how this authority is grounded in the relations and conditions that enable agency. In the following, however, I turn to the critique and curtailment of the authority of law and punishment initiated by Hegel in "Spirit of Christianity" and extended in the *Philosophy of Right*. I will draw on sections of the *Philosophy of Right* that lie beyond Hegel's explicit analysis of crime and punishment in "Abstract Right," since, given Hegel's method, the parts of a text are only understood when they are indeed understood as parts of a whole.

While Hegel's account of crime and punishment changes somewhat between the two texts—the "Spirit of Christianity" essay (treated in more detail in chapter 1) and the *Philosophy of Right*—his critique of penal law in "Spirit of Christianity" provides a good introduction to that of the *Philosophy of Right*. We saw that the ground of agency is found outside of the agent, and hence this agent misconceives her agency if she considers it solely her own doing. However, this is also true of *law itself*. That is, the ground of law is found outside of law, in the living relations of substantial life, and we misconstrue the law if we consider it capable on its own of identifying and supporting what is just. If law and the way in which it responds to crime are accorded authority above human inclinations, love, and the "wealth of living relations," then law essentially commands separation from the actual emotive and spiritual conditions that motivate genuine ethical behavior and make self-authorship possible in the first place.[13] In a passage cited already in chapter 1, Hegel rather starkly claims that the only difference between those who obey others and the man who obeys his own command of duty "is not that the former make themselves slaves, while the latter is free, but that the former have their lord outside themselves, while the latter carries his lord in himself, yet at the same time is his own slave. For the particular—impulses, inclinations, pathological love, sensuous experience, or whatever else it is called—the universal is necessarily and always something alien and objective" (*ETW* 211). This "particular" is an integrated aspect of the human being, and, in opposing it, the "dutiful" human being becomes divided against himself. To the authority of law Hegel contrasts the "spirit of Jesus, a spirit raised above morality" (*ETW* 212), which undermines laws and attempts to strip them of their legal form. The ethic of love attributed by Hegel to Jesus shows the superfluity of the law in the face of a "wealth of living relations," the "richer, more living, fullness" of the "higher genius of reconcilability (a modification of love)" (*ETW* 215).

The *Philosophy of Right* raises a different set of challenges to the authority of the laws that protect freedom and dictate punishment than those posed by "Spirit of Christianity," but the basic impetus is the same. While Hegel arrives at a less dismissive criticism of law in the *Philosophy of Right*, and while the language of love and life becomes less prominent, he continues to represent law's authority as dependent on, and understandable only in connection with, the actual ethical situations and conditions that generate internal motivation toward ethically engaged behavior. Let us explore the various ways in which the authority of law is ultimately beholden to the authority of this ethical context.

The first challenge to law involves a distinction between the *principle* of law and its *actualization* (and all that such actualization requires). Hegel says that right must be posited in objective existence and that only thereby does it become law (*PhR* 211), "applicable to the individual case" (*PhR* 214). However, as posited and determinate it is also prone to intervention by "the contingency of self-will and of other particular factors" and hence may result in a situation in which "what is law may differ in content from what is right in itself" (*PhR* 212). Right must be *positive* or *posited*, which means that it has validity in and for a particular state, and it takes on the content it does on the basis of several changing and contingent conditions. Hegel has already described these conditions in the introduction to the *Philosophy of Right*: on the one hand, they are conditions such as "the particular *national character* of a people, its stage of *historical* development, and the whole context of relations governed by *natural necessity*," and on the other hand, conditions such as the way in which an actual "system of legal right" applies "the universal concept to the particular and *externally* given characteristics of objects [*Gegenstände*] and instances" and makes "*final* determinations . . . for *making decisions* in actuality" (*PhR* 3). The positive character of law means also that specific laws undergo evolution; "they are in need of further and continuing determination" by the legislative power, in the mode of responsiveness to the living, human world that they structure and organize (*PhR* 298). Guided by the constitution, which the legislature presupposes and thus cannot determine directly, the legislative power transforms laws so that they may be more appropriate to the particular situations to which they speak.[14] Because the law must be brought to bear upon particular situations, and because the full meaning and impact of the law will only be discovered through the process of its application to these situations, it may reveal itself to be inadequate to the spirit expressed in it and require "further development" in line with "the progressive character of the universal concerns of government" (*PhR* 298). Hegel writes: "Because a law, in order to be a law, must be more than just a commandment in general," it must be relatively determinate and specific. But it may thereby reveal an empirical aspect that is "subject to alteration when . . . implemented" (*PhR* 299R),[15] especially with regard to the "endlessly increasing diversity and complexity" of civil society's "relationships and varieties of property and contracts" (*PhR* 213).

Law can never exhaustively identify the ways in which it might be implemented; it can never recognize and formalize its own limits. The fact that law must be posited by and in a determinate political system, in the context of a determinate people, opens it to complexity, conditions, and situations of particularity that demand of it a certain dynamism not contained in its pure concept. It is true that the issues of legal transformation and interpretation are addressed to a certain extent *within* the confines and operation of the legal system, insofar as they are the functions of the legislative and judicial powers, but the need for transformation and interpretation signifies that laws cannot speak on their own and that plans of decision and action are not immediately derivable from them. Once the issue of interpretation is introduced, laws become vulnerable to contextually and culturally sensitive judgment that emerges out of particular, determinate contexts and in response to particular and determinate needs.[16]

A second way in which law is challenged and shown to be embedded in and accountable to the dynamic nature of a singular political system is identified in section 218, in which Hegel argues that if the given and communicated laws of a society are strong, if its will is firm, this society will be less susceptible to the damage done by the audacious "law-giving" of the criminal and thus can be more lenient in its punishment. The severity of punishment, that is, depends on the extent to which crime can do damage to a society,. which in turn depends on how healthy and secure that society is. As Hegel writes, the "stability of society . . . makes crime appear in a milder light, so that its punishment also becomes milder," and further, therefore, "a criminal code cannot be valid for every age" (*PhR* 218A). The assessment of the health of a society is not a matter for law as such, and hence the law on its own is not sufficient to determine the appropriate nature of punishment; there are thus considerations other than law that dictate the shape that response to crime should take.[17] This argument shows that we cannot look solely to what Hegel minimally says about crime and punishment in "Abstract

Right" in order to understand crime and punishment; that is, we cannot understand crime merely in reference to abstract individuals and their property. The nature of crime and of punishment is understandable only in reference to the actual conditions of ethical life, involving the conditions that sustain and support individuals as individuals.

To explore this point more thoroughly, let us look at section 218, portions of which we have cited already, in its entirety:

> Since property and personality have legal recognition and validity in civil society, *crime* is no longer an injury [*Verletzung*] merely to a *subjective infinite*, but to the *universal* cause [*Sache*] whose existence [*Existenz*] is inherently [*in sich*] stable and strong. This gives rise to the viewpoint that an action may be a *danger* to society. On the one hand, this increases the magnitude of the crime; but on the other, the power of society has now become so sure of itself, and this reduces the external *importance* of the injury and so leads to greater leniency in its punishment. (*PhR* 218)

This new priority identified in section 218, that of the stability of society, is different from the priority of law, and in introducing it Hegel shows that there are contexts and considerations beyond law that have something to say to the approach to crime. This is a strong challenge on Hegel's part to the immediacy of the relationship between crime and punishment articulated in the concept of retribution, and it occurs, appropriately, not in the section on abstract right but in the context of civil society, the arena in which crime and punishment are developed in relation to the idea that any given form of ethical life has determinate ethical standards, characteristics, and needs. This challenge expresses a value that is different from that of following the law—namely, the vitality of the social institutions, practices, and conditions that ground agency as such. The formal universality of law is held accountable by and measured against the singular, given conditions according to which a crime has a particular significance. When a society is healthy, the social relations that sustain individuals are well developed, and individual action and acquisition are largely consonant with and expressive of "social patterns of mutual respect and recognition."[18]

It is important to add, however, that this particular consideration cannot be systematized or itself made into a rule or law. Since such a consideration requires assessment of the relative health of a particular society, every situation calls for its own unique assessment and treatment.

There can be no rule that would unequivocally determine the correct way to deal with any and every situation, since any such determination would be a practice too *ad hoc* to qualify as law. Indeed, to attempt to establish as a law that "each situation must be dealt with uniquely" would simply be to abandon the very notion of a law. The just deployment of law, then, necessarily depends upon something extralegal.

But whereas these first two considerations—the fact that laws must be adapted to their particular and changing situations and the fact that they may be disregarded if the society is healthy—are largely internal to the operation of the nation-state, there is another consideration that emerges from its finite status, from the fact that there is a reality external to the nation-state. This third indication that law cannot be authorized and sustained solely on its own terms lies in Hegel's analysis of the specificity and the history of nation-states or their coming-into-being and passing-away, which manifests the ultimate groundlessness of legality in the face of history. First, states and their laws *come into being*; Hegel explains that "it is the absolute right of the Idea to make its appearance in legal determinations and objective institutions" even if "the form in which it is actualized appears . . . as violence [*Gewalt*] and wrong. This right is the *right of heroes* to establish states" (*PhR* 350). What this means is that a system of law must be initiated or posited, and it can only come into being through this a-legal act of positing; law is brought into being in and relies for its existence on a set of actions that it cannot retroactively affirm or justify, that in principle lie outside of the scope of its authority and legitimating power. Further, while states and laws come into being, they also *pass away*; Hegel says that nation-states, which "emerge with their own *particular and determinate principle*," are "the unconscious instruments and organs of that inner activity in which the shapes which they themselves assume pass away, while the spirit in and for itself prepares and works its way towards the transition to its next and higher stage" (*PhR* 344). Through history, that is, lessons are learned about how to live together, and this project of living together, its nature and its demands, has priority over the particular legal forms of organization of each individual state. In sum, law takes shape only in the context of a determinate political system, and what is revealed in the initiation and demise of that political system are its limits, its impermanence, and its specificity.

It is Hegel's challenge to explain the forces and extensions that cultivate and constitute individual human beings—to think through the massive historical, interpersonal, and political realities to which human identity, activity, and thought are indebted. *Geist* or "Spirit" is his name for this reality that is our ground and the arena of our becoming, but that is simultaneously beyond us. It is not law or the specific constitution of a particular nation, then, but "spirit"—in short, the massive complex of historical, interpersonal, and political realities that constitute and cultivate individual human beings—that has ultimate authority with regard to the forms that collective life takes and the legal organization it has. In this sense, then, spirit, in its very authority, is criminal or transgressive with regard to given, posited laws. The transitory character of any given system of right holds such a system open to history, which transcends the particular ways in which freedom is embodied and determined in particular forms of legal and political organization.[19] If laws are the determinate accomplishments of those historical structures, they cannot be truly understood apart from history and the different shapes these structures take in history. The appearance and disappearance of nation-states, the fact that law takes a determinate form and is not self-founding, suggest that it is impossible to hold the foundation of accountability itself accountable, to authorize authority, to systematize laws that find their reason for being in an a-systematic network of developing individuals engaged in processes of discovery of themselves and others, processes of determination of themselves and the world. Crime chips away at the social conditions of action; punishment is the attempt to restore them; but it is necessarily the case that healthy and life-giving structures of interaction may require new laws and forms of legal authority, by which our understanding of and attitude toward crime and punishment may change. As Hegel says, reason itself "recognizes that contingency, contradiction, and semblance have their (*albeit limited*) sphere and right" (*PhR* 214R).

Law, therefore, must answer to terms it does not set and over which it does not have authority. It is couched by historical demands beyond that of its own self-consistency that require of us a broader understanding and a reconceptualization of the nature and significance of law. We see this broader understanding at work in a fourth indication of the inadequate authority of law in the *Philosophy of Right*: namely, in Hegel's identification of the sovereign's power to pardon. In his analysis of the rational form of the state, Hegel argues that it is appropriate that this power is installed at the pinnacle of the nation-state, as a kind of unsystematizable bulwark against the ultimate incompleteness of law.[20] Because of these foundational indications of the nonabsoluteness of law, we find the capacity to suspend law, by means of pardon or forgiveness (*Begnadigung* and *Vergeben*), at the very apex of law's guarantee and representation—in the person of the sovereign, that figure in which the legitimacy of law is grounded and through which the identity of the legally organized nation-state is articulated. This apex of the nation-state's authority becomes, in pardon or forgiveness, the voicing of a commitment to the idea that the authority of law will not always be assumed to be absolute, that the nation-state will remain open to the possibility of the appearance of an "absolute" that is different from its current governing structures. Hegel writes that "the sovereignty of the monarch is the source of the *right to pardon* [*das Begnadigungsrecht*] criminals, for only the sovereign is entitled to actualize the power of the spirit to undo what has been done and to nullify crime by forgiving and forgetting [*Vergeben und Vergessen*]" (*PhR* 282). Operative in the one who is the head and symbol of the identity and character of the nation-state is the capacity to suspend or subvert that legal procedure by which penal justice is carried out against crime. The ultimate symbol of the inadequacy of law in the specification of punishment is the "right" of the monarch to transcend right, a right that is unique in that it cannot be incorporated into any system of right. Its very authority lies in its status as an exception, as an indication of the fact that law is not ultimate, in its transcendence of the system of exchange depicted in crime and punishment.

We have worked through the ways in which the *Philosophy of Right* shows about the authority of law that it lacks absolute ultimacy, and we have described alternative priorities and sources of authority that accompany law. We turn now, however, to discussion of two further points or consequences of the analysis so far: first, law has and legitimately claims authority, and hence those conditions in tension with it can in fact be transgressive; and second, because of the fact that law and the conditions in tension with it each claim authority, but in a way that is opposed, human responsibility is located in discernment that is situated between them, a discernment for which there could never be a reliable rule.

FORGIVENESS AND CRIMINALITY

Pardon or forgiveness, however, can itself become criminal, in the sense that it can involve negligence of the legal conditions that enable and support action and agency and dismissiveness with regard to the justice distributed by law. The singularity of such an act of forgiveness, its incapacity to be universalized, and its suspension of the law suggest that it in fact could be the very *opposite* of justice. To refer to Vladimir Jankélévitch's account of the matter, noted in chapter 5, choosing to forgive the criminal "may mean the establishment of the reign of the hangmen for one thousand years."[21] In other words, to embrace the power of forgiveness is to risk abandoning the rule of law and falling back on the relations of force that accompany the arbitrary rule of personal will. This objection notwithstanding, the demands of justice require that it remain the case that, if the criminal injures herself in that she undermines the conditions of her own agency, restoration to those conditions through forgiveness has to be an option, as long as this restoration does not, in its unfairness, do too much to undermine our trust in the stable structure of that collective life. This, to repeat, is not a consideration capable of rational systematization.

Forgiveness is a particularly challenging and interesting matter precisely because it points to the imperfectibility of law, the presence of alternative sources of authority, and the limits to reasoning with regard to political and legal structures and concepts. Heterogeneous to the system of universal right, forgiveness cannot be given an exhaustive theoretical justification, and its applicability to given situations cannot be assessed prior to insight into and understanding of them in their specificity.[22] But, though the authority of law cannot be asserted as prior to those actual conditions that enable agency and authority, its essential status can also not be denied. Jankélévitch writes that "the obligation to annihilate evil . . . is no less imperious than the duty to love; of all the values, love for humans is the most sacred, but indifference to crimes against humanity . . . against the essence and hominity of the person is the most sacrilegious of all misdeeds."[23] Both law and forgiveness make demands on us, yet they can be inconsistent with each other; the seamless reconciliation of these two absolutes—law and forgiveness, the demand for respect of personhood and the demand to attend to singularity—is impossible.[24] Their tension cannot be ignored or eliminated, and with this *return* to what could be construed as crime, in the form of forgiveness, *we find the lack of closure that afflicts spirit in its objective form*—or, in other words, we find that the solution to any given political situation cannot be given in advance. What is lawful and what is criminal cannot be finally decided or determined, since their very openness to determination *and* to transformation is *a mode of the appearance of justice.*

The demands posed by law and forgiveness are demands that pull us in different directions, but they awaken a sense of the significance of *human* responsibility; the tension between them shows that our principles will not do the work of living together for us. Law's incapacity to exercise absolute authority, or at least to exercise authority as the sole absolute, demands a willingness to take up responsibility in that it does not relieve us of the need to work through a situation's and a criminal's determinate singularity, the gap between the universal on the one hand and the particular way in which it is determined on the other. The law's lack of absolute authority and the agent's dependence on the authority of the social terms and conditions of her existence render the extent of responsibility indeterminate. Co-ownership and authority with regard to ethical life, and its authority with regard to us, radicalize the extent to which we may be responsible.

Hegel's account of the various conditions that situate and limit law illuminates the urgency of consideration that must take place outside of the safe and secure answers given by law. Hegel interrupts and undermines the formula of law, crime, and punishment—crime's cancellation and law's reconciliation with itself—with something that cannot be subsumed under a formula, since our very capacity to formulate is owed to it. If the law distracts and detracts from the exigent demands of the particular situation, if it is the occasion for reticence, or if it is invoked to prevent openness to a newly defined future, then it, like crime, results in the undermining of authorship on the part of all those whom it is purported to protect. While laws mediate our relations with each other, relations that teach us the demands of ethicality immediately, they cannot replace or stand in for them. When the law entails the assertion of closure and the attitude of indifference, it denies that which motivates ethical concern in human beings—the sense that our identities are tied up in those of others, that our relationships sustain our capacity for agency.

As punishment is a *demonstration* of the fact that, indeed, the victim has a right, forgiveness risks evading such a demonstration. But it demonstrates something else of irreducible significance: the priority of sociality to individual agency. Hence it restores to the criminal that which the criminal denied but upon which she depends. Law, in its abstraction from the singularity of any given ethical agent and situation, must take guidance from those particular, affective, and differentiated relationships that foster and educate the capacity for authorship. It is indebted and subordinated to the authority of those conditions out of which the very possibility of authorship emerges, and it operates because of our concern for these conditions.

CONCLUSION

In pardon or forgiveness what is explicitly identified is the authority of the social and material conditions of our interaction, as well as the fact that a final and ultimate answer to the question of the nature and meaning of singularity cannot be given. Through pardon or forgiveness, the foundation is laid for restoration of the relationships that are recognized to sustain these singular identities. It is a symbol of the fact that we cannot locate authorship, control, and agency in any one single agent or abstract universal—that authority is ungroundable, unjustifiable, and yet impossible to live without. The highest norm or standard turns out to be that which allows for the possibility of authorship in the first place; the very conditions under which action is possible turn out to be what is authoritative.

Freedom must be made concrete: it must be actualized in the body, in objects, in one's environment, and ultimately in the institutions of ethical life and in recognition from the human agents who sustain and live on and in them. The free agent employs institutions and agents as tools, so to speak, to write her life and actualize her agency; in that sense they belong to her and she to them, and in transgressing them she transgresses the conditions of her own agency. But, while criminal action fails to conform to the universal and is thereby identifiable as crime, and punishment returns the one who committed the crime to the conditions of the existence of selfhood and self-authorship, law itself must ultimately be beholden to the singularity of those conditions that situate, educate, and enable agency and authority. Authority in the *Philosophy of Right* belongs to a certain extent to law, but also and significantly to that social realm to which I, in my identity as an author of my life, am indebted and in which my sense of responsibility and obligation is fostered. This kind of authority is an authority that forgiveness shows us cannot be systematically developed and defended, an absolute that is plural, and in the face of which our authority falters and infinite responsibility is required.

CONCLUSION TO PART 2

In part 1 we explored the separate priorities of ethical life, law, and conscience, noting their independent significance, the tensions between them, and the ways in which they supplement each other. We saw that the role of each one is to take as its priority to respond, in the name of justice, to something significant in human life and in doing so to recognize implicitly the ways in which the others do as well.

In part 2 we approached the issue of the relations among these priorities from the point of view of a closer examination of the *actuality* of law, or law as determinately enacted in the world, in contrast to law in principle; we discussed its legislation, interpretation, and execution. For that purpose we looked at Hegel's treatment of the French Revolution in the *Phenomenology* and his treatment of crime and punishment in the *Philosophy of Right*. In following the shape that law takes in its actual enactment, both of these discussions show the way in which law must grapple with the concrete realities represented both by particularity and by singularity—the local specificity of any given legal apparatus or system of enactment, and the singularity of the situations and people to which it must somehow speak. Laws must be determinate, the product of singular insight into the character and needs of a particular population, and they must be held answerable to the social relationships and material conditions that constitute our singular agency, which can demand the suspension of laws. Hegel's treatment of the structures by which law is enacted and by which it is executed—systems of governance and of punishment—shows again the significance of the activities of interaction represented by the inheritance of ethical life and ensured by the phenomenon of individual singularity.

Now, in part 3, we will address the relations among the priorities of ethical life, law, and conscience in the interest of exploring their relevance to contemporary ways of articulating and understanding the nature of political life. Hegel's treatment of these three themes has the capacity to speak powerfully to the political thinking and practices of our time, and I begin to demonstrate that capacity here, in relation to two central contemporary frameworks of political thought: the politics of liberalism and the politics of recognition. Each has developed into an important mechanism by which the ideal of justice is conceptualized, and each has captured something about contemporary political practice and has influenced that practice; hence they are ideal sites for demonstration of the continuing political significance of Hegel's work. Chapter 8 treats the issue of liberalism, and chapter 9, that of recognition. The conclusion of the book describes the tensions that characterize human life in light of Hegel's insight into the themes of ethical life, law, and conscience, showing how Hegel's work can contribute powerfully to a phenomenology of everyday life.

PART 3

HEGEL AND CONTEMPORARY POLITICAL LIFE

8

THE POLITICS OF LIBERALISM

At various points in the *Phenomenology*, Hegel shows how the attempted enactment of law encounters obstacles, such that law itself shows that it requires supplementation; it cannot do the social and political work for which it is designed solely on its own. The factors of its supplementation, as I have argued, are the social and relational work captured by the notion of ethicality and the work of transgressive singularity captured by the notion of conscience and its forgiveness. In this chapter, I explore specifically the relationship between law and the idea of forgiveness, for the purposes of illuminating the significance and also the limitations of the culture and politics of liberalism, of rights-based agency and the political authority that bolsters it. In my interpretation of the relationship between forgiveness and law, I am oriented by an issue that is alive in contemporary political thought: the opposition between the emphasis on individuality and the emphasis on community, captured differently in the tensions between liberal and communitarian thought, on the one hand, and between liberal and (for lack of a better term) poststructuralist thought, on the other. Hegel's treatment of law and forgiveness, which allows these two concepts to be seen in their mutual complementarity, illuminates the possibility of the co-existence of independent, singular selfhood and collective identification. Hegel identifies the significance of human relationships, human interaction, and human formation by external forces in a way that is consistent with basic liberal commitments and with the idea of modern, conscientious selfhood protected as such by the authority of law. His analysis is thus informative for any contemporary political thought that attempts to describe political agency in such a way that relies neither on the idea of an irreducibly independent and self-transparent subject nor on that of a romantic, unmediated communality that precludes reflective critique of its norms. It can thus contribute to the myriad attempts to put the problems associated with liberal conceptions of law on the political and theoretical agenda, but in a way that genuinely acknowledges the significant accomplishments of modern law.

I begin this chapter by reviewing the specific nature of forgiveness as Hegel describes it, and the issues in the *Phenomenology* to which it is meant to respond.[1] Second, I explain what kind of relationship between universal principles and singular individuals is possible in light of Hegel's analysis of forgiveness, showing how the possibility of being responsible exists only by virtue of the tension between them. Third, I discuss the political and theoretical consequences that this concept of forgiveness entails for a liberal society increasingly organized and constrained by the discourse of rights. Following Hegel, and with reference to the various resources offered by communitarian, Marxist, critical theorist, and feminist critiques of liberalism, I construct a case against specific liberal strategies such as the following: a) the impoverishment of the public realm through the relegation of politically charged issues to the private realm; b) the idea of a "universal moral consensus" undermined by most of political life and its deep-seated conflicts; c) the politics of the individual that precludes a politics of participation; and d) the presumed neutrality of the state as the executor and arbiter of rights. This critical analysis of liberalism does not contain a proposal for a particular political regime or for an "ultimate" form of human community. Rather, what Hegel's philosophy and his discussion of forgiveness offer us is a new understanding of the relation between the individual and a social whole organized in terms of laws and common practices that could allow us to better shape the *existing* political communities in which we find ourselves.[2] There is no final *political* solution to the relationship between the individual and the sociopolitical realm; or, rather, the ongoing negotiation of the tension between them—between being one's own, so to speak, and being a part of something bigger than oneself—*is* the political solution.[3]

THE LOGICAL AND INTERPERSONAL SIGNIFICANCE OF THE CONCEPT OF FORGIVENESS

There are multiple aspects—logical, interpersonal, and historical—to Hegel's conception of forgiveness.[4] First, with the idea of forgiveness Hegel shows us something about the logic of individual action and about the relationship between a conscientious individual's action and universal law and custom; this is the logical aspect.[5] Second, with forgiveness

Hegel explains how individuals only come to mutual recognition and understanding, to creating and inhabiting a shared reality, by acting and communicating with each other from different, finite, partial, and opposed perspectives that can come into conflict; this is the interpersonal aspect. Third, Hegel uses the concept of forgiveness to identify the way in which the wide variety of human action is integrated into a meaningful and coherent human history and further, how the development of a meaningful social life is accomplished by seemingly idiosyncratic individual action; this is the historical aspect.[6] In its various aspects, Hegel's treatment of forgiveness is a major, culminating theme of the *Phenomenology*; as Hegel says, forgiveness is essentially spirit, as the mutual recognition between the universal and the exclusively and irreducibly individual.[7] In what follows I will focus primarily on the first two aspects: the logical (or what the concept of forgiveness shows about the logic of action in relation to universal law or custom) and the interpersonal (or how the concept of forgiveness illuminates the political and social significance of responsiveness in interpersonal relations).

For clarification of the logical aspect of forgiveness, we can turn again, briefly, to the subject matter of chapter 5, the basic goal of which was to explain and identify the significance of Hegel's discussion of conscience and forgiveness in the *Phenomenology*. Hegel uses the concept of forgiveness to explain the relationship between individual action and universal law, between conscientious action and legal and social structure, highlighting the significance to each of the other. To review, there are two figures involved in his discussion: the singular action of "acting consciousness" is judged as evil by "judging consciousness," because, as an interpretation of what law, universality, or duty requires, action essentially represents a departure from them, or an assertion of authority over them. "Every action is evil," Ludwig Siep explains, "in the sense of self-isolation from the community insofar as the action results from a withdrawal into one's own inner sphere of convictions and personal scrutiny."[8] In judging, however, the judge takes himself to represent the law, universality, or duty, judging in the name of these standards and refraining from action; Hegel calls this judge a "beautiful soul," a figure that takes itself to be unbesmirched by the dirt and mire of everyday reality (M658, S484). This judgment, however, is hypocritical, since the beautiful soul commits the same wrong as that committed by acting consciousness.[9] Ultimately, it is incumbent upon both acting and judging consciousness to recognize that realizing the good requires their singular action and insight and also that singular action and insight can always be rightly accused of being one-sided and contingent. Ultimately, they must recognize *the essential significance of singularity* through a shared practice of communication. In Hegel's description of the scenario, both the actor's confession and the judge's forgiveness express recognition of the demand, logically inhering in the nature of action, that each of us be conscientious and that we be committed to sustaining, understanding, and forgiving the conscientiousness of others. Hegel thus says that forgiveness, "the reconciling *Yea*, in which the two 'I's let go their antithetical *existence*, is the *existence* of the 'I' which has expanded into a duality" (M671, S494). "I" is always more than one; to be an I, and to take oneself seriously as an I, with all the responsibility that entails, is also in principle to be committed to the existence of other such Is.[10]

The incapacity of both acting and judging consciousness to identify fully with law, universality, or duty brings us from the *logical* aspect of forgiveness—or the logic of the relation between individual action and universal law—to the *interpersonal* aspect of forgiveness. This development can be understood if we look at both the accomplishments and the shortcomings of law and universality as such. Law—and with it, rights—essentially functions so as to accomplish or institutionalize a certain kind of recognition and reconciliation among individuals; it is a highly mediated response to the demand for recognition, a central mechanism by which we become reconciled to each other and able to live in a world that, because of its order and organization, allows for the cultivation of complex and sophisticated human practices. Universals in the form of laws and rights are essentially the sedimented result of practices of mutual recognition, of our finding ourselves in our experiences of interaction with others, of our recognizing that we come to be individuals through the action, judgment, and significance that others offer to us, and of our capacity to institutionalize all of this—all the while understanding ourselves to be of irreducibly central significance in that our singular, unshareable self-consciousness is that through which the world appears at all.[11] Law is essentially self-conscious and human, having its origin in human history, in human deliberation about how to live together, and in the human construction of institutional life.[12] Law is also, however, an essentially universal structure, so it can never perfectly live up to its own motivating demand, that it accomplish recognition among individuals. It is employed to do so in the abstract: it structures the human environment so as to facilitate and regulate human interaction, but it does not present exhaustive answers to the question of what shape that interaction should take and what consequences it should have. It reconciles individuals to each other in their universality, and hence it facilitates the reconciliation of human beings in their singularity but leaves them to accomplish that task on their own. Single individuals, therefore, are always in part irreducible to the legal principles and structures that are supposed to accomplish their reconciliation to each other, even though their very capacity to stand outside of these principles and structures is partly due to the way in which they stand inside of them. Their recognition of each other as singular is enabled by its recognition of them as universal, but these two are also irreducible to each other.

Hence the significance of the *further* practice of confession and forgiveness among these individuals: if we owe our being to the being of others, if we find meaning and significance in the interaction between our partial, transgressive individuality and theirs, then the transgressive character of that individuality is something that we need to engage and not ignore or suppress in the name of universality or law. Our differences, our singularities, are the site of the possibility of meaning, and hence we are in principle dedicated to supporting them in each other, to considering the possibility of reconciliation to them. This is a *living imperative*, not an abstract rule, which impinges upon us in our everyday interaction. We are called upon as individuals to reconcile ourselves to other individuals, to establish with them the parameters of sharing.

This attempt to communicate with and reconcile ourselves to each other in our difference is a witnessing to our mutual dependence. In other words, we inevitably act individually, in ways that often need to be explained and justified to other people, and when we can communicate to them the meaning behind our action in ways they can understand, and when they can communicate that to us, we bring about a kind of integration—a forgiveness—between our action and reality in a way that is an accomplishment for both us and for our shared world.[13] We bring into being a shared and developed reality that is empowered to house all of us and to further support our cooperation with each other, which allows us to be more than what we immediately are on our own.[14]

This is "the word of reconciliation" at work (M670, S493). The forgiving community—the community constituted by conscientious individuals who practice in their interaction what is demanded by the very nature of action—would be one that recognizes the significance of individual identity, expression, and communication to language, law, custom, and social practices, and the forgiving individual would be one that recognizes the significance of language, law, custom, and social practices to individual identity, expression, and communication.

This view of forgiveness—understood both logically and interpersonally—is potentially significant for understanding political life. The principle of conscientiousness and its forgiveness calls for recognition that the political arena is properly understood when it is understood as an arena for transformative negotiation between the authority of established norms and the authority of individual conscience, the negotiation of these two different forms of answerability that lie potentially in tension with each other. But these concepts are also intertwined, as Siep notes: first, "conscientious action deviating from universal laws and public customs *belongs to the common spirit of a moral community* and has to be recognized as such," but, second, "the individual acting according to its conscience has to recognize that its decisions must be intended and understandable as such interpretations of common rules, values, and institutions. The agent *has to place himself within a recognized and therefore comprehensible pattern of actions*."[15] Neither aspect of reality can be understood solely on its own terms, in the absence of contextualization by the other; neither extreme—the overarching community or the "rugged individual"—is real on its own. Modern political life includes or incorporates attestation of the significance of transgression and forgiveness to it. Its own terms—the instruments and institutions of sharing by which it is articulated—attest to and support possible transgression. It is a *self*-sundering whole, a whole that relies for its articulation and existence on people who may refuse identification with it, who may challenge and transform it, though who in doing so recognize that they live, think, and act from within it.[16] Through the influence of society I become a person, one it identifies as capable of rewriting the determinations it affords me.[17]

From this picture we can see that two dangers face conscientious action and hence political life. First, conscientious action can dissipate and disappear under the pressure of conventional life. Indeed, not all modern action is conscientious; instead, the legal and institutional character of the modern world can be *committed in principle* to the value of conscientiousness, while particular laws, institutions, and people can oppose it. Modern selves, for instance, are broadly legally free to choose their own values, but they may fail to acknowledge and appropriate that freedom and instead give it away to inertia in the face of the authority of convention. They may *deny* the reality of conscience, the absence of infallible guidance coming from outside themselves, and the persistent presence of risk. The second danger is that conscientious action can undermine the social conditions of its very existence in opposing them; it can, like criminal action, damage the broader social context that supports the very possibility of conscientious action.

Concerning the danger of the disappearance of conscientious action, Bernstein wonders whether the fact that we are grounded as conscientious selves only within a community of conscientious selves entails, as he puts it, the *elimination* of all conscientious action and its replacement by *sittlich* or ethically and communally constituted forms of action.[18] In response to this danger, he attempts to construe the centrality of the social constitution of individuality in a way that also does justice to the singular and free nature of that individuality, since both are real and powerful. He attempts to develop, and to identify in Hegel's work, a theoretical framework that could express the co-existence of conscientious action, on the one hand, and, on the other, a sense of one's indebtedness to social reality or a sense of the significance of belonging to it. It is Bernstein's view that such a framework is available when one generalizes the model of tragic action explicated in ethical life: Antigone's deed has a significance that should be understood as shared by the modern self, according to Bernstein, in that it "makes the moments of individuality (apperception) and universality (community) come to be focused on the question of who she is in relation to the community to which she belongs."[19] Siep says, similarly, that "the philosophically enlightened person acting from conscience knows instead that he has to act both according to public rules and from inner convictions . . . [H]e has to preserve the spirit of the whole in his own integral person—like Socrates and Jesus."[20] The meaning of individual identity and action is resolved and decided only by reference to the social sphere in which identity and action develop, and it is the dynamism and significance of this relationship that the concept of forgiveness construes as the ultimate issue.

Bernstein also explores the second danger, concerning the way in which conscientious action can undermine its own conditions of possibility. Here he invokes again the case of Antigone, whose action individuates her and transforms the meaning of both laws—the one in whose name and the one in disobedience of which she acts—in such a way as to radically undermine the grounds of possibility of her own identity. Similarly, he says, modern conscientious action both individuates the actor and transforms the field to which she belongs, but also, since the conscientious individual thus changes the fabric (that is, the universals, laws, institutions, etc.) in which she enacts the project of self-determination, her action undermines her *own* stability. In carrying out her individuality the individual endangers that individuality. What is involved here is what Bernstein calls the *inevitable* "criminality" of action or the "causality of fate" described in Hegel's early essay, "The Spirit of Christianity and Its Fate."[21] In this essay, as we have already discussed, crime is defined as an injury to the broader life in which the criminal shares, and thus is fatefully self-destructive; in this way crime brings with it its own punishment. Modern conscientious action is similar to criminal action in this sense: because it is inevitably an assertion of the self over the law and others, it disrupts the basis of the identity of the self who performs it.

Bernstein's response to this danger is that this disruption is tragic but inevitable: by acting as an individual, the conscientious self destabilizes the ground of its own individual identity, the universals that situate it in a life with others, and the others with whom it engages in the project of being human, but the being and sustenance of these others and universals are dependent on this self's destabilizing activity, on its carrying out of its own individuality and life. Conscientious action—action undertaken by modern, conscientious selves—is a transgression of the others and of the ethical life that gives action and agents meaning and significance, but also something that is collectively supported, and because of which others have a human world full of resources for their own conscientious action. To attempt to act safely and without the possibility of blame, or to think of individual action as capable of perfect consistency with universality, is, as Bernstein argues, to want to try to deny all contingency in ethical life and to ignore the role of action and communication in "*engendering* moral universality."[22] All human, transgressive action *creates* meanings and selves in a way that changes the universal—which is, at its root, emergent from and committed to the mutual recognition of tragically, transgressively, and conscientiously acting individuals. As this mutual recognition, universals and laws depend on conscientious action; they do not logically pre-exist the identities and actions of the characters whose lives they uphold, as they are assumed to do in Greek ethical life. They reflect the continuous interaction between self and substance, the continuous attempt on the part of the self to establish and shape an identity in an active, dynamic, and meaningful world. Laws are not the outcome of a transcendent self or system that would render them above all judgment; throughout the *Phenomenology* such an idea is Hegel's target. Ethical life's Creon, the "one lord" of the condition of right, and the judging consciousness of forgiveness show us the inevitable one-sidedness, particularity, and self-interest of any purportedly transcendent and neutral source of law and authority. The principle of forgiveness simply identifies the tension between conscientious action and law, and their answerability to each other, as the ultimate and undeniable social reality.[23]

In their relationship, conscience and the norms and laws of political life can be understood as constantly answerable to each other. Law should be shaped in such a way that makes it responsive to and reflective of the significance of conscientiousness, and conscientiousness itself should be expressed in a way that reflects recognition of the social, legal, and political work that had to already have been done for conscientiousness to be a possibility for us. In this way, both law and conscience would reflect a fidelity to the actual terms and conditions of their existence. Conscience may show law, so to speak, that significant versions of individual specificity have not yet been able to make themselves visible in these legal terms; law may show conscience the profound weight and significance of the history of human interaction, a history the conscientious self could never adequately recognize or appreciate.[24] What the principle of forgiveness demands of the legal framework through which modern individuals are limited, protected, and enabled is that it rediscover fidelity to the dynamic between the universal and individual, that it be vigilant regarding the unexpected appearances of individual significance, instead of rendering us stagnant, reticent, and inactive, connected to each other merely abstractly, our "intersubjectivity" already accomplished by a law positing our formal identity. The principle of conscience and its forgiveness turns our attention to the politics that grounds and gives life to law, that transforms it, and that often undermines its abstract "rule" by hosting heated contestation over issues it does not substantively touch or resolve. Hegel's theory of forgiveness gives some indication of how, to use Bernstein's formulation, to supplement the work of establishing normative universals with the work of critique.[25] If the liberal idea of an "overlapping moral consensus," a consensus on principles of justice that will defray religious and moral conflict, "scarcely reflects the condition of contemporary democratic societies," as John Gray writes, then "the murky compromises of politics" must be politically and theoretically engaged.[26] I will now turn to a discussion of the ways in which the concept of forgiveness might aid in such social and political engagement, beyond the limits of a purely legal framework.

HEGEL'S CRITIQUE OF LIBERALISM

With the foregoing account of the circumscription of law and conscientious action by that which the principle of forgiveness represents, we can begin to articulate a three-part critique of the culture and politics of liberalism and thus show the potential relevance of Hegel's work to a reconfiguration of the fundamental terms by which liberal societies are delineated. Inasmuch as the liberal paradigm a) represents or imagines the universal and individual as already achieved and as stable, it b) denies the particularity and self-interestedness operative in existing "universals" and c) fails to motivate (or actively prevents) the conscientious, transgressive, and solidaristic action necessary to the genuine achievement of the universal and its fidelity to a dynamic human population. That is, the self-certainty of the conscientious self and of the social fabric in the liberal context, a self-certainty that Hegel challenges throughout the *Phenomenology*, dissipates the motivation to act conscientiously for the sake of a new and more inclusive legal and social structure that would manifest greater fidelity to the identities and interests of all conscientiously acting and dependent selves.[27]

There are, of course, a variety of manifestations of the liberal paradigm, the characteristics of which I will explore in the course of laying out Hegel's critique, and there are many challenges to it, the outlines of which I will briefly sketch here, simply to establish the context in which Hegel's thinking might resonate.[28] The communitarian critique challenges what it construes to be liberalism's presumption of an "unencumbered self" with no precommitments, who contracts with other autonomous and unencumbered selves to create social and moral standards out of nowhere.[29] Communitarian critics seek to prioritize a politics of community over the politics of the individual that they ascribe to liberalism of the type defended by theorists such as Kant and John Rawls. The critique developed by critical theorists also targets the methodological individualism at play in liberalism but, instead of a politics of community around integration or reconciliation, demands the development of a politics of participation, designed to counter the "loss of political agency and efficacy" that it sees to be a consequence of liberalism.[30] David Hollenbach seems to take a certain kind of communitarian critique in this direction when he challenges liberal theory and culture for engendering a loss of political agency; in so doing, however, he opposes what is usually considered a basic communitarian idea, that of a harmonious community developed around a common conception of the good, while acknowledging the significance of common forms of identification available in civil society.[31] Seyla Benhabib argues that this loss of political agency stems from "the contradiction between the various spheres which diminishes one's possibilities for agency in one sphere on the basis of one's position in another sphere," a contradiction that she says liberal theory tends to ignore.[32] The critique she invokes here resonates with that of some feminist and race theorists as well, who argue that liberalism's attempt to keep certain issues out of public space works against the interests of women and ethnic and racial minorities, whose lack of access to and mobility in the public sphere makes the actual exercise of rights much more difficult than the theory would profess.[33] They also accuse liberalism of entrenching existing inequalities by developing or emphasizing those rights that would allow those in power to continue to exercise that power, unsusceptible to any intervention on the part of less powerful groups or individuals. Finally, a fourth type of critique that might be called Foucaultian challenges the liberal dependence on law for draining substance from highly contested political issues, instantiating and supporting certain forms of identity that become entrenched and leave little room for the development of new forms of identity, presuming a neutral state unimplicated in techniques of domination and subject-formation, and evading (in the name of an abstract equality) transformation of the concrete social powers that produce real inequality.[34] Wendy Brown identifies a variety of these problems when she writes that "subjects are brought into being through subjectifying discourses"; they are "not simply oppressed but produced through these discourses, a production that . . . [occurs] through complex and often fragmented histories in which multiple social powers are regulated through and against one another."[35]

In different ways, these various critics of liberalism have the view that the starting point of political philosophy should not be the established and discrete individual, but the individual as a complex product of social relations of recognition and power; that the liberal reliance on tolerance and rational discourse simply ignores imbalances in power that make liberal virtues such as tolerance and rational discourse a more desirable and feasible option for some than others; that the nature of our political life manifests serious disagreements whose depth and volatility are simply ignored by the positing of, for instance, a Rawlsian "overlapping consensus" and a rigid distinction between public and private.[36] Most would challenge what Rawls identifies as the possibility of a shared political conception of justice in which we try, "so far as we can, neither to assert nor to deny any religious, philosophical, or moral views, or their associated philosophical accounts of truth and the status of values,"[37] as well as Richard Rorty's similar suggestion that we "reserve . . . for private life" religious and philosophical convictions and in so doing protect them, as well as people who do not hold them, from coercion.[38] In these accounts, the material of public negotiation is already decided, and the individual is importantly separable from it; what belongs and what does not belong is clear; what goes on in the realm of the public is free from influence by the activity and transformation that occurs in the context of private life. Similarly, law is construed as immune to that which takes place outside of the scope of its authority; law and the framework of public authority are considered independent of private issues and interests, whose freedom and autonomy they are supposed to protect while remaining indifferent to them.

We can begin to identify here some points of continuity between the critical approach to liberalism delineated above and Hegel's descriptions of law, action, and forgiveness. Briefly, focus on the individual, on a "hands-off" liberal tolerance, and on a firm opposition between private and public precludes the kind of engagement with others that could continue to contribute to the development of the "universal" and the "individual." These factors disavow the formative role played by this engagement with others in fostering a sense of obligation and mutual commitment in the first place, prior to any disengagement from it. Further, the liberal framework seems to presume that the state, the executor and enforcer of rights and the decision maker in the case of conflict, is morally neutral, lacking any interests that would interfere with its fairness. They fail to question, that is, the possible particularity of the executor of the universal.

These reflections lead us back to the three-part critique of liberalism that I have argued is entailed by Hegel's theory of forgiveness: the liberal paradigm: a) represents or imagines the universal and individual to be already achieved and stable; b) denies the particularity and self-interestedness operative in existing "universals"; and c) fails to motivate the conscientious, transgressive, and solidaristic action necessary to its real achievement and its fidelity to a dynamic human population. Let us begin by addressing a), the idea that liberalism represents the universal (for instance, law and the integrity of state authority) and the individual (for instance, the autonomous rights-bearer) as already achieved, thereby discouraging individual input into the life of the universal and collective input into the life of the individual.

Both the individual moral agent of liberal thought and the universals operative in the liberal community that seeks to protect her and to regulate her behavior are sites of excessive self-certainty and self-assertion. What seems to be missing in the case of the individual is a sufficiently profound account of the nature of action and identity. Acting is never done on the basis of absolute certainty about the meaning of one's action and about the conformity of one's action to the principles with the help of which one conceives of it. Individual moral agents presume such certainty if they are not alive to the possibility that they are indebted to others for their identity and agency in a way that law could never reflect and that they could never adequately honor. Individuals must *discover* what their actions mean by being attuned to the others around them; the action of intersubjectively constituted agents is not simply their own and should reflect their awareness of their dependence and impact on others. Such action is weighty and difficult: through it individual agents construct the universal with others and thus should be attentive to how their action, identity, and position in the world have consequences for these others. This *uncertainty* of self calls for solidaristic action, action as an expression of concern for the impact of one's individual position in the world on that of others, action as a question—about who I am and who we are, about what is meaningful and why—that is opened to the answers and input of others. It suggests a solidarity and a collectivity the centrality of which liberalism seems to have trouble conceptualizing.

We can refer again to Bernstein here, who writes that "liberal ethical thought is constituted by its stoical desire to place the worth of self and community beyond reproach or blame, to make the good will unconditionally good," and to shelter moral worth, choice, and rationality from contingency and thus from history.[39] Bernstein refers here to Kant's moral law, Habermas' Principle D, and rationality for Rawls, or, that is, to the possibility that a *procedure* could categorically determine the right or wrong of any plan of action, such that an individual could safely commit to it and rely on the procedure to make the ethical or political decision for her. Such an approach is comparable to that of the judging consciousness, who takes itself to be a pure representative of law, unembroiled in the contingencies of action; it is in effect a refusal of ethical agency, not the assumption of it.

Self-isolating self-certainty not only is evident in the individual agents of liberalism; it is also evident in legal universals and the community that upholds and defines itself through them. In the culture and politics of liberalism, it is presumed that liberal principles and universals will resolve any indeterminacy in action and interaction, that action is free and safe and has merely private impact because these principles and universals are solid and secure. The uncertainty of action, and the way in which through it we take guidance from our historical roots and from others, is concealed by claims to the security of legal universals, claims to their neutrality, impartiality, and fitness for every context. But the very meaning and desirability of these universals is what is being worked out through action and elaborated over time. There are no principles or universals that could *secure* the fate of individual actions, choices, and worth, since the principles or universals at work by which we regulate, coordinate, and judge action and choice are tied to and emerge from the shifting terrain of recognition. Whenever they describe and constitute the singular individuals to whose interaction they are beholden in a way that disables recognition and the expression of singular value, they should be challenged. The community and its universals exemplify self-certainty when they are regarded as beyond reproach and challenge by individuals, beyond the necessity of being recognized as such by individuals, and beyond all particularity of interest or origin or prior to any possible action or negotiation. Both the individuality of action and the universals through which action is justified are condemned to uncertainty by virtue of our inability to restrict rationally the possible outcomes of action and by virtue of the possibility that universals, as expressions of a particular society's particular self-understanding, do not have the privilege of absolute stability and permanence. These universals, that is, are beholden to the vicissitudes of transgressively acting individuals and may describe and constitute these individuals in a way that in fact forms and restricts their self-understanding.

This brings us to the second tier of the critique, or b), that the liberal paradigm denies the particularity and self-interest that operate through existing "universals" and the historical social relations through which these universals came into being. Hegel's critique of law in his discussion of ethical life is helpful here. In it he illuminates the social relations and their history that make already existing laws and practices meaningful and that make the "naturalization" of laws a disingenuous move on the part of an already acting and interpreting society. His observation here is that laws and social arrangements are always the product of human culture, and the assertion that they are *natural* and immediately authoritative is a *cultural* move. A historical myopia similar to that afflicting ethical life is sometimes operative in contemporary discussions of rights: the discourse of rights is the product of a particular world and a particular history, implicated in the good and bad aspects of that history and operative for particular kinds of beings produced in that history, and it would be improper to think of ourselves as the lucky recipients of *the* answer to the question of how human beings ought to live together. Indeed, many societies with which rights have been affiliated have imposed answers to the question of how to live together on others, and this history is as much to be explored as is the history of the discourse of rights. Our laws, rights, and social arrangements—both inwardly and outwardly—may express the interpretations of a society with a particular historically grounded framework of privilege and disprivilege, from which they are not separable.[40] Hegel's account of forgiveness brings our attention to exactly that exchange between historical social relations and the universals developed through them, opposing neglect of the historical social relations through which these particular rights came into being and in relation to which they were justified.

Unwillingness to explore or investigate the *particular* aspects of the claims to universality expressed in laws and rights—the specificity of the history that brought them into being, for instance—can also be manifest as an unwillingness to think through how they are actually accessible to and exercised by people. That is, the fact that rights only actually mean something when they are exercised means that their nature is not fundamentally decided in the realm of principle, but *only in the field of their enactment.* To assert and uphold the value and efficacy of rights demands that we follow them into this field, exploring what hinders and what encourages their actual invocation by actual people. The ability to exercise rights is in fact imbalanced; it increases or decreases depending on one's social, economic, and political mobility and leverage. The history of Western thought itself contains resources for the elaboration of this suspicion: Rousseau and Marx, for instance, describe how laws, rights, or universals in general cannot be effectively separated from the desire to entrench existing inequalities, protect property against the possible demands of the propertyless, and conceal the original brute expropriation that grounds much Western ownership of property.[41] The invocation of rights must be accompanied by critical reflection on the inevitable presence of specific economic and political interests and differing gradations of power, which motivate particular descriptions of the nature of selfhood and its dependence on rights.

What Hegel identifies with his account of forgiveness is the fact that universal and individual will never be finally reconciled to each other but must be continually negotiated. This is far from the idea that modernity is preparing us for a final reconciliation and designing an ultimate political regime, a stereotype that is sometimes attributed to Hegel. With the concept of forgiveness, Hegel articulates philosophically the priority of flourishing human lives to social practices, institutions, and laws and the idea that a universal is the always imperfect expression of the actions and interests of individuals acting together and recognizing one another. The liberal portrayal of universals and laws does not similarly identify the dynamic character of the universal and articulate the means of negotiation between the universal and single individuals. While purportedly *protecting* the individual's right to turn around and challenge her environment, it does not provide resources sufficient for identifying and criticizing its *own* specificity as a particular form of social organization that provides specific possibilities for political agency and social and cultural interaction.

This fact brings us to the third point of criticism: c), the idea that the liberal paradigm fails to motivate, or actively prevents, the conscientious, transgressive, and solidaristic action necessary to its real achievement and its fidelity to a dynamic human population. While supposedly supporting the possibility of individual freedom in action, liberal thought precludes the possibility that such action might make a change in the universal, since the stability of that universal is purportedly necessary for the protection of this capacity itself. The liberal representation of an already achieved and stable universal, while supposedly protecting individual action, disempowers this action from the start by construing the universal as indifferent to human contributions and participation in its formation.

Here we see the way in which the liberal paradigm resonates with that of the condition of right described in chapter 3. Hegel's analysis of the condition of right shows the right allotted to the human person to be the occasion of its disempowerment, for by means of it the person is separated from the world in which its freedom might be enacted and meaning might be elaborated and from the others with whom it could meaningfully develop its freedom. Most resonant in this context, however, is the fact that its separability from all contexts of determination means that there are no elements that would mediate its relationship with the power required to hold this society together—in this case, the lord. Like the lord of the Roman Empire, the universals of the modern world disempower persons if persons are construed as the ultimate source of authority and legitimation, the ultimate character of which is purported to be required for their effectiveness in upholding freedom. Further, these universals disempower persons if they individualize persons to such an extent that the institutions that mediate the relationship between persons and universal principles—the arena of civil society, for instance, and its variety of mechanisms of local organization—become impoverished. The particular contexts and other people with whom individuals elaborate their freedom must also be counted as authoritative and capable of transforming the overarching universal principles of social and political organization. Like the condition of right the liberal paradigm discourages recognition of the interrelatedness and mutual influence of subject positions and actions, since its account of the individual character of human agency generally works against meaningful articulation and exploration of this codependence. This is to work against the genuine actualization of freedom, which relies on the rich resources presented by human interaction.

Another way in which the liberal paradigm, especially through the notion of rights, fails to motivate the action necessary to its actual achievement, to its actual protection of real, dynamic, human individuals, is that it risks reifying or solidifying the often contingent shapes that identities take, inhibiting the possibility of new forms of identification and action. Wendy Brown gives this critique concrete shape when she says that rights for women

> secure our standing as individuals even as they obscure the treacherous ways that standing is achieved and regulated; they must be specific and concrete to reveal and redress women's subordination, yet potentially entrench our subordination through that specificity; they promise increased individual sovereignty at the price of intensifying the fiction of sovereign subjects; they emancipate us to pursue other political ends while subordinating those political ends to liberal discourse; they move in a transhistorical register while emerging from historically specific conditions.[42]

In her account, in these various ways, rights can repress agency instead of enabling it, and suppress growth and transformation instead of inspiring them.

To express Hegel's alternative, we must return to the paradoxical character of human action, that it is 1) individual and transgressive of the universals that ground and give meaning to those around me but at the same time 2) social and solidaristic, since in acting I come face-to-face with my indebtedness and responsibility to others and the ground against which but also with the help of which I act individually, unable to simply and directly express my intentions externally and control their consequences. Unlike the action of ethical life, which implicitly opposes *conscientiousness*, or action as it is construed by the condition of right and modern liberal society, which implicitly opposes *society*, Hegel's theory of modern conscientious and solidaristic action offers a platform by which the possibility of their co-enactment can be articulated. By developing an account of how they interact, Hegel allows us to imagine the co-existence of the dual poles of conscientious individuality and the community of conscientious selves. The real task of social life is presented not as the private elaboration of an individual life that is safely in conformity with abstract universal principle, but as the constant negotiation of ways of living together on the basis of shared commitments that are responsive to our unpredictable singularity, which in turn is made recognizable to ourselves and to others only in our interaction. With his account of forgiveness, Hegel illuminates the social repercussions of individual action and the interconnections that make possible transgressive, singular action; he conceptualizes the place of solidarity and community in a way difficult for liberal legal and political thought.

CONCLUSION

Hegel's account of the equivalent priority of conscientious transgressive action and the community structured by universals that ground the relationships among actors does not demand the abandonment of the legal apparatus but merely its reconceptualization. The problem is not, for instance, with rights as such, since they identify something that is true and significant of us—that is, that we "count" simply on the basis of being human, not solely on the basis of our particular characteristics, and that this is true of everyone. Even while I may be tempted to think of my identity as singularly important, even while my communities and groups may assert their particularity as singularly important, law presses me and my community to recognize that persons and communities have equal weight. It resists the pull of singularity and community and forces individuals and communities to self-consciously arrange, structure, and revise themselves, not simply allowing the force of habit and tradition full sway. Further, laws are one meaningful expression of the larger reality that situates us in relation to each other, and they implicitly express our obligations to each other and the common ground of our identities, in such a way that we can take for granted a certain degree of stability and an implicit and basic degree of recognition. We are respected, through the liberal legal framework, as having a profundity and significance that extends deeper than the merely visible qualities that declare of us that we belong to particular communities or groups, and our capacity to move in space and communities not defined by them is protected. We are acknowledged as in principle capable of reshaping the communities and norms that have powerfully shaped us. The legal framework introduces a kind of automatic responsiveness into our institutions, which ideally prevents them from being enacted on behalf of arbitrary preference, and it expresses of us that we have accomplished a kind of shared recognition of human dignity, asserting the significance of that recognition when it is absent and enlarging its scope when it is restricted. It prepares us for making connections with others, cultivating a kind of stability in the world that makes it hospitable to our forays into unfamiliar environments. Indeed, many of our criticisms of law and universality are made by means of appeal to the *principle* behind them—that they be universal and inclusive. In criticizing them we often implicitly condone the value of this principle. In all of these ways and others, it should be apparent that rights, or legal universality as manifest in rights and their institutions, are not problematic in principle and across the board. Rather, the problem lies in using rights as trump cards, prior and superior to any other forms of critical leverage and perfect in their present forms, and hence in avoiding the difficult, unending work of shaping a social and political life together.

This work, the work of political life, demands that we express in more concrete ways the similarities and differences between us, the possible solidarity and conflict that comes from being both independent and dependent, from recognizing that the law does not provide ultimate answers to the question of what shape our life together should take. In Hegel's notion of forgiveness we see the demand to conceive of laws as accountable to a critique grounded in the practices of individuals who mutually recognize their at once transgressive and social natures. There will always be a gap between universal norms and subjectively contingent action, but there are other realities at play besides universal norms to which the subjective agent can look for guidance; action is always a gesture in an intersubjective space, a move in a world of intersubjective communication, that inspires the evaluation of others. It is the gap between universal norm and finite action and the authority and judgment that exist in the context of this gap that Hegel answers to with his account of forgiveness. The gap in a sense infiltrates the universal norm itself, since it is posited and applied by human agents. Hence these universals that ground individual identity and enable cooperation and solidarity cannot be considered finalized and must tolerate in principle mechanisms that could lead to their transformation; the identities and relationships they ground, and in response to which they have been formed, themselves shift. It will always be possible that our current universals express and categorize human identities in restricted ways and that the development of new or "more universal" universals is necessary for the recognition of new forms of human identity and solidarity. The universal principles of social and political organization must be made hospitable to our future transformation, and for the sake of this possibility of transformation we should not presume that they can accomplish all our dealings with each other for us. Laws and universals give us an explicit "third term" by which we make sense of our own action and responsibilities to others, but this third term must shift to account for the changing relationship between the single self and others or for the ways in which we respond to the living imperatives of communication, recognition, and reconciliation. Conscientious action takes place within and is motivated by a given context, with all its existent standards and values, and through its vulnerability to this action the persistent possibility of its *own* transformation becomes clear. Laws and universals should allow the priority of collective well-being and development to be on the mind of the modern conscientious self, not prevent that priority from being concretely acknowledged and enacted.

In conclusion, Hegel's concept of forgiveness identifies the fact that we must be attentive to the particularity of interests that something supposedly "universal" represents, and we must know the history of these laws, the ways in which they have been shaped. We must develop formal and informal avenues through which action expressive of solidarity may have an impact on the universals upon which it depends, construing the universal as something we *achieve*, not as achieved or given and expressed already in the laws we happen to have. The concept of forgiveness, by identifying the significance of solidarity, by expressing the universal as the identification of what is singular in all of us and not already achieved, provides some indication of how this can be done—of how the poles of modern conscientiousness and community can coexist in theory and in practice.

9

HEGEL AND THE POLITICS OF RECOGNITION

Ideally, political life is oriented toward organizing human beings in relation to each other, such that the satisfaction of their various needs and desires might happen smoothly, but also such that they may benefit from the collective character of this life and in turn sustain it. Some of these needs and desires that require satisfaction and the aid and support of a collective life are related to the human being as a natural being—the need for shelter, for food, for good health, and so on. But Hegel shows that there is another need that emerges from the nature of the human being as a specifically *human* being, as something other than natural, and that is the need for recognition. This need is not immediately available to our perception; it cannot be discerned merely by observation of the physical body.[1] This need exists because of the way in which human beings live somehow *outside* of themselves, the way in which their identities and agency emerge in and through the space that exists between them or as a consequence of their relating.[2] The experience of each human being is not strictly had or made by that single human being; it is, rather, an experience made with and by others, directly and indirectly, and thus each human being is, in some particular sense, dependent on those others, *needy* of those others, for its own sense of self.[3]

The project of this chapter is to explore Hegel's account of recognition, for various reasons. First, Hegel's conception of recognition is one of the categories of his thinking that has had the most substantial impact on contemporary thought, so a work on his political insight cannot fail to address it. Second, and more significantly, ethical life, law, and conscience are all matters of recognition, such that to understand them we should also look at them through the lens of the idea of recognition. Third, the two different aspects or kinds of recognition I identify in this chapter show the significance of the tensions among these three concepts—ethical life, law, and conscience—but they also provide yet another conceptual framework through which to perceive the mutually necessary character of these concepts as ingredients of a theory of justice. Finally, this discussion of recognition is intended to set specific standards for contemporary political thinking with regard to how to think about recognition in an accurate and powerful way and should be taken as independently valuable with regard to that contemporary discourse, regardless of its interest or lack of interest in Hegel. In the following, I identify two different aspects or kinds of recognition in Hegel's account and show how these two aspects of recognition themselves illuminate the nature and tasks of social and political life. The first section identifies the two aspects of recognition discernible in Hegel's account: first, the *fact* of recognition, or the idea that it is something that has always already occurred; and second, the *demand* for recognition that makes itself manifest in our actual encounters, or the way in which recognition has *not yet* occurred and impinges upon us as a goal yet to be accomplished. In the second section I suggest how these two aspects of recognition set the agenda for the organization of human beings in relation to each other, or the organization of social and political life, and how they should impact our understanding of law. The purpose of this chapter, like the last one, is to venture into contemporary political discourse, so I also address the ways in which the issue of recognition has been taken up in the context of contemporary political philosophy and feminist philosophy, showing how both aspects of recognition are often obscured in them and showing how this articulation of the nature of recognition has powerful consequences for political thought and practice. This rather lengthy detour through contemporary political thinking concludes by addressing the fact that both aspects of recognition pose challenges to social life and individual agency and that they exist in tension with each other, but also that their problems are addressed and the tension between them reconciled in the idea that both exist for the purpose of bringing about expanded and deepened human interaction. That is, both aspects of recognition—the fact and the demand—exist for the purpose of bringing about relations of recognition.

THE NATURE OF RECOGNITION

THE FACT OF RECOGNITION; OR, RECOGNITION IS ALWAYS ALREADY HAPPENING

Hegel writes about self-consciousness that "it is a *self-consciousness for a self-consciousness.* It exists, in fact, only through this" (M177, S144), and "self-consciousness exists *in* and *for itself* by virtue of the fact that it exists in and for itself for an other; that is, it exists only as one who is recognized [*ein Anerkanntes*]" (M178, S145). This is the first thing to understand about recognition—the fact that a human being can only be explained on the basis of events and relations of recognition that have always already occurred—and it can be explained in a quite straightforward way. Each human being lives not only in the first-person position, but in second- and third-person positions with regard to others. For a single person, to be an "I" is the most obvious and immediate reality, but to be a "you" or a "he" or "she" is also overwhelmingly significant for the formation of this I, even though any given I is essentially blind to the way in which she exists for others, in the second or third person. This reality of being a "you" or a "he" or "she" is and has been formative for the I in a way in which she could never comprehend or control—the agency of others in the formation of the I is in an essential way out of one's hands. To be taken up as someone who exists in the second and third person is to be the recipient of a fund of meaning that is not self-produced. This formative reality beyond the I is extensive, involving more than simply interpersonal relations: each human being lives in and through mechanisms of sharing that situate her in relation to others; each inhabits and acts in a space constituted not by her own agency but by greater forces such as language, institutions, social practices, and laws that speak of the agency and presence of others in her formation and agency.[4] Experience and agency are thus intersubjectively constituted, so each human being *relies on* others to allow it to be a valid participant in experience or to *recognize* it as a human being, as one who belongs to this particularly human, intersubjective experience, who is allowed and entitled to take up the mechanisms of selfhood that exist "outside of" the self. If a self emerges in the context of an intersubjectively constituted experience, if it gets its coherence and integrity only in relation to that which is "outside" of it, then it is a self only with the cooperation of others. In other words, other people must confirm that my reality as a self is not merely inward and subjective, or merely for me, but has objective, concrete reality and is part of the true, shared world. I rely on their confirmation that I am real; indeed, the way in which they take me up confirms that I have both an inner, subjective orientation to the world and external existence and impact. My sense of the world and of myself relies on and is developed in connection with the sense that others have of me and of my sense of the world.

The significance of this aspect of recognition can be seen especially in the context of human development, learning, and growth.[5] Human beings must *learn* how to grapple with reality, and they rely on others to confirm that their interpretations, choices, and agency—the media they have for grappling with reality—are effective and significant. These others embody the criteria to which single individuals refer in order to assess their interpretation of reality, their agency in reality. Others typically make themselves available as resources for answers to the questions: Am I right in what I see? Is this really what I think it is? Does my action in the world have the effect and the significance that I think it has? The world itself does not speak directly to us about such things, and we do not enter into it already knowing. We rely on others to make themselves available to us as our organs of interpretation, and their intervention, ideally based on care for us and/or for the reality they represent, is imperative. They are the necessary reference points that empower us in the development of our own understanding and criteria for effective engagement with reality.[6] Through their confirmation, our subjective certainty about our value and impact becomes objective.[7]

Our reliance on others for the development of a sense of self, however irreducible our self-relation is with regard to these others, shows that our reality as individuals is an abstraction from a more primordial reality, an interpersonal situation. It is a heavily mediated reality, an accomplishment, not a starting-point. While we can see already how this recognition is something that is constantly needed in the course of the development and life of a person, it is also important to recognize that this reality of recognition in some essential sense exists in the past, as already having happened. Any relatively competent operation in the world on the part of single human beings is *evidence* of the fact that this recognition has occurred; discrete and relatively stable identity is an accomplishment of this fundamental reality of recognition. We cannot see clearly or understand thoroughly the nature of this history of recognition, since it is what brought about our ability to see and understand. It exists as the past or history of identity, as a fact or a facticity that has already given shape to identity.

R. D. Laing describes how we rely on others to give us a sense of what he calls "ontological security," an idea that is very close to Hegel's understanding of recognition. A person is ontologically secure if he has a sense of "his own being as real, alive, whole; as differentiated from the rest of the world in ordinary circumstances so clearly that his identity and autonomy are never in question; as a continuum in time; as having an inner consistency, substantiality, genuineness, and worth; as spatially co-extensive with the body."[8] A person is ontologically secure if he feels like a functioning and integrated piece of a larger reality, capable of having impact on it, if the *actual* character of this larger reality matches up to his *own* understanding of its character. Ontological security involves having both a sense of one's own stable and integrated self and a sense of the world as reliable, substantial, and positively oriented to one: it involves a sense that one is continuous in time and located in space, part of the integrated fabric of reality yet not "swallowed up" by it. To experience oneself as differentiated from the world and as having an impact on it and being valued by it is to experience oneself as both part of it and irreducible to it. Ontological security involves feeling both related to and separated from others, genuinely real, whole, and continuous in one's own right, but in a way that enables one to meet others who are the same.[9] It is not established on one's own; indeed, Laing talks most centrally about how parents must aid children in having an impact on reality, both communicating to the child *how* to have such an impact and confirming to the child *that* it is having an impact. They can also refrain from such aid, communication, and confirmation or engage in it in a way that is confusing and unclear. The child's ontological security depends on this basic aid and confirmation.

Hegel's development of these issues in the *Phenomenology* begins by articulating the *concept* of recognition and then, parallelling Laing's study, continues with a more detailed discussion of the *experience* of it. Let us turn to section 177, in which his discussion of self-consciousness begins, so as to see Hegel's articulation of the basic idea of recognition and his identification of the distinction between this and the experience of recognition:

> It [self-consciousness] is a *self-consciousness for a self-consciousness*. It exists, in fact, only through this, for only herein does the unity of itself in its otherness come to be for it . . . A self-consciousness, in being an object, is just as much "I" as object. With this, we already have before us the concept of *spirit*. What will later come to be for consciousness is the experience of what spirit is, this absolute substance that is the unity—even in the perfect freedom and independence of their opposition—of the different self-consciousnesses that exist for-themselves: *I* that is *We*, and *We* that is *I*. (M177, S144–45)

The idea of recognition can be expressed as the unity of two different and indeed alien things: the sense in which I am an I and the sense in which I am an other to other Is, a "you" or a "he" or a "she," intimately defined by significance that is not self-defined. This is the *concept* of spirit, as Hegel says—or the bare conceptual bones of the idea without the richness of treatment of a concrete, developed sociohistorical reality. It is the conceptual articulation or kernel of the concrete *experience* of recognition and of spirit, which Hegel investigates through consideration of the historical development of the shape that human interaction takes in norms, practices, and institutions—the subject matter of the chapter on spirit.[10]

The *experience* of being for another, of being self-conscious through being acknowledged, can first be seen in the context of familial upbringing; Hegel says that the positive end of the family is the production of the individual (M451, S331). The individual does not make himself but is *made* by an already constituted set of social relations; he *is* on the basis of the concern that others have for his being and existence. Hegel distinguishes the community and the family, calling the family "the immediate or existing substance" and the community "substance as its conscious, actual action" (M450, S330). To be part of a family is to have been formed already by the recognition of others in a way that one no longer has the freedom to take up explicitly, because who one is is a result of that recognition. The relation the individual has to the formative power of the family is immediate; the relation he has to the family as "other" is a self-relation, a relation to the sources of his own selfhood. But Hegel also calls the family "the universal possibility of the ethical sphere in general" and says that it "equally contains within it the moment of self-consciousness . . . [It] expresses the ethical sphere in this element of *immediacy* or of *being*, or . . . is an *immediate* consciousness of itself both as essence and as this self in an other—i.e., as a *natural ethical* community" (M450, S330). There is a sense in which, in the family, there is a separation between self and other and a recognition of the significance and claim of the other in relation to oneself, but this separation is situated in identification and in ethical orientation; to be me is to be responsive to, or ethically oriented by, my intimate familiars.

We also find a description of the dependence of self-consciousness on acknowledgement or recognition in Hegel's definition of spirit as

> *ethical actuality*. It is the *self* of actual consciousness, a self that spirit—or, rather, spirit as objective, actual *world*—confronts, but as a world that has lost all the significance of being alien to the self, just as the self has lost all the significance of being a dependent or independent being-for-self separate from the world. As *substance* and the universal, self-identical, and abiding essence, spirit is the unmoved, concentrated

> [*unaufgelöste*] *ground* and *starting-point* for the action of all and their *purpose* and *goal*, as the thought *in-itself* [*gedachte Ansich*] of all self-consciousnesses. This substance is equally the universal *work* that is produced by the *action* of all and each as their unity and identity, for it is the *being-for-self*, the self, action. As *substance*, spirit is unwavering, just [*gerechte*] *self-identity*; as *being-for-self*, however, it is the dissolving [*aufgelöste*], self-sacrificing, and benevolent essence, in which each accomplishes his own work, rends asunder the universal being, and takes from it his share for himself. (M439, S325)

"Substance" and "being-for-self" share in their being: the ground for the self's identity and action is the world, which as such is not outside of the self at all but inside it, and the action of that self, while introducing something new into that world, is also effectively the world's action, since this world in a sense has made the self who acts. And this substance is nothing other than the work that is produced by *all*, the significance that others bring and have brought into being. It is on the basis of these others, then, that the self has its being, identity, and action.

With spirit we have in front of us the "self-supporting, absolute, real essence" of which "all previous shapes of consciousness are abstractions" (M440, S325). The reality of the "we"—as historical, social, cultural, and political—undergirds any action of any "I." And while the self is the irreducibly individual mode in which any experience must be owned and claimed, it is authentically self-aware or enacts awareness of the source of its selfhood in its communication with and accountability to others and to the context they share with it. "The reconciling *Yea*, in which the two 'I's let go their antithetical *existence*, is the *existence* of the 'I' which has expanded into a duality, and therein remains identical with itself, and, in its complete externalization and opposite, possesses the certainty of itself" (M671, S494). This "reconciling yea" signals the acknowledgment on the part of each "I" of the significance and centrality of others to it, of the fact that it is real because they are real and they acknowledge it.

This phenomenon—that we rely on the recognition of others to become and to be human—affects us both positively and negatively.[11] On the positive side, because the resources and powers of social life constitute individuality, we find "outside" of ourselves what seems to be profoundly our own and find "inside" of ourselves what is profoundly other, in such a way that it is possible for us to live more or less comfortably "outside" of ourselves in the context of the rich environments of social life. Further, since the process by which we become human is an already social process—or since it was on the basis of an unreflective and original interaction that we were brought into being in the first place—ethical imperatives governing our interaction with others and our engagement in a world already make sense to us in a very concrete way. Additionally, since the ingredients of ourselves as individuals come to us from outside, our individual reality is much richer than it would be if we were responsible for being human solely on our own. There are concrete goods that come into being through such forms of identification, goods that provide people with resources with which to develop meaningful lives, and goods that can only be common or attained and sustained merely by individuals or on the basis of individual agency (even though they are not necessarily universally shared).[12]

On the other hand, however, because we rely on others to recognize us in order to be able to develop as human beings who are significant and capable, because they can insert themselves forcefully into our development before we have the capacity to discern whether their intervention is positive or not, or because our identity is as it were strewn out in pieces in the world around us, we are significantly vulnerable to others and their visions for us and shaped by their values and expectations, all of which could be fundamentally misguided. Desiring to be recognized, and to *belong*—motivations that we may not even explicitly recognize as such at the time—we respond to those values and expectations, learning how to act and communicate in ways that make sense to those upon whose recognition we depend. Sometimes the modes of behavior we learn in one place or group can handicap us for meaningful human interaction in another place or group, or can develop in us certain prejudices or biases that prevent us from being able to see the value of other values, standards, and expectations. A human good, to be recognized and valued by people who are significant to us and to learn certain ways of moving around and engaging in the world, can turn into a human "bad," to be prevented from valuing and recognizing, and from being valued and recognized by, other people and to fail to learn other valuable and productive ways of moving around and engaging in the world.[13] While we must become human somewhere, and while we will inevitably take on particular habits of perception, action, and interaction, we can thereby be prevented from being human differently, with other, perhaps better habits. The contexts we inhabit, because each is one among many, have an ambivalent significance: they encourage a kind of participation that either equips or hinders us from participating in other such contexts. What gives us the capacity to be human also threatens to take it away.[14]

Here, however, the power of the second aspect of recognition and the possibilities it presents become evident. We are human in a particular and determinate way or in relation to specific and determinate communities that draw us into human life by virtue of their recognition of us, but we are also irreducible to these ways and communities and can always be propelled out of them and beyond them in situations of growth and confrontation with other ways and communities.[15] We are open to possibilities of determination that lie outside of our immediate contexts of determination; indeed, the various contexts of human life operate as contexts of determination but also as contexts of exposure or propulsion out into the world. This leads us to the second way in which recognition is operative in our lives, linked as it is to this idea of the infinite possibilities of determination that lie in our futures.

The Demand for Recognition; Or, Recognition Is Always Not Yet Happening

We have seen that recognition is always already at play in our lives, having already shaped us to be the people we are, through a history of recognition that is not fully accessible to us. We have explored how we rely on the recognition of others to become who we are and how in receiving or inheriting our identity we inherit both great cultural and social wealth and a certain discourse about identity that can cut us off from certain possibilities for ourselves and from certain possible interactions with others outside of our inherited ways of life. There is a second aspect at work in Hegel's concept of recognition, however, which is that it is also *still to be* accomplished. We live also with a *demand* for recognition; it is always also operative as a goal, as something that we want from others and that we have yet to offer to them; we are open to various forces of determination beyond those that immediately shape us. While recognition is a fact that operates prior to our development and in a way that enables this development, as we have just been exploring, it is also a *demand* imposed upon us, one that makes itself manifest in our very singularity and our irreducibility to the ways of life and interaction that we inherit, one that we actively and consciously adopt and enact. And it is a demand that we can and do refuse or ignore on the basis of the fact that we are shaped and formed into a particular way of being human. In other words, we will see that the fact of recognition can be at odds with the demand for it.

We can see the demand for recognition operative in the kinds of formative contexts treated in the previous section; or, that is, the contexts associated with the *fact* of recognition can also operate in a way that is open to transformation in the name of the *demand* for recognition. First, the contexts we inhabit, or to which we feel we belong, may not necessarily be completely closed off to the possibilities presented by different forms of human agency and interaction and may be populated by people who take a critical attitude toward the determinacy of these contexts. Their inhabitants may, in their practices of recognition, hold and communicate the standard that to belong they must adopt habits of openness to other ways of life and action and revise their own habits and practices of interaction when these habits and practices are revealed through certain situations to be inadequate. That is, we could belong to a group or a community or a way of life a central commitment of which is to be self-critical, convinced that it does not and cannot hold the ultimate answer to the question of what being human requires.

Second, throughout the course of our lives we encounter new situations in which the values and practices to which we are accustomed are not operative and in which the people we confront have different basic understandings of the nature of reality and interpret and react to our actions and assumptions in ways that surprise us and that call us to see those actions and assumptions in a new light. Many situations in human life bring about such consequences and give us the opportunity to see our lives and actions differently, such as leaving home to go to college, moving to a new city, changing jobs, and beginning a new relationship. We should note here the important point that this possibility is often granted to us by others; it is not simply an accomplishment of our own.

There is a third important way in which this tension at the heart of the issues of belonging and recognition is addressed and mollified. While the first could be called personal and the second social, the third is formal and political, involving the general standards that govern our action and interaction with each other as members of a polity. These standards, articulated in laws and rights and the institutions that represent them and carry them out, implicitly state of us that we belong to a larger sphere than the ones in which we immediately find ourselves and the ones we find personally compelling, and they compel us to identify with a reality beyond the determinate reality through which we were brought into being. They remind us of our extension beyond our immediate personal and social spheres; they bring us into contact, in principle, with a larger reality and with people who "belong" elsewhere. In principle, at least, laws and rights assert and foster in us the attitude that *everyone* belongs, which opposes itself to our commitments and partial communities. In living according to these laws and rights, we indirectly express or indicate our recognition of others who live by them as equal and equally entitled to belong here with us, regardless of their particular affiliations and specific commitments, and when that recognition is inadequate they cultivate it in and demand it of us.[16]

These examples show the emergence of the demand for recognition out of ordinary human circumstances, just as Hegel does; let us explore some of the details of his consideration of what it is to experience and to act in the world, to live and to desire. To be human is not simply to be constituted by others and the world, but it is also to be confronted by a world that is *for oneself*, in the sense that one can make it over into the means of one's own satisfaction and fulfillment, that it takes on the character it does by virtue of the nature of one's orientation to it.[17] For the human being, the world is in some way ordered around her perspective, values, and desires in that they are the ineradicable media through which she approaches it. This ordered and interpreted world is the arena of her subjectivity and her action, her identity and transformation; it is not a simple, inert set of objects but gets its orientation from her. It takes on a certain character as a result of her identity and agency in it, and she acts on it in that light, thereby making it conform further to her vision of its significance. This means that her experience of herself is as a being that is fundamentally capable of overreaching the world, so to speak. She can cause it to signify new things; she can read or interpret it differently; it takes on a nature according to her terms.

In the context of this world as the medium or arena filled with things that get their significance and orientation from her, however, the human being encounters *other* such human beings, beings for whom the world is the medium and arena of *their* subjectivity and action, identity and transformation, and from whom that world and its things obtain a different kind of significance. These other beings do not allow themselves simply to be made over into the means of *her* satisfaction and the puzzle pieces of *her* world, since they are the kind of beings that do the same thing as she does—that make the world over in light of their orientation, interpreting, organizing, and consuming it.[18] These human beings are irreducible to the objects in the world, in that they are all *also* the kind of beings who make the world come to be meaningfully in relation to themselves, who overreach the world and its terms. Such beings cannot be made to acquiesce to the centering force of others; they cannot be forced to assume a purely objectlike status and give up their own centering force. If they accommodate themselves or acquiesce to her, they inevitably do so on the basis of their own initiative, their own power. Hegel shows this by observing the slave's attempt to accommodate himself and acquiesce to the master: it turns out that he cannot simply obey the master's will and bring that will about in the world—or, that is, his acquiescence is something that *he* and not the master does.[19] Further, the slave must interpret and carry out the master's will, which leads him to work on and in the world and develop a relationship with it that is essentially outside of the master's determining power, not essentially subordinate to someone else's will but capable of himself in turn giving his self real existence and essential shape in the world.[20] He simply cannot avoid being the kind of being who determines himself, who approaches the world with his own sense of its significance, fundamentally and inevitably opposed, consciously or not, to the idea that someone else's power could be all-determining.[21]

Hegel is mostly oriented to describing the *tension* between would-be centers of reality here; his indication of the ways in which this tension is resolved is only implicit here and will be made explicit later, in the context of spirit, or in his discussion of the developed social life and institutions that human beings have construed in order to deal with this tension. This tension is due to the fact that we all in some fundamental sense take ourselves to be the center of reality and to be the center is to implicitly posit others as peripheral in a way that is at odds with their self-conception; hence our relationships and interaction can be the site of conflict. In addition to simply not being *able* to understand the experience another has of being the orienting center of a world in which we are in turn peripheral, we may also want our way of seeing the world and our power of shaping it to be taken as authoritative, and we may find the fact that others have the same power—and with it the tendency to consider us as peripheral—to be threatening. In response, we may deal with their power dishonestly or violently, trying to ignore it or stifle it. Also, given that our views of the world and of the significance of our action in it are shaped in a particular way by a particular, inherited discourse about what it means to be human, we can be quite antipathetic toward others who are shaped by the force of other discourses, since our very sense of ourselves may rely on thinking of our way of being shaped as essential.

If we look more closely at the fact that being human entails giving a particular orientation to the world, however, we finally come to the point at which we can see explicitly the emergence of the second aspect of recognition—the *demand* for it—in the form of the demand to recognize the shaping power of others. First, the world to which we give our orientation *is* a world of other people—it is *for* them—and if our interpretation of it and existence and action in it are to be effective and real, we have to recognize it as something that is given orientation by others. That is, to live out our own reality as real and to live as forces of orientation in the world demands that we accommodate ourselves to similar aspects in others. To deny the interpretive and shaping power of others is to deny the conditions under which we ourselves live, thus to hamper our own ability to live in the world and to find ourselves as real in it, as having the impact we intend in it. To understand ourselves and our situations accurately, and to act effectively, we need to recognize that we live in the world with others who are not simply ingredients of the orientation we give it and who similarly cast the world in their own terms. Second, we have the human world that we do because of the fact that others *take* it to be their world—the world of their development, growth, and significance. Only because it is already human, already thoroughly infused and made meaningful by multiple human orientations, can the world allow me to be human and to find rich resources for significance in it. That is, I have resources for my own agency and life because I am an *other* to and for others and because it is possible for me to operate in a space that is already structured and elaborated. Thus, I *rely* on the force that others have to make the world over in relation to themselves; I rely on the fact that they take up the world in the light of their own commitments, which means that I rely on the fact that I am an other to others, on the fact that I am peripheral in relation to their status as centers of world orientation. I can be an independent center of reality because they are independent centers of reality.

This is how the *demand* for recognition makes itself manifest, beyond the mere actual fact of recognition. The task that this reality sets for us is dual: on the one hand, we have to take up ourselves as the centers of reality, and on the other hand, we have to reconcile this with the fact of the centrality to others of themselves. For both myself and an other, the terms of reality fluctuate depending on our approach to them, such that no determinate term or manner in which we signify our reality can be used to define us conclusively. Each of us will always be presenting our social reality with things it does not yet have the capacity to accommodate, and each of us will always also be a part of that social reality to which others will present things that cannot yet be accommodated. The way in which we deal with the unique kind of being that each of us is will be different from the way in which we deal with worldly being: it is the kind of being that demands that we refrain from simply moving it around, so to speak—from telling it what it is, from taking it up merely as an immediate aspect of our own projects. In every way, that is, this human kind of being demands that we refrain from thinking we can impact it immediately and trying to do so. We respond to it by developing ideas about the proper treatment of such a being, ideas we can share and that make themselves manifest in standards, norms, and rules. We develop various terms and mechanisms that mediate our interaction with it, that will do both of us justice at the same time by recognizing us equally to be the kind of being that shapes itself. And we develop institutions and structures that will allow us to develop our capacity for interaction on the basis of the engagement of *willing* and *thinking* and that will allow us to avoid relying on our physical capacity to influence the bodies of others directly.[22]

We began by exploring the *fact* of recognition—that we emerge as human out of determinate sites of recognition. We also saw the fact (and the significance of the fact) that we are propelled into interaction and growth outside of those sites, a phenomenon of which the fact of recognition can never give a full account. We have seen, that is, that recognition is the fundamental *context* out of which human individuality emerges and that recognition is a fundamental *demand*. On the one hand, recognition is associated with particularity, or with the fact that we belong *somewhere*, and on the other hand, it is associated with singularity, in that recognition is owed to each as one who is singularly irreducible to the orientation others give to the world.[23] We are human in a particular *way*, *and* in a way that can never be exhaustively determined by someone else; we are particular and singular, both characteristics of which belong to us universally. Recognition is operative as a fact in our constitution and as a demand in our action, and because it is a fact in our constitution it is two-fold as a demand: first, that people be recognized in their particularity and their unique attachment to the particular ways of life out of which they emerge, with all the historical significance that attaches to such ways of life; and, second, that people be recognized as infinitely transformable and as giving the world an orientation that is traceable only to their own singularity and inexplicable in reference to any present and determinate condition.

This leads me to a final issue. We are characterized by particular and unique attachments to certain ways of life, with all the historical significance that attaches to them, but we are also characterized by the singular capacity to give the world an orientation that is irreducible to any present and determinate condition; now, what does this dual nature, and the tension between these two aspects, demand of *political* organization, of attempts to define the place and significance of recognition in political life? In response to these questions I will show that the ultimate goal of recognition is the happening of human interaction and communication. That—and not the significance of the characteristics to be recognized—is the ultimate goal behind any particular practice of recognition and any attempt to institutionalize it.

RECOGNITION AND JUSTICE; OR, HOW POLITICAL LIFE IS ANSWERABLE TO RECOGNITION

With this analysis—with the fact and demand of recognition—we have a basic framework with which to understand or categorize the various ways in which recognition is mobilized as a medium of political critique or empowerment and thus also a basic framework by which to treat the issues and challenges that arise in it. I begin this section by laying out the way in which the two aspects of recognition could form the basis of a powerful way of thinking through the tasks and responsibilities of the political framework and political institutions. Second, I will use this basis to critically analyze other ways in which the theme of recognition has been developed in contemporary political thinking. Third, and finally, I explore the relationship between law and recognition, showing how this relationship clarifies both the nature of law and its responsibilities.

THE POLITICS OF RECOGNITION

Political life, in response to the fact that recognition has always already happened, must in some way enforce acknowledgment and recognition of established terms. Recognition of *me* is recognition of a self who already means certain things, who is defined in certain ways by a particular world, and this history must be acknowledged as real by the political framework that organizes and negotiates my relations with others and structures and enables my agency. We are always already recognized by a determinate community that in recognizing us inducts us into a certain way of being human; it is significant, in various ways, that I am Muslim, trans, white, a mother, Chilean, male, South Indian, straight, middle class, tall, a construction worker, an activist, an entrepreneur, and so on. Hence these aspects of us must get some satisfaction in the context of our living together.[24]

But this phenomenon and its recognition by the political framework exist in tension with the *demand* for recognition, which political life must also acknowledge and address. I may want these characteristics and qualities to be seen and valued *differently*; I may find that others' ways of evaluating their significance do not match up with mine; I may want this history of signification to have a different future; I may want to challenge the link between specific characteristics and the social expectations based upon them. Various issues can come up here: the world's habituated practices of valuing may have determined certain characteristics to be undesirable or may have determined that certain characteristics merit certain expectations, and my response may be not to suppress these characteristics but to dissociate characteristics from expectations or to take them up and assert their value and significance, as well as the significance of the fact that human beings are human differently, and so on.[25] In various ways, I may seek to have my capacity to rewrite the terms of significance be recognized: in addition to having specific characteristics, I am *also* a dynamic and creative source of meaning, capable of projecting myself into the world in such a way as to reveal in it a new significance.[26] The political framework that organizes and negotiates my agency and relations with others must recognize and protect the openness of my reality as well. While political life must support acknowledgment of existent terms, it must also support the possibility of changing those terms. Recognition does not leave the individual the way that she is; its very occurrence is an occasion for this kind of singular, unpredictable transformation, and political life in turn must support and sustain the practices of recognition that propel this transformation.

These two aspects of recognition, as well as the tension between them, give us a powerful platform upon which to ground a politics of recognition. What this dual framework identifies is the fact that particular social and political frameworks have made particular characteristics significant and that to respond effectively to this fact is, on the one hand, to *acknowledge* this reality and, on the other, to *refuse it* lasting or permanent significance. Mechanisms that reflect our recognition of each other's capacities for infinite determination must not foreclose the possibility of asserting of the significance of particularity, and insistence on the significance of particularity must not foreclose the possibility of rewriting the terms of significance. With this introductory account of the potential political relevance of these two aspects of recognition and of the tension between them, let us now look at how recognition has been construed in political thought.

THE DISCOURSE OF RECOGNITION

We can see what this tension entails if we consider some of the criticisms launched against employment of the discourse of recognition in contemporary political philosophy, which Charles Taylor calls the "politics of equal recognition" (or against political moves and arguments that do not rely on the term "recognition" but look similar to this discourse).[27] The central challenge it faces is launched against it by virtue of its tendency to perpetuate a certain picture of what it means to be human and thus prevent the appearance or emergence of new values, forms of identification, and possibilities for human interaction.[28] This accusation is made in multiple ways. First, it is said that to be recognized is to be recognized by *someone*, and thus to be dependent on actual persons who invoke particular standards by which to recognize, or who only recognize people if they accommodate themselves to expectations as to what is recognizable.[29] Typically, those whose recognition *matters* are already in a dominant position and liable to recognize only those characteristics that are compatible with the position of the dominant. Additionally, in a system characterized by domination and subordination, the desire for recognition from actual dominant persons can be pathological, for to desire recognition from those in a position associated with domination is to in a sense keep intact the system by which one is subordinated. Such patterns of recognition may contribute to the suppression of other standards and characteristics; what is recognized is simply what falls inside the familiar standards and values of the framework of the one who takes herself to be a recognizer, or the person who is recognized is one who makes herself look the way the one who dominates her wants her to look.

Frantz Fanon speaks to this issue as it manifests itself in the postcolonial situation, and his discussion of this issue shows the fact that the above criticism is somewhat misplaced. First, the issue: Fanon asserts that what needs to be treated is the "black man's desire," since it is problematically oriented toward all that belongs to the "white man" and desiring of recognition from that man; hence it is desiringly oriented toward the conditions of its own subordination. A central political task in such a case is to train one's desire to be different, to develop different objects of desire, to make meaning and value beyond the borders of the "recognizer's" framework—that is, to refuse the goal and dissipate the desirability of being recognized by the "white man."[30] The challenge to the prioritizing of recognition that one could develop from Fanon's work is (at least) two-fold: first, Fanon challenges the idea that freedom could be *granted* by the one who dominates, through the act of recognition, for the idea that it requires *granting* is a product of the unequal relationship and reinforces it. He illustrates this issue by saying that "the upheaval reached the black man from the outside. The black man was acted upon.

Values that were not engendered by his actions, values not resulting from the systolic gush of his blood, whirled around him in a colourful dance. The upheaval did not make the black man different . . . As master, the white man told the black man: 'From now on you are free.'"[31] In this context, the acknowledgment of the humanity of the black man by the white man turns out again to erase the significance of the black man's agency. Second, instead of advocating a relationship governed by the goal of recognition, Fanon advocates a *departure* from the world of the white man, from the pathological relationship. To refuse recognition and its desirability is Fanon's strategy for bringing about a reality in which actual relations of recognition could be possible in the future.[32]

But the importance of recognition does not by any means go unmarked in Fanon's work: it is only in the context of their relationship that the meaning of each identity has emerged, that black and white exist in the terms in which they do and with the significance that they have. Again, first we have the mere *fact* of recognition: relations are the occasion for the development of identity; our characteristics only have the significance they have in the context of comparison and relation (though this comparison tends to be diminutive and this relation unequal). Second, however, we have the *demand*: Fanon says that the person demands to be noticed as one who is not immediate, who is not an inert thing signifying nothing. And Fanon adds a third point: what it means for me to be human, also, is that I be able to struggle for a human world *with* others, that to struggle *with* is the way in which the world becomes human. I struggle for a world in which the other is *not* an "object" or "instrument" whose role is merely "to allow me to achieve my subjective security."[33] I struggle for a world with others, in which we live in a way that is faithful to the possibility of our continuing transformation beyond the way we are now. In illustration of these second and third points, Fanon writes: "I ask that I be taken into consideration on the basis of my desire. I am not only here-now, locked in thinghood. I am for elsewhere and for other things. I demand that an account be taken of my negating activity insofar as I pursue something other than life, insofar as I am fighting for the birth of a human world, in other words, a world of reciprocal recognitions."[34] He identifies the significance of being recognized as someone who is capable of becoming defined in the future in different ways but who does so in the context of being with others, only *with* them.

The lesson here, for the critics of recognition as much as for its defenders, is that genuine recognition has a certain *nature*, and this nature is simply not accomplished in the context in which the one who wants recognition has to accommodate herself to a particular framework or set of expectations as to what is recognizable; this is not genuine recognition. To be able to genuinely recognize someone requires that one recognize both the significance that her particular characteristics have accrued through the movement of history and her reality as a site of possible future significance, and it is to recognize *oneself* as situated in, and to recognize one's perception as colored by, the context of a particular significance but also as potentially distinguishable from it. Many practices that are purported to be practices of recognition do not qualify on this basis, and many criticisms of recognition are not in fact criticisms of this, the *ideal* of recognition. With the dual idea of the fact of and demand for recognition, we can understand both the one-sidedness of our identifications and capacities for recognition and the persistent demand that we recognize in each other the real ways in which we are seeing something *whose nature cannot be made clear to us in an ultimate or final way*.[35]

A second criticism that the contemporary politics of recognition faces is that claims for recognition made on behalf of a determinate quality or characteristic may lend too weighty a significance to such a characteristic, which could have the following effects: a) frustrating the goal of greater liberation in *self*-determination; b) erasing or underemphasizing the historical development that brought that significance into being; and thus c) reversing the general political purpose of the discourse of recognition, which was to liberate people from restricted possibilities for self-definition and to reveal the shape that history has taken to be the contingent result of thinking and behavior that was misguided or problematic. When feminists, for instance, demand legal protection for particular characteristics that attach to women or demand recognition of female specificity, they may run the risk of entrenching definitions of "womanhood" or femininity that are the result of a historical process they criticize, in relation to which a more ambivalent attitude might be more appropriate.[36] Wendy Brown's suspicion of rights is transferable to this issue of recognition as well: the demand for recognition of women as women, for instance, could "secure our standing as individuals even as [it] obscure[s] the treacherous ways that standing is achieved and regulated"; it could "entrench our subordination" by revealing, specifying, and asserting the characteristics with which it is associated; it purports to move "in a transhistorical register while emerging from historically specific conditions."[37] Similarly, the liberal advocacy of toleration and of multicultural discourse tends to operate on the basis of an assumption that identities in interaction are fixed, that discourse involves the traversal of boundaries between identities but has no effect on the nature and location of those boundaries themselves.[38] Fanon implicitly articulates this challenge to the discourse of recognition when he explains how black and white are relational concepts, understandable only in reference to a particular history out of which they emerged as oppositional and codependent. Recognition of blackness, then, is not simply innocent of the history of colonialism and valuable on its own terms; it invokes the troubled relationship out of which its significance emerged and cannot be straightforwardly and unproblematically advocated. The nature and meaning of "blackness," the characteristic to be recognized, needs to be discovered, filled out, and elaborated in the context of, and with hope for, a different future.[39]

Let us summarize the problems that have been attributed to the "politics of recognition." It can set in stone the framework that, or person who, recognizes, as well as the thing that, or person who, is recognized. It can treat them as isolated and inert terms, failing to fully acknowledge their capacity for interaction and the potential transformation that occurs on its basis. It can thus cripple future transformation instead of enable it and eclipse rather than illuminate the historical developments that have brought certain kinds of significance into being. The general political purpose of a politics of recognition—that is, to reveal the inadequacy of this historical development to the ideal of recognition—is thereby undermined. The focus of the discourse of recognition may prop up those who have the power of recognizing, or the determinate characteristics recognized, instead of sustaining the process of recognition through which we come into contact with each other and have our ways of seeing, thinking, and judging changed. The social reality that hinges on and changes in relation to our interaction is the site through which objects, qualities, and characteristics obtain their significance. To emphasize recognition of a being the significance of which is fundamentally and finally established, or recognition by such a being, is in a sense to refuse from the start the kind of interaction that would bring about the true goal of a politics of recognition: a better awareness and understanding of those who are different from ourselves and with whom we live.

The idea of genuine recognition, however, addresses these problems. Genuine recognition is recognition of a being who is characterized by becoming, and its real purpose is to allow for interaction that will change our understanding of who each of us is, interaction that prevents us from being able to ultimately answer the question of who we are. The demand for recognition should not simply be oriented around recognition of stable and enduring characteristics or essential modes of being in the world, in the context of which all particular forms of identification are construed as stable and prone to being held at an arm's length. Each of us takes up the world in a particular way, but in a way that is also dynamic and alterable in response to interaction with others. Struggles for recognition should not seek to close down the elaboration of new meaning, significance, and forms of identification. If claims for recognition of particular forms of identification are made, they can and should be made in the name of supporting civic and social capacities and powers that will in turn support and propel people into *interaction* with each other, in the context of which their identities, desires, and claims may change. That is, recognition should be conceived as preparation for ongoing transformation or as an inauguration of relationships through which those who are related may bring about each other's transformation.

In sum, the discourse of recognition should be developed around a more explicitly social conception of human identity, in which what we look for is not simply recognition of our discrete identities and determinate characteristics as individuals, but recognition of the *significance of dynamic relations of recognition* for those identities. The goal of genuine recognition is not the assertion of the significance of ourselves and our own identity, but assertion of the significance of human interaction and human collaboration, out of which immanently emerge norms for our engagement, for our action and interaction. Thus the real insight of the discourse of recognition is that to better acknowledge the significance of each other's determinacy and the unconceptualizable weight of each other's determinate singularity would be to make significant steps toward improved human *interaction*, in which neither being defined by the world nor being defined by ourselves has the upper hand, but in which both are mutually enabling. In interaction with the person of another, who carries with her both her own singularity and the determinate characteristics of the history of human interpretation, we may *receive* our capacity to be our singular selves; our interaction leads to the discovery and formation of singular human identity.

The arenas and structures of social and political life exist *because* of the fact of recognition, because experience is collectively constituted, and because we rely on each other for our identity, agency, and value. Ideally, they are structured also in response to the demand for recognition—that is, they are structured not only around the satisfaction of natural needs, but also around the satisfaction of the social need for recognition. The structures of social and political life take their orientation from the goal of negotiating the fact of plural points of orientation, plural and conflicting centering forces. They represent the organization of giving and receiving, of autonomous initiative and dependence; they provide the structure in which we can express recognition to each other and can receive from others, and from our interaction, what we cannot ourselves create or sustain. While social and political life operates on the basis of the fact of recognition and in response to the demand for recognition, it must also, as I have just argued, explicitly take up the project of supporting the different kinds of human interaction that are the genuine purpose of recognition.

We have looked at the issue and nature of recognition, articulating how it should be understood and why and in what form it should be desired. This discussion has in various ways made reference to law—on the one hand, as a medium of response to the difficulties we face by virtue of our embeddedness in communities of recognition, and, on the other hand, as an institutionalized expression of our actual recognition of each other and of the demand that we recognize each other as self-determining. I now explicitly turn to an investigation of law, exploring how our discussion of recognition can illuminate the nature and goals of legal discourse.

RECOGNITION AND LAW

One of the ways in which the political realm answers to the fact of and demand for recognition is through the institution of law. In principle, at least, law formally expresses the recognition, *as* persons, of all who are protected and governed by it; it is a formal reflection of the fact that we have adopted broad-ranging practices and habits of recognition, in principle asserting that all are worthy of and should be included in participation in intersubjective experience. On this account, law is a tool employed in the name of recognition and emerges from the fact of recognition and the need for it. While it is at least a result of the recognition that we are all orienting centers capable of giving significance to the world, it can even be construed as a result of the historically accomplished realization that human beings rely on each other for meaning, fulfillment, and development. And it aids in the *development* of individuals who participate in and contribute to reality by the very fact that it aids in the development and sustenance of a collective perception that *sees* individuals as so capable.

Further, each of us, in living according to law, implicitly expresses recognition of all who are protected and enabled by it. In living out of law we implicitly indicate that we are living out of a shared reality, and we implicitly acknowledge the importance of the orienting perspectives of others to our own orientation. Law provides support for our cooperation and makes the fact that we are each centers of orientation in our own eyes the occasion not for our self-isolation but for our mutual growth and enrichment. Law is a formal, habituated, and habituat*ing* expression of my recognition of you as a person and your recognition of me. We live through others and depend on their recognition of us in order to have experience that is coherent, integrated, and meaningful. Law articulates this dependence and enables its smooth operation.[40]

We have explored two characteristics of recognition that lie in tension with each other: what demands recognition is the human being as the infinitely determinable and dynamic source of meaning, *as well as* the human being as a being with determinate characteristics, which are given determinate significance by the world that she inherits and inhabits. These two characteristics—dynamism and fixity, indeterminacy and determinacy—can also shed light on the nature of law, as well as on challenges to it. Law recognizes and protects the human being's capacity to contribute to reality and to intersubjective experience—her capacity and desire to participate in the construction and elaboration of meaning and value. It identifies the abstract concept "human" in every person, protecting a central essential characteristic that accrues to them: that they are capable of construing significance, of making meaning. But it does so by one-sidedly identifying and protecting determinate forms of collaboration and determination, for that is the only kind of collaboration and determination that human beings have. Similarly, in protecting the human capacity for determination and the particular achievements of determination, law must itself be both fixed and dynamic. As the protection of something dynamic, law must be responsive to its dynamic nature, and the particular expressions and forms of law may be required to change in relation to the changing demands and needs of the human beings it protects. A static instantiation of such recognition might transgress the dynamism it is invoked to protect. Law must also, however, be stable and fixed if it is to effectively protect such a nature, if dynamic human beings are to securely and assuredly take up individual and collective projects in the world. And law must be stable and fixed also in order to respond adequately to the determinate aspects of human identity, to the determinate ways in which human identity and activity have been articulated in and by a particular world, to the determinate values and practices we have established as human beings. It must protect the real things that we actually do and value, in order to have real impact on the lives of real people. This tension between the need for dynamism and the need for stable determinacy is one that cannot be resolved, but it continuously characterizes the operation of law and the negotiation involved in legal determination.

The challenge facing law is that it must take particular form, like the human being it protects, that only by being fixed can it effectively protect indeterminate and dynamic human identity and activity, as well as determinate human values and activities, but that in its very fixity, and in protecting determinate values and activities, it might be unfaithful to the dynamism of human identity and activity. That is, the legal universal must be stable, and must protect determinate values and activities, in order to effectively respond to the dynamic character of human beings; if it is to protect their dynamism effectively then it must to a certain extent be itself impervious to it. Thus, while law is key to the institution of recognition, it can, in the particular shapes it takes, be inadequate to such recognition. In order to operate justly, it must be in tension with *itself* in the same way that recognition is in tension with itself, in being both recognition of dynamism and recognition of fixed determinacy.

Many of the criticisms of law can be linked to the fact that law is invoked in the name of recognition, but it cannot adequately reflect and enact the demands of recognition or cannot adequately negotiate the tension between dynamism and static determinacy—that it errs on the side of static determinacy, identifying and entrenching characteristics of human being that have been made significant and valuable by a particular and not unproblematic world. Throughout this book we have explored many of these criticisms: while I will not rehearse them in any detail here, I will briefly mention some in the context specifically of their relation to the issue of recognition. First, legal discourse and practice are challenged for their production of subjects who can deny or repress their character as social, a character that the above account of recognition has shown to be essential. If law operates in the name of recognition—that is, if it is a formal articulation of our interdependence, reflecting and institutionalizing our perception of each other as valuable—then it must not take a shape that conceals this interdependence. Individuals should be conceived not as autonomous, isolated, self-accomplishing agents, but as beings whose independence and effective agency are a social accomplishment, sustained by the continuation of social cooperation and recognition. A second challenge to law, essentially an extension of the first one, is that the way in which law is justified and shaped aids in *weakening* the social ties that support individual agency, further repressing the significance of recognition. In other words, the cultural and political construal of individuals as fundamentally individual, and not fundamentally captured in and shaped by various kinds of social and familial relationships, is accomplished partly by the forms that law takes, whereas law could be recast in particular ways to recognize the significance of social ties and in so doing witness to the operation and centrality of recognition. A third criticism is that the formal procedures of law are relied on too much, to the reduction or elimination of our perception of the need for actual political agency, interaction, and transformation, and that these procedures thus reduce or preclude occasions in which the dynamic possibilities of transformation of those who are recognized through it could be enacted. In other words, the way law operates, and the way we rely on it, does not encourage but discourages participation in the realms of public discussion and political negotiation. Fourth, law can conceal the ways in which access to public discourse and interactive reality is hindered by imbalances and inequalities accruing to people by virtue of their cultural and socioeconomic status. The assertion of political and civil rights, for instance, is popularly understood to be enough to ensure participation in the political and civic spheres, when in fact such participation might be prevented by cultural and socioeconomic powerlessness and inequality. Fifth, the legal apparatus is linked to what is often presumed to be a neutral state, a mere "administrator" of law and rights. Such a presumption conceals the ways in which the state itself emerges in response to the demand of recognition and is not merely administrative of right but is actively invested and operative in the production of certain relationships of recognition among its citizens and of a certain conception of subjectivity and political activity. A particular state can never pretend to be equivalent to the "universal will"; it is not a neutral administrator, but it enables and disables certain possibilities for interaction and recognition. In order to give these particularities and modes of recognition room to develop and be transformed—to act in their service or to act in the service of democracy—a particular state must confront its own particularity and the partiality of its attempts at justice. To conceal its own partiality and masquerade as the benefactor of a universal, neutral justice is simply to repress other possible shapes that justice could take and to silence demands for them.[41]

In sum, legal discourse is implicated in various ways in the injustice that it is invoked to redress, partly because it is not perceived as it should be, as a mechanism of recognition and thus accountable to its demands and committed to its sustenance. Law could be made to be *more* faithful to the dynamic and shifting self-understanding of the human beings it protects, and to the significance of intersubjective recognition in the production of individual subjects. Like recognition, if it is conceived in the name of participation in collective experience, or in the name of the sharing that is necessary for individual experience, then it must serve that participation and that sharing and not hinder, discourage, or conceal it. It must operate in the name of encouraging entrance into public relations with others in a public space, in which context *new* conceptions of value and worth might appear, to which it would have to respond. If, by entrenching individual separation, isolation, and atomism, it prevents the establishment of organization, cooperation, and interaction that leads to the transformation of intersubjective relations and the collective development of humanity, then it acts against what is human and against potentially more sophisticated, fulfilling, and productive forms of human interaction.[42] It must serve human interaction and be accountable to it; it must be adequate to the idea of the fundamental sociality of human being, according to which human self-creation is a creation of the many, and in the context of which every human being is irreducible to any particular shape that such self-creation takes.

CONCLUSION

What Hegel's account offers us, essentially, is the idea that the demand for legal and other forms of recognition must be enlivened by the tension between the capacity for infinite determinability and the actuality of finite determinacy, between the dynamic and the fixed. Given the dependent, interactive, and dynamic nature of human identity, the structures and practices of social life must be oriented toward allowing new conceptions of value and worth to appear, so as to ensure that established senses of the "universal" character of humanity and its organization not prevent the *appearance* of what must then again be taken up, protected, enabled, and valued in the name of justice. This means that a legal or recognitive framework, principle, or process cannot be construed as complete and just in its own right and finally but must be the open ground for action and interaction that may lead to its transformation. It means that the assertion of rights or the insistence that a particular difference is worthy of recognition must be accompanied by attentiveness to the dynamic capacity of human beings to determine themselves in new and unpredictable ways. Similarly, individuals must not be oriented toward simply asserting what their actions and standards mean in the context of the intersubjectively constituted social space, but toward *discovering* this meaning, by interacting with others and being attuned to the ways in which they are situated in relation to these others.

We find here a certain measure of justification both for universalist discourses, such as those that demand equal rights and recognition for the sake of inclusion in a universal humanity, and for particularist discourses that seek the recognition of difference. However, neither rights and laws nor cultural, religious, sexual, racial, and other forms of identification are impervious, stable, purely objective, or permanent; rather, they both serve a complex variety of interests, are indeterminate with respect to particular situations, and vary depending on the demands of the dynamic, relational context in which they operate. Our task, if we are to be answerable to the demand for justice, is to attend to these interests, situations, and relational contexts in the process of elaborating the nature of the life and co-dependence of the social body. Universalist and particularist discourses are attached to and transformed through this social life that is bigger than they are and that is capable of transforming their significance at any moment. The human interaction that inaugurates and inspires transformation and resignification always has the last word and gives us the task of working toward a world, as Carole Anne Taylor writes, "in which relationality not yet recognized as such might renegotiate what agency names and what theory does," in which we are answerable to the future and its possibilities.[43] What the phenomenon of recognition draws our attention to *most* centrally is the significance of dynamic relations of recognition for any accomplished and developing identity, and thus to the need to enhance, encourage, and explore such relations. Valuing determinate qualities or elaborating universal standards and laws, while purposeful for the removal of such obstacles, should not then stand in the way of the transformative power of interaction. Justice requires that we prepare for a future, which may look different from the present—for a world in which new meanings and values might be produced out of our constitutive reality, the reality of recognition. But it can only do so in this determinate present, in attentiveness to the real dynamics and relationships that structure it and orient it to that future.

CONCLUSION TO PART 3

Part 3 has aimed to show the continuing relevance of Hegel's work to contemporary political thought, using the philosophical resources under development throughout the book to portray the strengths and shortcomings of the contemporary discursive frameworks of liberalism and recognition. Hegel's work enables us to capture meaningfully the significance and weight of modern law and in so doing it is helpful for liberalism's project of self-understanding and self-legitimation, but it also makes clear that law can never be the ultimate and decisive factor in the construction of ways of living together and in so doing it is helpful for liberalism's project of self-critique. With his discussion of conscience, Hegel identifies the significance of answering to the dynamic norms at play in our singular interaction by constructing practices, principles, and institutions that are responsive to the new possibilities of identification and agency that emerge in that interaction. Further, Hegel's discussion of recognition illuminates the demand for a kind of responsiveness to the possibility of new value and significance, such that our established sense of what it is to be human does not preclude the revelation of new forms of identification. Recognition is twofold: it is recognition of what is determinate and identifiable, and hence recognition of how our particular situations have shaped our identity as individuals, but it is also recognition of the dynamic capacity of human beings to make new meaning, to determine and define themselves in new and unpredictable ways.

This treatment of the discourses of liberalism and recognition shows, again, the significance of developing a theory of justice that is answerable to the variety of ways in which human life takes shape. Modern law operates in powerful ways to identify and protect human beings as beings of value, and the demand for recognition of persons as members in a universal humanity powerfully affects our behavior in relation to each other and sustains our cooperation. These universalizing discourses, however, do not support a sufficient recognition of difference and of the ways in which our situatedness in particular communities and as particular kinds of people affects the shape that our lives take, whereas justice requires this recognition—hence the significance of curtailing the operation of law and universal recognition in the name of the recognition of particularity. And law and our awareness of the significance of human value should not be used to put a stop to the exploration of human possibility and the expression of new forms of human identification and cooperation—hence the importance of instituting forms of law and forms of recognition that can be held open to the appearance of the new.

In the conclusion of this book, I will consider the genuine pressures and tensions that characterize ordinary human life and show how the topics we have dealt with in each chapter, as well as the central concepts that Hegel elucidates and employs, emerge as strands or aspects of this general description. My goal is to tie the various pieces of this analysis together in a simple and clear picture. It is to give an account of the different elements of human life and corresponding aspects of justice that have emerged as themes throughout the book—the idea of belonging somewhere, the universality of law, and human singularity—but to do so in a way that emerges out of a description of everyday life. I aim to express thereby Hegel's capacity to speak powerfully to the terms of everyday life and to the ongoing value of projects that translate his insight into these ordinary terms.

CONCLUSION

THE ETHICS AND POLITICS OF CONSCIENCE

All of us somehow find ourselves in a tradition of some kind; we inhabit a way of life that carries the traces of its history within it. These traces are found in the way that people think, act, and feel, in the way our institutions, businesses, and governments are organized, in the attitudes we have toward different days of the week and of the year, in our physical characteristics and their significance, and so on. The immediate world is heavily mediated by this history; every surface is replete with significance that is not immediately available to us in the terms of the present.

Our action—however independent and singular we might think it is—is especially heavy with this accrued significance. Meaning that is not solely our own creation is enacted through us. We may try, for instance, to wear clothes and use words that express our unique identity and sense of style, to act in a way that is respectful of others, to play a good soccer game, to make a tasty meal, or to teach a class in a particularly gripping way, but our ideas of what counts as good in each case and the resources we have to accomplish such goods are always at least partially inherited and learned, unconsciously and consciously.[1] A tradition's meanings act *through* our action; they determine what shape agency will take and what significance it will have. We act in and through an inheritance; our action is always expressive and reflective of this "ethical life."

But if it were not for our action as individuals—action that we take to be in a sense independent and singular, at least to the extent that it requires our initiative—the inherited way of life would not exist. The one who inherits, that is, must enact that inheritance in order to sustain it as a real thing in the face of new demands and situations. Further, as individuals we can never simply repeat or reproduce what we inherit, even if that is all we want or intend to do. In every attitude we take toward our inheritance—whether positive or negative, whether fervent, accepting, or critical—we both express it *and* change it, sustain and contaminate it.

There are two sides to all action; it is mediated by this inheritance, and it does not merely repeat but disrupts what precedes it. An inherited way of life, with its laws, norms, attitudes, expectations, and common practices, is, strangely, both bigger and smaller than we are. It is bigger in that it precedes, shapes, and houses us and others we care about, and in ways that we cannot comprehend. It also, however, relies upon us, as individuals, to shape it, to carry it out, and to make it speak to new situations. In this way it is beholden to and smaller than us; without our commitment it could not exist.

In this concluding chapter I want to explore this tension between shaping and being shaped—between the authority of an inherited way of life and its laws, norms, and practices, on the one hand, and the authority of the single individuals who enact such things and maintain their existence, on the other. This tension is more than just conceptual; it is often existential as well. We struggle to discern the ways in which our traditions act through us when we think we are acting independently; we struggle to free our action and self-understanding from the aspects of our traditions that we do not like; we struggle to interact effectively with others from other traditions and make perceptible the ways in which we have been one-sidedly shaped so as to do better at that interaction. We struggle to find ways to make our traditions speak to our unique identities and with the sense of alienation that ensues when we fail. We struggle with the guilt of feeling unfaithful to our traditions or with the pleasure of being free of them, with the disappointment that arises when we recognize their flawed character, when others take them up in a way that we think is wrong, or when others judge our relation to them in a way that we think is inaccurate.

In interpreting the requirements of an inherited way of life, our obligations to it, and the flaws that characterize it and that need correction, every human being risks *transgression*—both of the inheritance and of the demand to act well and justly. What I want to argue here, however, is that this risk is necessary and inevitable and that traditions, laws, and complex social realities live and flourish only through people who take it. Even further, I want to explore the possibility that acting in the service of an *inheritance*—defined by laws, norms, common practices, and so on—requires going beyond it, creating it anew, and making it speak in new ways. I want to explore, that is, the *risk* of action and the *necessity* and the *necessary risk* of interpretation.

THE MEDIATION OF ACTION: TRADITION AND LAW

The weight of tradition and of history makes itself apparent and known in the action of individual human beings. In many ways we are simply conduits of meanings that are bigger and broader than us, even though we might think of our action as simply our own—as independent, self-defining, and expressive of our free and pure inner reality. Action is inherently mediated by an inherited way of life: the ways we walk, talk, dress, greet each other, house ourselves, organize our schedules, "balance our priorities," express our care for each other, shape our careers, and take up our responsibilities are fundamentally shaped by the ways in which we have *learned* to do so and by the standards for which we have been taught. We learn how to act and what to value even before we are able to consciously reflect on our acting and valuing, before we are able to choose the ways in which we would like to act and value things. Indeed, we inherit our ability to consciously reflect, and the habit of thinking of ourselves as individuals, from a tradition and a particular history. We are already involved in living in and sustaining a set of common practices by the time we come to develop capacities with which we can evaluate them. In a sense our agency fundamentally belongs to these practices and forces and not merely to ourselves; or, said otherwise, we ourselves are instantiations and expressions of these practices and forces.

This idea can be elaborated in its relation to the notion of ethical life explored most explicitly in the first and second chapters. Hegel gives the name *Sittlichkeit*—ethical life or ethicality—to this inheritance of a determinate way of life, action, and identity that has taken shape in the world over time; that gives us a context through which we engage with specific things, people, and events; and out of which emerge demands and obligations to which we find ourselves immediately responsive. Sociopolitical life must be organized in a way that is responsive and alive to the priority of such fundamental ethical relations and ways of life, because they are the terrain—they provide the medium and the resources—in which our individual capacities are cultivated, and because they provide us with a sense of familial and cultural belonging that is directly linked to our sense of purpose and level of comfort in the world. Indeed, we typically search out these kinds of contexts, even as we emerge from them; we often want to live in such a way that we *find* ourselves obliged by people and situations, needed or valued in a relatively immediate way, because that contributes to our sense of our own significance. If, on the contrary, we lived lives in which we simply chose all of our commitments and obligations, we would probably feel alienated from the things and people to which we would be committed and by which we would be obliged. As I have argued, concern with issues of "ethical life" is a central aspect of justice: justice requires that ethical bonds and relations and their agency in the construction of ethically capable human beings be recognized. Justice, therefore, cannot be reduced to the universality of law nor to recognition of the human being in her singularity, even though law and the recognition of singularity are themselves necessary for justice; it must also respond to this significant aspect of human living, its traditioned and collective character.

A significant part of any given way of life or ethical life that acts through and shapes individual action is its mode of social, political, and legal organization. All societies operate according to certain standards and procedures whose operation is more or less invisible depending on the extent to which they have become internalized and habitual. Laws can become conventional or traditional in this sense—accepted in such a widespread and automatic way that they become more or less invisible—and we in turn unconsciously reveal and confirm their authority in our habituation to them, in every move we make. I walk down the sidewalk confident of its friendliness to my aims, so to speak, and I trust that other people will allow me to move freely on it, that we will cooperate in our shared use of the sidewalk, that I do not have to fight with them or to negotiate with each of them a new agreement that would allow both of us to use the sidewalk at the same time. This capacity is a legal, social, and political *achievement* involving the establishment of shared public space, our shared recognition of each other as valuable by default, and the emergence of a legal apparatus to sustain and respond to transgressions of norms and laws governing public and private space. Here again, simple actions, if observed closely, reveal their reliance on and mediation by collective and historical social, legal, and political accomplishments, and they are understood incorrectly if understood in abstraction from these accomplishments.

But with modern law we also see something more than simply ethical life at work, in several ways, which makes it into an independent, second ingredient of justice. A central aspect of modern law is the requirement that it be transparent and communicable to more or less rational human beings. It does not operate *merely* unconsciously or habitually but can also be described and explained and can cross borders and operate in various different contexts, being not necessarily incompatible with different *kinds* of ethical life. It is not simply the same as tradition because it says about itself that it is in principle applicable to any and all individuals, no matter what their particular cultural, religious, or political alliances—that is, no matter what kind of groups with which they align themselves or no matter what the nature of their "ethical life" is. It is also different from tradition insofar as it acts as the leverage by which individuals can remove themselves from damaging and dangerous traditional and customary relations. But, like tradition or ethical life, it is a significant shaping mechanism, a massive complex that the individual brings into motion with every action and that most often lies beyond the scope of visibility, of conscious, reflective thought. As Hegel's analysis of the French Revolution also reveals, any modern, universal legal apparatus is reliant on particular, exclusive nation-states, on a particular political terrain and singular political judgments as to the shape its operation should take. It is dependent on shared ways of living together that have become habitual and customary and in which we find our ethical concern mobilized by our proximity to each other. Law, in sum, is in actuality tied to ethical life and tradition but in principle separate from them, and this tension in it is a significant aspect of its operation.

In both modern sociolegal structures and inherited traditions, meanings that are both bigger and older than us are being enacted in everything we do, think, and say, and this is not a reality that we can deny or escape. Even our attempts to unearth, reflect on, and challenge these meanings are colored and more or less enabled by them. Indeed, to try to discard the terms by which we enter *into* reality, the terms by which we become real and human, is in a sense to give up on our own reality or to endanger our sanity and our self-understanding, as well as our capacity to relate to others.

Let us look more closely at this last point, which has been at work already implicitly throughout the above discussion of the mediation of action—that our relationships with others are also implicated in the mediation of action by tradition. Our action is an enactment of significance that extends beyond this action and beyond our intention, and because of this significance is opened to being shared with others in ways that they recognize. Being real and making sense to others relies to a certain extent upon our acting in accord with this inheritance. In this context, therefore, the phenomenon of *recognition* also becomes relevant. Others identify, recognize, and accept us as human beings like them if we show that in our action we are participating in a reality that they also know and share with us, and we show that we recognize them by acting according to the terms of their reality. Our explicit expressions of recognition are only a minor way in which recognition is operative. The broader and older meanings enacted in our actions situate other human beings as well, and by virtue of our enactment of these meanings we receive recognition by them and express in turn our recognition of them, as having a reality in common, as capable of supporting each other's projects, as being reliable participants in this world and not radically disruptive of it.

By now we have looked at the idea of inheritance from the point of view of several different aspects or points of focus: tradition and history (or ethical life), legal and political organization (or law), and recognition. With these resources in hand, we can clarify also what Hegel means by "spirit": spirit is essentially the *relationship* between individual action, speech, and thought, on the one hand, and tradition, history, convention, law, and recognition, on the other; it is the term that Hegel uses to invoke the entirety of these various aspects and the intimate relations between them. Spirit is the conventions and shared history that define and determine our actions in ways of which we are often unconscious. It is the consciously formulated, promulgated, and accepted laws and norms by which we structure our social and political interaction. It is the rich and complex traditions that allow us to do things that we could never accomplish without them. It is the recognition that all of these things-in-common reflect and enable. It is, that is, the *vast complex of significance* that we reflect whenever we act, speak, or think, the reality we miss if we do not look closely at our actions, speech, and thinking—if we do not see realities enacted through them that extend beyond what we may think to be our personal boundaries. But the individual and her singular action are an essential aspect of spirit; they are the vehicle for the cultivation and transmission of shared histories, values, and lives, the medium through which this complex reality is expressed and exists. The protection and celebration of this individual and her action make up the third ingredient of justice, and we will turn to it now.

THE SINGULARITY OF ACTION AND THE CHALLENGE OF RESPONSIBILITY

Notwithstanding the force of the inheritance that one mobilizes in every action, action is also characterized by the disruption and transgression of this inheritance.[2] Tradition, law, and inheritance in general do not constitute a purely self-defined and inevitable force but require for their force that we make ourselves into their conduit. Further, they are executed by singular and different people in a way that is irreducibly perspectival. Action reveals the presence of a person with a singular and partial understanding, who automatically and inevitably takes herself to be the center of reality and who finds herself answerable to both singular others and to the broader world, as it shows itself to her within the rubric of her particular perspective. In multiple ways, in other words, action sets us sets us sets us apart or distinguishes us from others or from what is held in common—a tradition, a history, a set of laws and institutions—and presupposes and casts the world as something that is *for us*. While it is true that action always invokes shared resources and significance that presume our commonality and our co-dependence and that sustain in us the ability to share our resources, action is an assertion of a seemingly opposed point as well: that my singularity, my sense of my obligations, and my view of the world from the point of view of myself as the center of it are fundamentally and primally unshareable and unknowable. There is nothing in the world that could be used to exhaustively explain why I am the way I am, and there is no way that my singularity could be exposed, investigated, and understood, even by me. In every action I undertake, I bring this singularity to bear upon a reality that cannot explain, predict, or appropriate it, a reality that is permanently, therefore, at the mercy of my action and myself.

So there are two sides to action: it is mediated by broader significances couched in laws, institutions, and traditions, and it is irreducibly singular. The question that emerges here is, How do we act responsibly, given these two aspects of action? How can we deal with both the mediation of action and its inevitable separateness in trying to act in situations that require our response? In other words, how can we act in such a way as to avoid conceiving of ourselves as purely determined and ruled by tradition or by law or conceiving of ourselves as purely and naïvely free—acknowledging the weight of both tradition and singularity? In what follows I will attempt to articulate the *relationship* between these two aspects of action, identifying how responsibility involves accurately apprehending their equal necessity and their relationship. What we will see is that it is *only* in disrupting and transgressing a tradition and a sociolegal framework—only in acting in a fundamentally singular way—that any history, tradition, laws, institutions, and social patterns of recognition are sustained. These two aspects of action, that is, are mutually implicated, and their tension is negotiated in everything that we do.

The remainder of this section is divided into three parts. In the first I discuss the incapacity of any given moral law or tradition to spell out what responsibility entails and the ensuing need for human interpretation: the idea that only in accepting the risk of interpretation can people in fact act morally and responsibly. The second part is devoted to exploring the incapacity of law to articulate the boundaries of responsibility in the specifically political realm and the nature of its relationship with conscience. The third part addresses the risk involved in keeping societies responsive to and responsible for unique, conscientious persons and asserts that enacting a community, a tradition, and a shared social world requires most importantly that we be open to the very human creativity and transgression that could undermine them.

LAW, TRADITION, AND INTERPRETATION: THE ETHICS OF CONSCIENCE

A tradition typically carries with it certain obligations and expectations that those who honor it try to meet or that articulate what a person would have to do in order to exercise responsibility. Moral and posited laws are specific expressions of these obligations, as are the "unwritten laws" of custom. Exercising responsibility through obedience to such obligations, however—the site at which tradition or law meets singularity—is more complicated than it might first appear. Let us begin by considering the example of a command that could be moral or legal: "Do not steal."[3] This command—do not take for yourself what belongs to another—seems unequivocal, but its simplicity is deceiving. One could describe, for instance, at least two opposed interpretations of it. The standard one might look like this: when something belongs to someone, it is not up for grabs; leave the things that belong to others alone. But another person could with good reason think that having "private property" already involves a kind of theft, when it is regulated by political and economic systems and supported by corporations and states that have turned a blind eye to exploitation and unjust appropriation. For this person, "ownership" in the modern world might already count as disobedience of the command, and to support private property would be to support theft and disobey the command. This example shows that interpretation is needed to determine what exactly the command requires. It does not include a definition of its terms, and the world in which it speaks is extraordinarily complex, so figuring it out calls for interpretive intervention, and interpretations could conflict.

Another issue requiring interpretive intervention on the part of singular human beings is that of what *specific* action is appropriate as a response to a command that is universal. By virtue of their universality, moral and legal commands make no reference to specific situations and single actions, but a single actor needs to determine what specific situation, and, indeed, in what situations she should get involved in the first place. To illuminate this issue, let us consider an example of a moral command: "Love your neighbor as yourself." The command sounds decisive and certain, but it gives very little guidance. What the unique needs of my neighbor are and what I might do to meet them are not issues resolved by the command, so in trying to follow it I have to bring my own knowledge and imagination to bear on the situation. The law is not precise enough to command me to love, for instance, Aron and Rachel, by babysitting their children for the day; I in my own committed way have to figure out how follow it, to figure out by what *kind* of obligations my particular situation is constituted, and to figure out whether it is right for me to *be* in this situation. Also, loving one "neighbor" could make it difficult for me to love another "neighbor"; following the law "here and now" could make it hard for me to follow it "there and later." With this example we see again the necessity of interpretation and discernment in fulfilling obligations and exercising responsibility. The details that law cannot provide are precisely the terrain of moral action and decision; they are where my moral obligations lie and where the moral value of my action is established.

In both of these examples, obeying a command requires that I submit the command to my own interpretation, so as to bring a universal law to bear on a particular situation to which it does not speak directly. If, as in the loving example, we have to decide on a particular action and choose someone to love, then our thinking and decision making operates, and must operate, outside of the boundaries of the law's explicit authority and guidance. If, as in the stealing example, we rely on our own interpretation to determine what the law prohibits, then in a sense we are asserting our *own* authority over that of the law. This is, however, exactly the opposite of what it commands—namely, that we submit to *it* and to the others in the name of whom it speaks. In order to follow these laws, I must go beyond them, into the domain of interpretive risk. Since they do not provide sufficient guidance on their own, I must, in order to be responsible, subordinate them in a sense to my interpretation.

We should not underestimate this point, since what it means, in a sense, is that we are actually required to *disobey* law and, indeed, that only in disobeying law can we obey it. At the most basic level law commands obedience; it demands that I simply follow it. In order to do so, however, I must interpret it and the situation to which I think it speaks, so I disobey its command to simply follow it. I submit not to its authority but to my own; I obey myself. However, if, in order to carry out the law, I *must* interpret the law and the situation—if law can only be obeyed through interpretation—then in another sense it *commands* me to disobey. To obey a command requires disobeying a command; being true to law entails being false to it. What this means is that not only do we break laws by following them, but we follow laws by breaking them. Our commitment to law can only be enacted through our interpretation of it, and this commitment is necessary for its continued existence. We confirm the authority and significance of law by interpreting and transgressing it.

What we see here, in effect, is that law, and any general obligation that appears to us in the context of a shared tradition and sociopolitical context, is only perpetuated through its violation. *Action always goes beyond the terms specified by law and tradition*, and the adherents of such laws and traditions, in order to be responsible for them and to sustain them, must take up the risk, on their own, of that action, the risk of carrying them out. Only in taking up this risk, responsibly and responsively, can we truly act morally, lawfully, and in a way that is responsive to our inherited traditions and ways of life.

Hegel gives the name "conscience" to that figure who has grappled with the question of how to carry out universal laws and how to act appropriately in a given traditional context and who has resolutely come to terms with the fact that situations are singular and accessible only through the terms of its own conviction. "Conscience" takes responsibility for its interpretation, knowing it cannot pretend that it is simply following the law. The conscientious self effectively says, "Here I am; I can think and do no differently. This is the situation facing me; this is how I understand it; this is what I must do in order to respond to it well." The conscientious self may be committed in principle to doing what is right, but she knows and accepts that she is open to the world in a particular way, incapable of knowing and being everything and responding indifferently to every situation. In general she may want to carry out her tradition and obey its laws, but they never speak specifically to her unique situation, so in attempting to sustain and apply them she knows she will challenge and change them. Thus her action is as much a challenge to these guidelines as it is an attempt to honor them.

The predicament confronting this conscientious self is that her action is both good and bad. While acting with an interest in what is right and with the intention of doing well by others, she leaves the mark of her self-assertion and self-centrality on everything she does. Her unique perspective, while inevitable, is in fact a moral and legal *problem*, because it entails that she asserts her own authority as central and her own interpretation as correct, that she asserts herself and not others as the point around which reality revolves, and that she asserts the situation in which she acts to be the most important one. In so doing, she is implicitly opposed to others and to the possibility of sharing a world and exercising moral concern. Her action is in principle divisive and antagonistic, even when her intention is to act out of concern for others. She exercises responsibility and transgression simultaneously, acting in obedience of law and in respect for shared customs out of concern for others and asserting herself over those others by acting out of her own conviction.

However, if this conscientious person does not act, she also disobeys the law and fails to express ethical concern and exercise responsibility, since it and the people around her require her to do something. To freeze and take the "safe" path of inaction, to refuse to "get one's hands dirty" like Hegel's beautiful soul (M664, S487), is to refuse to respond at all to the call of justice—perhaps an even more unethical act than that of responding but getting it wrong. Indeed, laws and traditions rely on individuals to make them effective in the world; they need individuals to take them up as authoritative in order to be authoritative; they rely on our collective recognition of them and on our interaction in their terms. Even in getting them wrong, therefore, we could still be enacting them and making them real and effective in the world, for ourselves and for others.

Let me try to clarify this double-sidedness, this moral dilemma, with an example, one that will also introduce the fact that action's inevitable and strident assertion of the singular self has a positive significance. Let us imagine the event of a university graduation or convocation. For each person in attendance, the reality of the situation is different. Each is there for different reasons and with different interests: maybe one person supports the school and attends every year, indifferent to who the participants are; another's nephew, sister, or grandson is graduating; another is on the board of the school and required to attend; another has a special interest in hearing the convocation speaker; another is a teacher of the graduating class. They all have very particular and self-determined ways of defining the situation, as well as the tendency to act in such a way that is consistent with and perpetuates their vision of the nature of the situation. They may very well be committed to making the situation a good one for everyone in attendance, but the strategies they use to accomplish this will emerge from their *different* ways of seeing it. Indeed, others might vehemently disagree with these strategies, to such an extent that they could instigate conflict, the opposite of what was intended. Even in trying to act appropriately and in consideration of the participation of others, even in supporting the situation in principle and the participation of all in it, they could undermine the experience others have of it.

But with this example we can also see the positive significance of this diversity of interest and of the inevitably self-centered shape that personal investment takes. The situation *is*—it exists—through these reasons, interests, and commitments; it becomes real through and because of them; it becomes valuable because of the value that people give it. It is not really the case that each one of them gets the situation wrong, because each makes the situation significant in the way that it is and thus sustains its existence. Since they bring it into existence as a weighty and significant event with their ideas about it and attitudes toward it, in a deep sense they cannot really be wrong. There is no bare, neutral reality upon which their expectations and interests are imposed, since this reality becomes what it is because of these expectations and interests. Hence in a sense they cannot be said to be accountable to a reality that pre-exists such expectations and interests, or these expectations and interests are more than just an incidental addition to an already concrete reality, and they are valuable to the extent that they *make* a reality.

Another positive aspect of this persistent difference among attitudes and commitments can be discerned in the idea that the stance of conscience is a possibility that exists for everyone. The conscientious person acts according to his conviction and defends himself by saying that this is the only way he can act responsibly, in response to moral and legal commands, which have weight because of their significance for other people. If, however, he defends himself in this way, then he is implicitly committed to allowing others that defense as well; he has implicitly recognized conscience as a norm for all. He thus recognizes others as justified in their conscientious action, and in supporting his own he must support theirs. Because it is required that he support them, the conscientious person must be more than merely tolerant of difference. He supports something that could be opposed to him; he is committed in principle to defending the existence of a point of view that could assert that he is wrong, that could challenge him. And he exposes his interpretation to the judgment of others in admitting that their judgment is fundamentally legitimate, just as his is.

The problem with conscientious action is that it is inherently and inevitably self-centered, involving the imposition of a singular interpretation on the world: in trying to care for others the conscientious person asserts himself. Hemmed in by his own powerful interpretive framework that gives the world an orientation around him, this person cannot really know what it is like to live through a different interpretive framework, and hence he cannot exercise perfect concern for others. But found in his commitment to opposing points of view, in his commitment to conscience in general, is a possible solution to this problem: in recognizing the legitimacy of these alien interpretive frameworks, he is in principle devoted both to opening himself to correction by them and to "forgiving" them their transgressive nature. He can do justice to them, that is, in confession of his singularity and in forgiveness of theirs. This open, forgiving attitude is the ground for a kind of identity between himself and others that is different from the one provided by law and tradition. It is a kind of living infinite requirement, which makes itself apparent in all of our interactions with others, to respond to such singularity, apart from the "safe" direction provided by law and other guiding structures and norms. Adequately responding to singularity requires engaging in dialogue with others so as to find out what it is that requires our response, dialogue that can be transformative, that can change our conceptions of our own action and identity. To recognize the permanent and inevitable mystery of conscience, in both ourselves and others, is to acknowledge that law, norms, and traditions do not give us an exhaustive account of the requirements of ethical behavior and interaction and that we must traverse beyond them into a process of communication, learning, and transformation with other singular selves, discovering from the situations in which we find ourselves what is required of us. In confessing and forgiving singularity, in acknowledging and responding to the unique identity and creativity of others, we establish a newly shared ground of communication upon which we can explain ourselves to and learn from each other: the ground for a future of sharing and identification.

The kind of social reality this form of interaction enables might be called a society of forgiveness. The society of forgiveness can only be lived, not conclusively formulated or given explicit legal shape, because it must be *constantly open and available for response*. Responsiveness is what is morally significant or what sets the groundwork for responsibility.

While reliant on law, the society of forgiveness exceeds the grasp of law: it cannot be given a recipe or formulation, for it always changes. We are share*able*, and this potential presents to us an infinitely compelling task.

Law and tradition, the already established terrain of our interaction, the structures of our present communities, are not the same as the dynamic negotiation of this new society in the process of being created. Stepping out from the protection and security of law and tradition so as to take the risk of action is always necessary, for each situation is new and each person singular. To assume that there is a guaranteed or formulaic answer to the question of how to respond is to deny this uniqueness and to fail to respond. Now let us turn to the issue of the politics of conscience and the question of what kind of place and impact the inherent singularity of action has in and on the specifically political realm.

LAW, DEMOCRACY, AND FORGIVENESS: THE POLITICS OF CONSCIENCE

So far I have argued that universal laws are insufficient to guide ethical interaction and that nevertheless we conscientious selves show our accountability to them and to each other by interacting in the modes of confession and forgiveness. In addition to asserting itself in the context of ethical interaction, conscience is of political significance as well; it is typically protected by democratic law in the context of liberal democratic nation-states. I will turn now to this political context and argue a) that it is in fact a strength of democratic political life that the authority of law wavers in the face of conscience, and b) that the tension between law and conscience, between universality and singularity, allows for the possibility of justice and responsibility in the domain of political life.

The liberal democratic tradition takes the protection of conscience to be one of its cornerstones. This is apparent, for instance, in Article 18 of the United Nations' Universal Declaration of Human Rights, which asserts that all have the right to freedom of thought, conscience, and religion; in the Canadian Charter of Rights and Freedoms, which describes as a fundamental freedom the freedom of conscience and religion; and in the First Amendment of the United States, which prohibits the making of any law that would impede the free exercise of religion. In protecting conscience, democratic law declares the existence of a space that is essentially beyond the boundaries in the confines of which the exercise of political authority takes place, in which people are free to believe what they want to believe and, to a certain extent, to shape their lives accordingly, under certain constraints that involve protecting the same right in others. What is especially interesting here is how any political regime that protects the right of conscience implicitly undermines itself. In limiting the scope of its laws in the face of conscience, a political regime authoritatively sets limits to its own authority. It declares the right of conscience, and thereby both exercises authority and announces the insufficiency or nonabsoluteness of its authority. Law builds, nourishes, and protects a space that it cannot enter.

We can approach this same point in a different way, by looking more closely at one of the purposes of law in the liberal framework: that is, to regard and treat all human beings as identical, asserting the value of each and protecting each from being unjustly used as means for the ends of others. In operating in this way the law is just in the sense of fair. But human beings are not in fact identical, and, since under law they are considered so, law does an injustice to their singular nature. The institution of a space for conscience allows for the exploration of differences that law cannot itself acknowledge, identify, and regulate; or, in other words, the legal protection of conscience protects human beings against the potential injustice of law. Law allows for the existence and exercise of a freedom that is supposed to compensate for law's own insufficiency and thus a freedom that is to a certain extent opposed to it. Thus does it acknowledge the irreducible complexity of the subjects it otherwise governs and whose interaction it otherwise regulates.

The most common sites of the protection of conscience are religious beliefs, moral commitments, and political views—those that would compel one, for instance, to refuse to accept blood transfusions, go to war, believe in the equality of women, or educate one's children in the public school system, or those that would compel one to disagree with a political decision or explore political, moral, and religious ideas that are in some way antagonistic to the principles and practices of one's own political, moral, and religious communities. The democratic state is described as neutral with regard to these commitments, beliefs, or ideas, though it cannot legislate neutrality. Indeed, in its support of conscience it indirectly supports the development of commitments regarding how to live that are not neutral and that actively influence action and interaction in the social and political realm. In its support of conscience this kind of political organization allows for the flourishing of different ways of imagining what life is and could be and thus prioritizes and is committed to the creative (and destructive) transformation of beliefs and practices.

But the intimate relationship between law and conscience also has consequences for law and the shape it takes. It is *not* the case that the liberal democratic state can and has ever been able to remain untouched by what happens in the space allotted to conscience, though the public significance of this so-called private space of conscience is often neglected. Law gives room to the development of unique selves who can in no way merely repeat their legal inheritance in a reliable and obedient fashion, who in fact continue to make new demands of it because of the new needs and characteristics they discover and cultivate in themselves and others, and whose singular agency is necessary to the continued sustenance of that legal framework. In the arena of conscience, unpredictable transformation takes place, entailing that the future cannot be guaranteed to look the same as the past, and law and political authority are not free from the consequences of this transformation. The essential characteristic of democratic law is that it leaves itself vulnerable to its own transformation and, indeed, is committed in principle to its own transformation in the name of democracy.

The same can be said about tradition and its practices and customs, which are similarly vulnerable to their adherents. Traditions are the sedimentation of a history of shared social, cultural, and political practices that shape the ways their members perceive the world and act in it, and they can have as much significance for how we act and think of ourselves politically as law does; indeed, much of our forms of legal organization have, by virtue of the habitual ways in which we are oriented to them, become traditional or customary. Nevertheless, traditions and their customs are operated and sustained only by free individuals whose interpretations of their obligations may differ from those of their predecessors. Traditions are sustained and extended into the future only by being brought to confront and speak to the ever-new demands arising in unique situations—that is, only by being harnessed by the authority of conscience. A tradition is vulnerable to the ways in which unique selves take it on as their inheritance, but it would cease to exist if it were not made to speak to the new demands of unique situations. A tradition is vulnerable to its own transformation; its meaning could in fact be different than earlier versions of it have asserted; it could find a richer or more impoverished significance in the future situations to which it will be made to speak. To live in and act out of a tradition—which we all do, at a basic formative level, even in our opposition to aspects of it—means to be committed to its dynamism, to its potential for change, to the possibility that is always part of its current reality. A tradition can change and develop in essential and significant ways; it could turn out to be resourceful enough to sustain its adherents in their unique and creative transformation; or, alternatively, its wealth and resources could be squandered by inattentive and disinterested adherents. Support for a tradition cannot involve a refusal to engage with what is new, and, conversely, critique of a tradition cannot involve a denial of its formative power.

The very vulnerability of law and tradition can be the occasion for social and political innovation, but this vulnerability could also entail transformation that is life denying and destructive.[4] This, however, is the *necessary risk* of the recognition and protection of conscience, and in this fourth and last section I turn to reflection on the kind of communities that are possible in light of this risk and this vulnerability.

The Risk of Forgiveness

The existence of law and tradition is a concrete manifestation of the fact that we are all answerable to a shared reality, one that expresses our recognition of each other and exercises formative power in our lives. Law and tradition presume our *identification* with each other, and they sustain individual development and social life by giving them stable ground and by giving us access to the activities and accomplishments of others. It is the task for the conscientious self to explicitly acknowledge the ways in which it is constituted as a singular and ethical agent by this broader reality. What I have tried to show here, however, is that law and tradition are on their own inadequate in their attempts to establish commonality or universality and to give final form to our shared life, because they cannot respond creatively to unique situations but need single selves to do that for them. Law and tradition can in principle never initiate anything, even though they are themselves the contexts in which such individuals are formed and express initiative; they always and inevitably follow in the footsteps of individuals. They do not exhaust the possibilities of human meaning and meaning-making, and they are only powerful and alive insofar as they are allowed to be propelled into uncertain futures by unique human beings grappling with the demands of unique situations. The possibility of identification that they are presumed to accomplish is only ever a task still to be completed, through the interactive negotiation of singular human beings.

What I have suggested here could indeed have troubling implications, however, since the incapacity of law and tradition to speak adequately and exhaustively to unique situations leaves these situations open and vulnerable to destructive and life-denying practices. The impossibility of finding formulas or final answers that will be exhaustive—laws and traditions, canons, norms, common practices—makes this shared life always risky and demands our vigilance over it. This risk, however, cannot be avoided or denied, and it should also be recognized that there is danger in too much security, in thinking that our traditions—indeed, our civilizations—already have all the resources they need. The measures we take to guarantee and protect a shared life could in fact bring about division and alienation from that life, since they could make us deaf to the unique demands of those for whom justice obliges us to care, of those with whom we engage in the creation and elaboration of a shared reality, of those who speak, uncannily, in the terms of a different world that is unimaginable in the terms of the present.

Confession and forgiveness, or acknowledgment of one's own inherently transgressive behavior and engagement with that of others, involve on the one hand the recognition of *difference*, and on the other hand, preparation for the establishment of a *shared* terrain through which we engage in new ways in the infinitely demanding project of living together. While risky, the communicative nature of confession and forgiveness brings about its own kind of universality—that is, the universality we establish together in our interaction in the attempt to elaborate new and newly illuminating forms of identification and communication.

In writing texts such as this one, we attempt to engage in this kind of communication. With the various discussions of conscience, tradition, law, and forgiveness, inherited philosophical concepts and projects and the terms of a given socio-political reality are transferred to new contexts, these concepts, projects, and realities are made to respond to different questions and points of focus, and the continuing significance of philosophical thinking is illuminated—or so I hope. We appropriate traditions of thought, philosophical practices, and politics in singular ways, trying to do them justice even as we make them speak to our concerns, and thus we selfishly transgress them. We also communicate with others who differ from these traditions, who will change, with us, our inevitably shared future in unforeseeable ways.

Hegel's *Phenomenology of Spirit* pursues the various ways in which human beings are differently engaged in a shared world, for different reasons and with conflicting interests. It casts these beings as living with the accomplishments of the past and preparing for the future, in dialogue with those who have transferred their traditions to them and with those who carry these traditions out in unpredictable ways. These various ways of life depend for their sustenance and transformation on creative interpretation, and they remain real, concrete, and coherent only in being transformed. The challenge of responsibility can be accepted—the new situations that could change shared life and that could make traditions different could be eagerly anticipated—or they could be the objects of dread and avoidance. But there are shared worlds partly because differences give life to them and to the extent that these worlds allow us to attend and be faithful to these emerging differences. Such shared worlds require human beings to be the *consciences* of their inheritance. Human commitment to these inheritances and to themselves as shaped by these inheritances is propelled by the promise of a future commonality that could house their uniqueness, a promise that demands continual response, continual reading and writing, acting, and judging. These communities require constant inauguration; the new must be continuously instituted even for the old to be sustained.

NOTES

INTRODUCTION

1. An eloquent (negative) articulation of this point is made in the preface to the *Philosophy of Right*, in which Hegel writes: "No other art or science [than philosophy] is treated with this ultimate degree of contempt, namely the assumption that one can take possession of it outright" (*PhR*, p. 15). Addressing this issue, John Russon observes that while the project of observing experience seems "to require . . . a stance of nonintervention, a stance of noninterpretation in which one 'clears one's mind' of any structures, plans, or expectations, . . . such a stance is in fact a stance without intelligence, a stance *unable to recognize* intelligence when it sees it. To see the world in its rationality, one must look at it rationally . . . It is through the *attempt* made by a given form of consciousness to describe experience that one is taught by experience how one *needs* to describe experience." John Russon, "The Project of Hegel's *Phenomenology of Spirit*," in *A Companion to Hegel*, ed. Stephen Houlgate and Michael Baur (Oxford: Blackwell, 2011), 51.

2. In a study of Hegel's notion of the family and of the significance to human identity and experience of intimate ethical relations, David Ciavatta illuminates the tension between the universality of law and the relations of particularity one finds in the intimate context of the family in the following: "the inherently particularized character of familial obligation—the fact that I immediately experience my familial obligation as being *exclusive* to *this particular, concrete other*, and not to this other as one representative of a universal type that includes all selves—puts the family at odds with other, readily universalizable sources of normativity." David Ciavatta, *Spirit, the Family, and the Unconscious in Hegel's Philosophy* (Albany: State University of New York Press, 2010), 12.

3. Jacques Derrida discusses this issue in terms of the separability of justice and law and derives from this separability a sense of "responsibility without limits" that gives us

> the task of recalling the history, the origin and subsequent direction, thus the limits, of concepts of justice, the law and right, of

> values, norms, prescriptions that have been imposed and sedimented there . . . One must be *juste* with justice, and the first way to do it justice is to hear, read, interpret it, to try to understand where it comes from, what it wants of us, knowing that it does so through singular idioms . . . and also knowing that this justice always addresses itself to singularity, to the singularity of the other, despite or even because it pretends to universality. Consequently, never to yield on this point, constantly to maintain an interrogation of the origin, grounds and limits of our conceptual, theoretical or normative apparatus surrounding justice is on deconstruction's part anything but a neutralization of interest in justice, an insensitivity toward injustice. Jacques Derrida, "Force of Law: The 'Mystical Foundation of Authority,'" tr. Mary Quaintance, in *Deconstruction and the Possibility of Justice*, ed. Drucilla Cornell, Michel Rosenfeld, and David Gray Carlson (New York: Routledge, 1992), 19–20

Justice "will always have it, this *à-venir* [to-come], and always has. Perhaps it is for this reason that justice, insofar as it is not only a juridical or political concept, opens up for *l'avenir* [the future] the transformation, the recasting or refounding of law and politics" (Derrida, "Force of Law," 27).

4. Ludwig Siep also identifies these three elements as mutually intertwined aspects of a single way of life or "ethical spirit": "According to Hegel, a concept of ethical spirit enabling such procedures and developments must contain at least three elements, corresponding to the 'moments' of the concept: the universality of rationally justifiable laws, the particularity of customs and traditions of a community based on common historical experiences, and the singularity of a conscience that interprets the laws and applies them appropriately in a specific situation." Ludwig Siep, "Practical Reason and Spirit in Hegel's *Phenomenology of Spirit*," in *Hegel's* Phenomenology of Spirit: *A Critical Guide*, ed. Dean Moyar and Michael Quante (Cambridge: Cambridge University Press, 2008), 179. These aspects are integrated as aspects of a single principle, according to Siep: "For Hegel 'the concept' is the systematic mutual generation and explication of meanings as determinations of a single thought or principle" (Siep, "Practical Reason and Spirit," 185).

5. While I am mostly interested in demonstrating the resonance between Hegel and Derrida's philosophy, Stephen Houlgate and Rocío Zambrana take an approach that could be equally legitimate: identifying Derrida's inadequate acknowledgment of his affinity with Hegel. Indeed, Houlgate seems to say that Hegel has greater success in enacting a Derridean project than Derrida does. See Stephen Houlgate, *The Opening of Hegel's Logic* (West Lafayette, IN: Purdue University Press, 2006); Rocío Zambrana, "Hegel's Legacy," *The Southern Journal of Philosophy* 50, no. 2 (June 2012): 273–84; Rocío Zambrana, "Hegel's Logic of Finitude," *Continental Philosophy Review* 45 (2012): 213–33.

6. A. V. Miller translates *der Rechtzustand* as "legal status" (discussed in M477–83, S355–59), but I will follow H. S. Harris in translating *der Rechtzustand* as the "condition of right."

1. THEMES FROM "THE SPIRIT OF CHRISTIANITY AND ITS FATE"

1. While Hegel will articulate the basic theme of the "Spirit of Christianity" essay in more complex and convincing ways in other texts, and most effectively in the *Phenomenology of Spirit*, this essay, as J. M. Bernstein writes, "presents Hegel's vision in its undiluted form . . . [I]t captures something about why ethical life matters, about how and why we have ethical concerns at all, about how the achievements and fatalities of ethical experience can appear as what matters most in a life." J. M. Bernstein, "Love and Law: Hegel's Critique of Morality," *Social Research* 70, no. 2 (2003): 393–94. The basic idea expressed in this essay, according to Bernstein, is that "the flourishing and foundering of each is intimately bound up with the flourishing and foundering of all. Social space is always constituted ethically, as a space in which subjects are necessarily formed or deformed, freed or oppressed through the structures of interaction governing everyday life . . . [Ethical life] is about the secret bonds connecting our weal and woe to the lives of all those around us" (Bernstein, "Love and Law," 394).

2. For a helpful discussion of the different order in which the *Phenomenology* and the *Philosophy of Right* place ethical life and morality, see Will Dudley, "Ethical Life, Morality, and the Role of Spirit in the *Phenomenology of Spirit*," in *Hegel's* Phenomenology of Spirit, ed. Dean Moyar and Michael Quante (Cambridge: Cambridge University Press, 2008): 130–49.

3. Hegel's critical attitude toward the Jewish people of the Old Testament seems rather one-sided here. In his discussion of Hegel in *Glas* Derrida invokes some significant Jewish motifs that Hegel does not mention—motifs that might better withstand his criticism. For instance, the Jewish motifs of exile, homelessness, and wandering could be analyzed as expressive, in a way resonant with Hegel's work, of an ever-deferred promise that protects against a dogmatic faith that believes in an already present good. Jacques Derrida, *Glas*, tr. John P. Leavey Jr. and Richard Rand (Lincoln: University of Nebraska Press, 1986). See also John Caputo, *The Prayers and Tears of Jacques Derrida* (Bloomington: Indiana University Press, 1997).

4. For a very helpful and concrete treatment of these issues, see F. H. Bradley, "My Station and Its Duties," in *Ethical Studies* (London: Henry S. King, 1876), especially the discussion that begins on page 111.

5. Hegel discusses these examples at *ETW* 208; they are described in the New Testament in Matthew 12: 1–14 (RSV).

> 1 At that time Jesus went through the grainfields on the sabbath; his disciples were hungry, and they began to pluck heads of grain and to eat. 2 But when the Pharisees saw it, they said to him, "Look, your disciples are doing what is not lawful to do on the sabbath." 3 He said to them, "Have you not read what David did, when he was hungry, and those who were with him: 4 how he entered the house of God and ate the bread of the Presence, which it was not lawful for him to eat nor for those who were with him, but only for

> the priests? 5 Or have you not read in the law how on the sabbath the priests in the temple profane the sabbath, and are guiltless? 6 I tell you, something greater than the temple is here. 7 And if you had known what this means, 'I desire mercy, and not sacrifice,' you would not have condemned the guiltless. 8 For the Son of man is lord of the sabbath." 9 And he went on from there, and entered their synagogue. 10 And behold, there was a man with a withered hand. And they asked him, "Is it lawful to heal on the sabbath?" so that they might accuse him. 11 He said to them, "What man of you, if he has one sheep and it falls into a pit on the sabbath, will not lay hold of it and lift it out? 12 Of how much more value is a man than a sheep! So it is lawful to do good on the sabbath." 13 Then he said to the man, "Stretch out your hand." And the man stretched it out, and it was restored, whole like the other. 14 But the Pharisees went out and took counsel against him, how to destroy him.

6. Cf. Alice Ormiston, "'The Spirit of Christianity and Its Fate': Toward a Reconsideration of the Role of Love in Hegel," in *Canadian Journal of Political Science* 35, no. 3 (Sept. 2002):, 505.

7. Cf. Alan Norrie, *Law and the Beautiful Soul* (London: GlassHouse, 2005), 184.. Also see Ciavatta's *Spirit, the Family, and the Unconscious in Hegel's Philosophy*, an excellent exploration of the way in which our capacity to relate to ourselves as selves and agents—our capacity to think, to judge, and to act—is inextricably tied to the identities of other selves. Ciavatta examines this issue particularly in relation to the family: "Through intimate familiarity, we come to internalize the particular perspectives of these other selves, along with their particular manner of interacting with us and with our world, into our most basic ways of relating to ourselves as selves and agents, such that we implicitly carry these others around with us in all of our dealings" (Ciavatta, *Spirit, Family, Unconscious*, 2). This is an experience of being at home, Ciavatta says—"an original modality of our experience of the world generally . . . that is more basic than our more detached, 'objective' experience of the world as a set of external objects standing out before us" (Ciavatta, *Spirit, Family, Unconscious*, 5). It is an experience from which we *emerge*, and hence one that irreversibly and often unconsciously informs the way we think, judge, and act in the world.

8. H. S. Harris says that, according to Hegel, "the conception of reason as an authority that gives laws to sensibility is fundamentally mistaken. From the beginning (in *Religion ist eine*) he was convinced that the enlightened idea of critical rationality and autonomy must be so interpreted as to refer to a harmony of all the faculties, propensities, and needs of human nature; and because of this he rejected from the beginning the Kantian opposition of reason and sensibility." H. S. Harris, *Hegel's Development: Towards the Sunlight 1770–1801* (Oxford: Oxford University Press, 1972), 322.

9. Bernstein, "Love and Law," 410–11.

10. Hegel brings similar focus on the way in which moral action must speak to *this* life and its conditions in the section on "conscience" in the *Phenomenology*. Conscience knows action to be morally valuable to the extent to which it brings the universal to bear on the particularity of its character, its situation, and the needs of those around it. See especially section 635.

11. H. S. Harris writes that "the law loses its form as law; for it is not right to speak of being obliged to do something when one is really doing it because one wants to . . . In place of the empty abstraction, 'Thou shalt not kill,' Jesus sets a willingness to be reconciled for which the command is superfluous; and indeed the 'rending' of life by the attitude of reflective neutrality, which is all that the law requires, is the one thing which the new attitude excludes" (*Hegel's Development* 342). See also chapter 10, "The Contradictions of Moral Life: Hegel's Critique of Kant," of John Russon, *Reading Hegel's* Phenomenology (Bloomington: Indiana University Press, 2004), 147–56.

12. Hegel writes about Kant that "his remark that 'love,' or, to take the meaning which he thinks must be given to this love, '*liking* to perform all duties,' 'cannot be commanded' falls to the ground by its own weight, because in love all thought of duties vanishes" (*ETW* 213).

13. Harris, Hegel's Development, 350.

14. Ibid.

15. Derrida discusses the topic of this constitutive and abiding tension and its relevance for a living notion of responsibility in *On Cosmopolitanism and Forgiveness*, tr. Michael Hughes (New York: Routledge, 2001), and in "Force of Law," although it is a theme that pervades his work more generally.

2. THE IMMEDIACY OF ETHICAL LIFE

1. Alice Ormiston identifies the immediate connection between the ethical order and human value when she states that "traditional societies, as in ancient Greece, are pre-reflective, according to Hegel, in the sense that they are not marked by radical separation between thought and existence. The ethical order is, rather, built upon the natural morals and sentiments of individuals; it is an extension of their being, and so their commitment to it is implicit and unreflective" (Ormiston, "Role of Love," 504). She notes that the transformation from this way of life to the next involves ". . . a radical separation between thought and being, self and ethical substance, abstract thinking ego and concrete individuality. The basis of the new political community, in such a scenario, becomes the 'abstract ego,' which Hegel sees historically manifest in ancient Rome" (Ormiston, "Role of Love," 504).

2. I am thinking specifically of Seyla Benhabib, "On Hegel, Women and Irony," in *Situating the Self* (New York: Routledge, 1992); Judith Butler, *Antigone's Claim: Kinship between Life and Death* (New York: Columbia University Press, 2000); Tina Chanter, *Ethics of Eros: Irigaray's Rewriting of the Philosophers* (New York: Routledge, 1995); Patricia Mills, "Hegel's *Antigone* Redux: Woman in Four

Parts," *The Owl of Minerva* 33, no. 2 (Spring/Summer 2002); and Heidi M. Ravven, "Has Hegel Anything to Say to Feminists?" in *The Owl of Minerva* 19,. no. 2 (Spring 1988). I am also thinking of Luce Irigaray, whose comments about Hegel can be found in many places, but especially in Luce Irigaray, *Speculum of the Other Woman*, tr. Gillian C. Gill (Ithaca: Cornell University Press, 1985) or *Speculum de l'Autre Femme*, Paris: Editions de Minuit, 1974). See also Luce Irigaray, *An Ethics of Sexual Difference*, tr. Carolyn Burke and Gillian C. Gill (Ithaca: Cornell University Press, 1993) or *Ethique de la Différence Sexuelle* (Paris: Editions de Minuit, 1984); Luce Irigaray, "Sexes and Genealogies," in Margaret Whitford, ed., *The Irigaray Reader* (Oxford: Basil Blackwell, 1991) or *Sexes et Parentes* (Paris: Editions de Minuit, 1987); Luce Irigaray, *This Sex Which Is Not One*, tr. Catherine Porter (Ithaca: Cornell University Press, 1985) or *Ce sexe qui n'en est pas un* (Paris: Editions de Minuit, 1977). These attempts to come to terms with Hegel's work have engaged for the most part with his representations of Antigone and the family in the *Phenomenology* and the *Philosophy of Right*.

3. Cf. Derrida, *Glas*, 151.

4. Other formulations of this line of thinking can be found in the work of commentators such as H. S. Harris, Heidi M. Ravven, Karin de Boer, John Russon, and Martin Donougho. Ravven and Russon, for instance, elaborate (independently) the naturalness of *both* forms of identification in ethical life. They construe the "natural" as the preeminent problem according to ethical life, characterizing this society as one that does not acknowledge the role of human spontaneity and social construction in its identity. See Russon, *Reading*, 241–42, and Heidi M. Ravven, "Has Hegel Anything to Say to Feminists?," 155. Hegel, for de Boer, shows that sexual difference is always already "permeated by cultural significance" and that "a culture that forces men and women to identify one-sidedly with either human or divine law is doomed to be ruined." Karin de Boer, "Hegel's *Antigone* and the Dialectics of Sexual Difference," in *Philosophy Today SPEP Supplement* 2003), 144. H. S. Harris argues that what is most significant to Hegel's thought on this topic is the instability of the relation between spirit and nature. The ultimate ground of destruction is, he writes, the unstable "'marriage' of Mother Nature to self-defining Political-Freedom." H. S. Harris, *Hegel's Ladder II: The Odyssey of Spirit* (Indianapolis: Hackett, 1997), 227. Martin Donougho locates "the heart of the contradiction Hegel discerns in ancient Greece" in the fact that "nature becomes spiritually (or culturally) mediated, while in turn culture is discovered to be based on a natural immediacy, sheer contingency." Martin Donougho, "The Woman in White: On the Reception of Hegel's *Antigone*," in *The Owl of Minerva* 21, no. 1 (Fall 1989): 85.

5. That is not to say, however, that there is no such division; it is merely to say that this particular division is based on a false principle, or, even more, on the denial of the fact that there is principle at work here at all. There *is* a real division between familial and political life, and it does concern Hegel, both here and elsewhere. David Ciavatta describes this division in the following passage, also cited in the introduction: "[T]he inherently particularized character

of familial obligation—the fact that I immediately experience my familial obligation as being *exclusive* to *this particular, concrete other*, and not to this other as one representative of a universal type that includes all selves—puts the family at odds with other, readily universalizable sources of normativity" (Ciavatta, *Spirit, Family, Unconscious*, 12).

6. The immediate way in which the ethical consciousness resolves to identify with its law, "the immediacy of its decisiveness[,] is a being-in-itself [*Ansichsein*], and hence has at the same time the significance of a natural being" (M465, S343). Hegel says that Antigone acknowledges these "unalienated spirits," these "stainless celestial figures," as "the *unwritten* and *infallible* law [*Recht*] of the gods. 'They are not of yesterday or today, but everlasting/Though where they come from, none of us can tell.' They are" (M437, S321–22).

7. I use the term "character" following Hegel, who writes that "the ethical consciousness, because it is *decided* for one of the two powers, is essentially *character* [*Charakter*]" (M466). He also uses the term "character" in M472, stating that each character belongs to one of the parts or powers. "Character" is interesting insofar as it captures the dramatic element of this section—its status as the analysis of a fictional representation of a social world—and insofar as it suggests that Antigone and Creon do not take themselves to be acting on their own initiative, but on behalf of a kind of "script" that designates and defines their roles to and for them.

8. "In this way, the two sexes overcome their natural being and appear in their ethical significance" (M459, S338).

9. This cannot be described as intentional; agents do not intentionally transcend nature and become aware of themselves as doing so. The tension in ethical action between "nature" and "spirit" only becomes clear after the tragic conclusion.

10. "The blood-relationship therefore supplements the abstract natural movement by adding to it the movement of consciousness, interrupting the work of nature and rescuing the blood-relation from destruction" (M452, S333).

11. The family "weds the blood-relation to the bosom of the earth, to the elemental imperishable individuality. The family thereby makes him a member of a community which prevails over and holds under control the forces of particular material elements and the lower forms of life, which sought to unloose themselves against him and to destroy him" (M452, S333).

12. Hegel mentions that Antigone's guilt is purer; it is significant that *only here* does reference to Antigone arise at all. "But the ethical consciousness is more complete, its guilt purer, if it *knows beforehand* the law and the power it opposes, if it takes them to be violence and wrong [*Unrecht*], to be an ethical contingency, and, like Antigone, knowingly commits the crime" (M470, S348).

13. Derrida, *Glas*, 176.

14. Martha Nussbaum, *The Fragility of Goodness* (Cambridge: Cambridge University Press, 1986), 80–81.

15. John Russon illuminates Hegel's analysis of Greek society's own self-unraveling in the following:

> Through Antigone, Greek society reads itself . . . In sum, because Antigone acts from a duty that is socially instituted, her act enacts the self-cognition of Greek society. Of course, the same could be said of Creon's act: indeed, Antigone and Creon fight precisely because they are each animated by a one-sided logic, and their logics are mutually exclusive. In this case, both readings are equally justified, since each is legitimately rooted in the necessary institutions of their social existence. This is Hegel's point: both do read justly, and the contradiction of the readings demonstrates the contradictions at the heart of this kind of traditional society. (Russon, *Reading*, 78)

In a footnote to this passage, Russon adds that "at the level neither of human nor of divine law is the question asked 'what is law?' There is likewise no element within either set of laws that aims at the development or transformation of the society in such a way as to produce individuals who could answer 'what is law?' Rather, it is a self-satisfied society that takes itself to simply be itself, naturally: it does not see humanity as an achievement" (Russon, *Reading*, 241–42).

16. Hegel writes:

> The union of man and woman constitutes the active middle term of the whole and the element that, while divided into these extremes of divine and human law, is equally their immediate union. It makes the first two syllogisms into the same syllogism, and unites into *one* movement the opposing movements: one from actuality down to non-actuality—the movement of human law, organized into independent members, down to the danger and trial of death—and the upward movement of the law of the underworld to the actuality of daylight and conscious existence. Of these movements, the former falls to man, the latter to woman. (M463, S341–42)

17. The fact that by acting in the way that she does Antigone essentially refuses participation in the sexual and reproductive duties expected of her conflicts with Patricia Mills' argument that Hegel's portrayal of Antigone is his response to the "problem" of female desire, "an antidote to the 'immoral' sexual seductiveness of womankind in general, meant to *neutralize* woman's sensuality, her erotic otherness" (Mills, "Hegel's *Antigone* Redux," 214).

18. Again, it is Hegel's purpose to show the instability of Greek society, not to advocate a particular kind of social organization that would allot different social roles to men and women. By tracking the inevitable decline of Greek society, he does not uncritically perpetuate its sexual division of labor; his observations are a diagnosis, not an endorsement. Seyla Benhabib, for instance, on the one hand accurately notes that Hegel's philosophy describes the way in which "the human, historical world of tradition, institutions, laws, and practices" and "the self-reflection of knowing and acting subjects upon . . . works

of art, religion, and philosophy" transform nature into a second world or second nature; "*Geist* externalizes itself in history by appropriating, changing, and shaping the given such as to make it correspond to itself, to make it embody its own subjectivity, that is, reason and freedom" (Benhabib, *Situating the Self*, 245). On the other hand, however, instead of following through on this position and recognizing that Hegel attributes the demise of Greek social life to its refusal to acknowledge its own inevitable power in transforming nature into a second nature, Benhabib says that Hegel "is women's gravedigger, confining them to a grand but ultimately doomed phase of the dialectic, which 'befalls mind in its infancy,'" and that "the dialectic will sweep Antigone in its onward historical march . . . the female principle must eventually be expelled from public life . . . [and] the serious transparency of reason will discipline women and eliminate irony from public life" (Benhabib, *Situating the Self*, 255–56). The work of Luce Irigaray, which may be valuable for its elegant descriptions of the costs of sociosexual hierarchy and its contributions to new ways of speaking and thinking that could change the terms of sexual differentiation, is similarly inaccurate as a reading of Hegel, whom she construes to be actively invested in the fact that Greek society is organized around a fixed conception of the significance of sexual difference.

19. The *Phenomenology* does not provide much direct or explicit indication of how to deal with the issue of sexual difference; Karin de Boer rightly notes that it does not "indicate how this development [beyond ethical life] allowed men and women to increasingly interrupt their immediate identification with either of the two ethical principles and the cultural values bound up with them" (de Boer, "Hegel's *Antigone*," 143). But the question of whether the *Phenomenology* says anything about sexual difference is different from the question of the usefulness of Hegel's work for thinking about sexual difference today. If the development of, to refer again to de Boer, "a conception of sexual difference that neither identifies men and women with their physical differences nor completely ignores the significance of those differences" (de Boer, "Hegel's *Antigone*," 140) is on the contemporary agenda, as it should be, then I would argue that we can think *with*, rather than *against*, Hegel—relying on, among other things, his rich discussion of ethical life. Also, as Harris aptly states, "things like the human significance of gender . . . must be settled by history (and all that philosophy can say is that *no* settlement will be absolutely permanent)" (Harris, *Hegel's Ladder II*, 207).

20. Here Judith Butler misreads Hegel. Butler understands Hegel to claim that kinship is the prepolitical realm that is "the condition of intelligibility for the social" (Butler, *Antigone's Claim*, 15). According to Hegel, however, the essential reason for the foundering of ethical life is that it does not *acknowledge* the mutual contamination of laws and ethical realms, of nature and spirit. Butler also sees Hegel as siding with Creon against Antigone upon the demise of ethical life and as allying himself with the state, through a "desire for the law to be the indisputable law" (Butler, *Antigone's Claim*, 21). Again, however, it is a diagnosis of ethical life that is at work in Hegel's reading, not an endorsement, and

in the very next section of the *Phenomenology*, the "The Condition of Right," Hegel in fact shows the problems with social organization based merely on law.

3. THE RIGHT OF PERSONHOOD

1. As noted above, while A. V. Miller translates *Rechtzustand* as "legal status," I will follow H. S. Harris in translating this term as "condition of right." It is worthy of note, however, that Miller's translation captures the standard Roman usage of the literal term "status" for the legal recognition of the individual.

2. In this chapter I will use masculine pronouns when Hegel does—first, so as to keep the general issue of his reliance on male characters alive, and second, so as to call attention to the fact that the "person" is male, which, though I will not explore the issue here, is at the very least historically significant.

3. Since the principle of self-possessed, free personality has become the basis of Western law ever since, the condition of right can be used to illuminate various other historical frameworks. Michael H. Hoffheimer suggests that "the abstract non-specific character of Hegel's discussion of the condition of right equivocally supports multiple historical referents" (Hoffheimer, "Idea of Law," 357). Hoffheimer argues, indeed, that Hegel conflates Roman law and the European law contemporary to him, employing Napoleon as inspiration for his description of the lord of the world and describing the condition of right in terms that would have been very familiar to a German audience experiencing French expansion. He argues that in addition to connoting "the appearance of the legal order of Rome after the decline of Greece . . . Hegel . . . also associates the establishment of the state of law [*Recht*] as prerequisite for culture and morality with the expansion of legal systems under Napoleon. The equivocal meaning implies that the dialectical development corresponds to no single linear chronological development. The parallelism of Rome and Napoleon that Hegel makes in his later lectures on the philosophy of history thus finds methodic and historic justification in the experience of law-based society in the *Phenomenology*" (Hoffheimer, "Idea of Law," 359).

4. Antigone's obedience in carrying out the law, that is, is a significant aspect of the operation and effectiveness of that law. John Russon writes that "the ethical self experiences its own identity as flowing from the laws, without recognizing that the laws owe their efficacy—their very identity as laws—to the single wills that accept them" (Russon, *Reading*, 139).

5. Hegel writes, further, that "the religion of Art belongs to the ethical spirit which we earlier saw perish in the *condition of right* or law, i.e. in the proposition: *The self as such, the abstract person, is absolute being*'" (M750, S546). The form in which it experiences this demise is comedy.

6. For an excellent discussion of the historical referents of Hegel's analysis in this section, see Patricia Fagan, "Philosophical History and the Roman Empire," in *Hegel and the Tradition: Essays in Honour of* H. S. *Harris*, ed. Michael Baur and John Russon (Toronto: University of Toronto Press, 1997), 17–39.

7. Terry Pinkard, "Spirit as the 'Unconditioned,'" in Stephen Houlgate and Michael Baur, eds., *A Companion to Hegel* (Oxford: Blackwell, 2011), 98.

8. Much of Stephen Houlgate's work is helpful for explaining Hegel's critical approach to individualistic conceptions of freedom. The basic point he seeks to defend is the following: Hegel's "criticisms of individualistic conceptions of freedom are not due to any prejudice in favour of state authority on his part, but arise during the course of a prolonged meditation on and determination of the proper meaning of *freedom* itself . . . the very meaning or concept of freedom itself requires us to recognise that freedom is not simply to be found in unrestricted individual choice or in the unregulated pursuit of self-satisfaction, but in living in accordance with law within a just political constitution." Stephen Houlgate, *Freedom, Truth and History: An Introduction to Hegel's Philosophy* (London: Routledge, 1991), 79.

9. Many readers of Hegel identify a connection between the condition of right and the contemporary order of right. Robert C. Solomon, for instance, writes that Hegel's characterization of personhood "reaches far beyond life in the Roman Empire and, indeed, includes most Western societies ever since" (Solomon, *Spirit of Hegel*, 550). Quentin Lauer argues that a rights-based conception of agency and political authority simply disguises authority and weakens agency, noting that "[o]nly too frequently the contemporary state can and does conceal from its members the absence of their true self-determination (freedom) by granting 'rights,' e.g., freedom of thought, which the state can regulate in such a way as to make said 'rights' ineffectual in any number of ways" (Lauer, *A Reading*, 217). Gillian Rose argues that the condition of right (as well as the spiritual animal kingdom) is a premonition of the false dilemma of modern societies—that between the rights of the individual and the rights of the state. She writes: "Modern law is that of legal status [*Rechtzustand*], where those with subjective rights and subjective ends deceive themselves and others that they act for the universal when they care only for their own interests. This is the spiritual-animal kingdom; it is comic, not in the sense of frank joviality or careless gaiety and self-mockery, but in the sense of bitter and repugnant intrigue by individuals who deceive others by seeming to share their interest and whose real interest is without substance" (Rose, *Mourning*, 73). For Rose, we are faced with a "modern legal status" (Rose, *Mourning*, 75), wherein individual rights are a smokescreen for the underhanded use of power on a super-individual scale and the loss of value. This is the "migration of ethical substance (objective freedom) into the hapless subject" (Rose, *Mourning*, 74), by which the legal person loses any relationship to the world, work, desire, and otherness (Rose, *Mourning*, 73). Rose contrasts the legal person to the slave as Hegel describes him in the master-slave dialectic: one of the unexpected aspects of the slave's condition is his opportunity to develop a meaningful and self-affirming relation to what is not himself—the world and the objects upon which he works in it. Steven B. Smith also connects the condition of right with contemporary political reality, arguing that both could be conceived as "a primarily passive and defensive posture having more to do with institutional protections against the abuse of

power than with access to power itself." Steven B. Smith, *Hegel's Critique of Liberalism: Rights in Context* (Chicago: University of Chicago Press, 1989), 122.

10. Allen W. Wood makes a similar point, saying that "Hegel is worried about the 'spirit of atomism' in civil society because he thinks that too little social structuring of individual possibilities and expectations (too much of what liberals usually value under the name of freedom) might actually frustrate the whole aim of subjective freedom. Hegel plainly fears that a market system without the sort of ethical structure he assigned to corporations might well be self-defeating in just this way" (258). He adds that Hegel's "claim is that what has the most value for individuals, what actualizes their freedom most completely, is the pursuit of a universal or collective end, not the pursuit of their own private ends as such. If a liberal state is one that has no universal, collective goals but exists only to serve the particular whims and desires of its individual members, then Hegelian ethical theory says that the members of a liberal state, for all their personal, subjective, and civil freedoms, are fundamentally *unfree*" (259). Allen W. Wood, *Hegel's Ethical Thought* (Cambridge: Cambridge University Press, 1991).

11. This is an important theme in Derrida's *Rogues*, in *The Other Heading*, tr. Pascale-Anne Brault and Michael Naas (Bloomington: Indiana University Press, 1992), and in *Politics of Friendship*, where Derrida writes about "the duty for democracy itself to de-limit itself . . . not only in the name of a regulative Idea and an indefinite perfectibility but every time in the singular urgency of a *here and now*" (Jacques Derrida, *Politics of Friendship* 105).

12. This discussion is found in M741–47 of the *Phenomenology* (S540–44).

13. "What to Stoicism was the *in-itself* merely in *abstraction* is now an *actual world*" (M479, S356).

14. In the context of his discussion of the religion of art Hegel explains the problem like this: "It is the return of everything universal into the certainty of itself which, in consequence, is this complete loss of fear and of essential being on the part of all that is alien" (M747, S544). Here he identifies the two sides to this accomplishment: on the one hand, there is no need to fear what is alien, since its power over the person has been dissipated, but, on the other hand, there is no significance or essential being to that externality, and hence a loss of meaning.

15. John Russon explains these two aspects in the following: "Thus, any social relation (call it 'traditional society') that treats the law as something existing in its own right in independence of the singular self-consciousnesses that obey the law is misconstruing its own situation." And "just as it is fiction to think of the law as existing in independence of the adherence to it of singular self-consciousnesses, it is equally false to posit a singular self-consciousness that does not exist precisely as the representative agent of a social system" (Russon, *Reading*, 161).

16. Aristotle makes this point powerfully in his *Politics*. Even though political structures of interaction and organization can only be accomplished

through our actions, and hence are not merely given to us, it is nevertheless "evident that the state is a creation of nature, and that man is by nature a political animal." It is natural for us to be part of a state, but the state does not occur by nature, since it requires human initiative for its formation and operation, because it is a phenomenon of creative thinking and deliberation. Aristotle, *Politics*, tr. Benjamin Jowett, in *The Complete Works of Aristotle*, ed. Jonathan Barnes (Princeton: Princeton University Press, 1984), 1253a3–4.

17. Robert Brandom expresses a similar point when he says that "self-conscious beings do not have *natures*, they have histories," in "The Structure of Desire and Recognition: Self-Consciousness and Self-Constitution," *Philosophy and Social Criticism* 33, no. 1 (2007): 128.

18. Bernstein, "Love and Law," 399.

19. "Objective Spirit" is treated in sections 483–552 of the *Encyclopaedia of the Philosophical Sciences*.

4. THE LEGAL CONDITIONS OF ACTION

1. See Richard Dean Winfield, "Freedom as Interaction: Hegel's Resolution to the Dilemma of Liberal Theory," in *Hegel's Philosophy of Action*, ed. Lawrence S. Stepelevitch and David Lamb (Atlantic Highlands, NJ: Humanities, 1983), 173–90, for a nice explication of the reliance of the free will on relationships of recognition.

2. In discussion of a similar point, John Burbidge writes, "[W]e discover our genuine freedom only when we act as members of a structured society. To be sure, we are free when we can do whatever we want. But if such action does not accomplish our interests, then such freedom is faulty. By working within the petrified passions of convension we are able to act, and develop our interests, in a way that can accomplish what we have in mind. We achieve our destiny when we accept our station and perform the duties that it imposes." John Burbidge, *Hegel's Systematic Contingency* (New York: Palgrave Macmillan, 2007), 6.

3. Thomas Hobbes, *Leviathan* (Cambridge: Cambridge University Press, 1996), 89.

4. As Judith Butler writes, "the staging and structuring of affect and desire is clearly one way in which norms work their way into what feels most properly to belong to me" (Butler, *Undoing Gender*, 15).

5. In discussing the role of contingency in history, John Burbidge gives an excellent example of a situation that seems to be different from what it really is and requires subtle perception. While traditions and customs may seem to be "restrictions on our freedom" and hence *opposed* to the passions, since "they certainly serve to hold our passions in check," they are actually the result of these passions or "the result of having the passions free play, of having them rub against each other until they became worn out. They are the result of abrasion" (John Burbidge, *Hegel's Systematic Contingency*, 6).

5. LAW, RIGHT, AND FORGIVENESS

1. In a description that in effect leads Hegel to the introduction of "spirit," and that is similar to his description of what is accomplished in forgiveness, he says that what is at issue here "is rather substance penetrated by individuality; *subject*, in which there is individuality just as much *qua* individual, or *qua this* individual, as *qua all* individuals; and universal, which is a *being* only as this action of all and of each, and an *actuality* in the fact that *this* consciousness knows it to be its own actuality and the actuality of all" (M418, S310).

2. For further exploration of the idea that law is the adoption of a shared interpretive standpoint as one's own, see "The Ritual Basis of Self-Identity" in Russon, *Reading Hegel's* Phenomenology, especially pp. 173–77.

3. The distinction between consciously posited laws and customary, unposited laws is a familiar and long-standing distinction, one made, for instance, in "Pericles' Funeral Oration." Pericles says, "We obey the laws themselves, especially those which are for the protection of the oppressed, and those unwritten laws which it is an acknowledged shame to break." Thucydides, *History of the Peloponnesian War*, tr. Rex Warner (London: Penguin Books, 1972), 37.19–22.

4. Hegel writes: "[C]onsciousness of right, therefore, in the very fact of being recognized as having validity, experiences rather the loss of its reality and its complete inessentiality; and to describe an individual as a 'person' is an expression of contempt" (M480, S357).

5. J. M. Bernstein and Kelly Oliver have argued that in Hegel's discussions of confession and forgiveness lies the resolution of Antigone and Creon's conflict in ethical life—the opposition between the single individual and universality. Oliver, for instance, writes that Hegel concludes spirit "with a discussion of forgiveness and confession that reconciles the Particular and the Universal, the unconscious and the conscious, which began in this section as the opposition between woman (Antigone) and man (Creon) that gave rise to the ethical order." Kelly Oliver, "Forgiveness and Subjectivity," *Philosophy Today* 47, no. 3 (Fall 2003): 281. Similarly, Bernstein writes that "the *agon* between acting and judging consciousness means to resolve the matter between Antigone and Creon, between individuality and universality, unwritten and written law . . ." J. M. Bernstein, "Confession and Forgiveness: Hegel's Poetics of Action," in *Beyond Representation: Philosophy and Poetic Imagination*, edited by Richard Eldridge (Cambridge: Cambridge University Press, 1996), 40. I follow Oliver and Bernstein here by looking at the conflict between Antigone and Creon through the framework of forgiveness, while adding the consideration that forgiveness is also importantly a way of responding to the problematic representations of personhood and agency at work in the condition of right and the spiritual animal kingdom, since such personhood and agency operate in ways similar to the judging consciousness of forgiveness and the contemporary rights-bearing individual.

6. Derrida writes, similarly, that "justice, however unpresentable it may be, doesn't wait. It is that which must not wait. To be direct, simple and brief,

let us say this: a just decision is always required *immediately*, 'right away.' It cannot furnish itself with infinite information and the unlimited knowledge of conditions, rules or hypothetical imperatives that could justify it. And even if it did have all that at its disposal, even if it did give itself the time, all the time and the necessary facts about the matter, the moment of *decision, as such*, always remains a finite moment of urgency and precipitation, since it must not be the consequence or the effect of this theoretical or historical knowledge" (Derrida, "Force of Law," 26).

7. "Morality" is also called "Spirit That Is Certain of Itself." Indeed, the "Spirit" chapter begins with "True Spirit" and ends with "Self-Certain Spirit," or advances from truth to certainty, from a world in which an "objectively valid law" is simply given for individuals to follow blindly, to a world in which the individual *must* rely on her own insight, having available no guarantee that she is doing the right thing. For an analysis of the significance of this movement from truth to certainty, see chapter 10, "The Contradictions of Moral Life: Hegel's Critique of Kant," in Russon, *Reading Hegel's* Phenomenology, pp. 147–56. Russon writes that "to be moral, according to Hegel, still means to be rational, but being rational means being led by the demands of our determinate situations—it means being unable to withdraw into an a priori morality that would somehow know what to do in independence of knowing the situation" (Russon, *Reading*, 155). A further point to emphasize with regard to this theme of certainty versus truth is that what is translated as "conscience" is *Gewissen*, related to *gewiss* and *Gewissheit*, which mean "certain" and "certainty," and that *wissen* means "to know." Conscience's all-knowing "certainty" is what is mobilized in conscientious action. While this conscientious self-certainty is recognized as necessary, in that there are no genuine alternative sources of guidance, we also find out that this certainty is precisely what is offered to the other through confession: the other is welcomed to alter the actor's certainty, to have something to say about the action.

8. As Hegel states, the actor brings about a "non-identity with the other [the judge], since this other does not believe it or acknowledge it" (M662, S486).

9. This consciousness "is aware of itself as this single individual [*Einzelne*], and is conscious of the antithesis between what it is for itself and what it is for others, of the antithesis of universality or duty and its reflection out of universality into itself" (M659, S485).

10. Hegel writes that "duty for duty's sake, this pure purpose, is the non-actual; it has its actuality in the deed of individuality, and as such the action has in it the aspect of particularity" (M665, S489).

11. This is "universal consciousness, for which the essential being is rather universality, duty" (M660, S485), but which sustains its alliance with universality by refraining from particular action (M664, S487).

12. Bernstein identifies the factor that each brings to the conflict in the following: the principles that motivate the judge's judgment refer to the "intentional content" of actions, which is one aspect of their content, but principles cannot be fully determinative of actions. Conversely, the virtues associated with

the actor refer to the "reflective expressive scope" of actions, which similarly is an important aspect of action but not the only one (Bernstein, "Conscience and Transgression," 64).

13. Robert Pippin is concerned with a similar theme in *Hegel on Self-Consciousness*—with the relationship between recognition and normativity. He writes: "To be norm-sensitive at all is then shown not just to be *open* to these unique sorts of challenges [from others], but to be finally *dependent* on some resolution of them." Robert Pippin, *Hegel on Self-Consciousness: Desire and Death in the* Phenomenology of Spirit (Princeton: Princeton University Press, 2011), 39.

14. Hegel describes this further: the judge "cannot attain to an identity with the consciousness it has repulsed, nor thereby to an intuited union of itself in the other or to existence" (M668, S491).

15. The judge "recognizes itself" in the actor's return from "its external actuality back into itself as essence" (M670, S492).

16. "The forgiveness it extends to the first is the renunciation of itself, of its *non-actual* essence, which it equates with that other which was *actual* action" (M670, S492).

17. Harris, *Ladder II*, 493.

18. The solidarity that is produced here is a solidarity involving people who are different. What we share with each other, what constitutes the "universal" in this domain, is our singular individuality, which means that what is common among us is what makes us different from each other. This is a radical notion, in that it suggests, as Kelly Oliver writes, that "Hegelian identification is precisely with the otherness of the other, with the other's difference. The identification comes with the realization of the particularity of individuals, a particularity so radical that it is only by virtue of the recognition of this universal property of individuality, of difference itself, that the judge and agent find any common ground. In one sense, Hegelian identification is already an identification with the impossibility of identification" (Oliver, "Forgiveness and Subjectivity," 282). This is emphatically *not* the formula of the condition of right, in which all persons are declared identical and whose individual difference is cast as irrelevant to the existence of the universal. (In keeping with the terms Hegel uses, we should think of the term "singularity" when Oliver, following Miller, uses the term "particularity.")

19. In this vein, Bernstein asserts that action is not directed to and motivated solely by the moral or legal universal, but to and by other selves (Bernstein, "Confession and Forgiveness," 47).

20. Kym Maclaren's discussion of Hegel and Plato in the context of a discussion of the nature of education resonates well in this context. She characterizes any context of learning as in a sense blind: "Precisely because the rational move forward involves a revolution in the terms in which things make sense, consciousness cannot, from the position of its familiar terms, immediately see the rationality of the new configuration of reality." Kym Maclaren, "The Role of Emotion in an Existential Education: Insights from Hegel and Plato," *International Philosophical Quarterly* 48, 4/192 (December 2008): 476.

"Conscientious learning," or learning that would bravely take on the experience of this kind of blindness, requires, according to Maclaren, that one "undergo the violence of losing one's current world and of being born into a new, more comprehensive world. One undergoes a world-collapse, the death of this way of being, in order to be carried into a new, previously unknown way of being that subsumes and is the truth of the previous way of being" (Maclaren, "Role of Emotion," 487).

21. In a powerful discussion of the political significance of these tensions, Vladimir Jankélévitch also identifies two conflicting absolutes: the one attached to law and requiring concern and punishment for crimes against humanity, the other attached to forgiveness and requiring infinite love. Law is universal, standard, stable, just; forgiveness, as an event, is fleeting, singular, irrational, and, in the terms of law, unjust. Law must disregard the singularity and particularity of those to whom it applies and refuse to enter into a personal relation with them; forgiveness pinpoints precisely that singularity in the urge to establish or reestablish a relation. Each absolute also carries with it a risk—the law that it will respond without love in violence and force, forgiveness that it will "establish the reign of the hangmen for one thousand years." Vladimir Jankélévitch, *Forgiveness*, tr. Andrew Kelley (Chicago: University of Chicago Press, 2005), 163. The human spirit, says Jankélévitch, cannot go beyond these contradictory triumphs; neither has the last word. He writes that "forgiveness is a principle of mobility and fluidity *for the law*. By the grace of forgiveness, this law will remain pneumatic, evasive, and approximate" (9, my emphasis); it will always defer any last word with regard to the accomplishment of justice. And it will remain evasive and approximate in the name of its *very own principle*, which is to be universal, general, applicable to every circumstance. In the absence, therefore, of full knowledge of its perfection as a universal principle, it can never be asserted absolutely. Žižek, similarly, says that

> when we criticize the hidden bias and exclusion of universality, we should never forget that we are already doing so *within* the terrain opened up by universality: the proper critique of "false universality" does not call it into question from the standpoint of pre-universal particularism, it mobilizes the tension inherent to universality itself, the tension between the open negativity, the disruptive power, of what Kierkegaard would have called "universality-in-becoming," and the fixed form of established universality. Or—. . . in Hegelian terms—we have, on the one hand, the "dead," "abstract" universality of an ideological notion with fixed inclusions/exclusions and, on the other, "living," "concrete" universality as the permanent process of the questioning and renegotiation of its own "official" content. Universality becomes "actual" precisely and only by rendering thematic the exclusions on which it is grounded, by continuously questioning, renegotiating, displacing them, that is, by assuming the gap between its own form and content, by conceiving itself as

unaccomplished in its very notion. Judith Butler, Ernesto Laclau, and Slavoj Žižek, *Contingency, Hegemony, Universality* (London: Verso, 2000), 102

22. It is the project of the *Phenomenology* to identify these ingredients of selfhood, to bring us to an understanding of who we are, and that involves an understanding of the social realities that have been powerful agents in our becoming.

23. Indeed, what is significant about ethical life and what is significant about the condition of right in a sense come together in the world that we inhabit: *modernity*, a world of abstract right, is in a way its ethical life, its particular culture, and where many of us find ourselves at home.

24. This idea is captured in Bernstein's argument that it is insufficient to develop rules and principles that will express the fact of mutual recognition; understanding right to preclude any further action or interaction on their part will simply enable individuals to refuse solidarity, which is contrary to the principle at the heart of law. This political strategy—employed, Bernstein says by "the Rawlsian veil of ignorance or . . . Habermas' principle D" (Bernstein, "Confession and Forgiveness," 36)—creates judging consciousnesses who merely "judge the correspondence between particular actions and collective principles" and who thus preserve their moral purity by not acting at all (Bernstein, "Confession and Forgiveness," 37). Individual reason and action unfold out of such institutions and relations, and the world, as Kimerer Lamothe similarly argues, must be transfigured in such a way that it allows for the emergence of individuals capable of bringing ethical relations into being that in turn support their individual capacities and claims to difference. Kimerer L. Lamothe, "Reason, Religion, and Sexual Difference: Resources for a Feminist Philosophy of Religion in Hegel's *Phenomenology of Spirit*," in *Hypatia* 20, no. 1 (Winter 2005): 139.

25. Bernstein introduces this possible reconciliation between law on the one hand and transgressive individuality on the other when he writes about law that it cannot be an abstract and "independent universal to which [one's] deeds might correspond or fail to correspond" (Bernstein, "Confession and Forgiveness," 44) or a "structure of universality indifferent to the claims of individuality," but neither can we simply assert "the claims of individuality and its 'unwritten law' against the . . . laws of community" (Bernstein, "Confession and Forgiveness," 40). What is necessary is a compromise between these two extremes of individuality and law, in which laws must allow for the continuous negotiation of our recognitional dependencies, not disavow them (Bernstein, "Confession and Forgiveness," 50). They must express and not deny the reality of human identity and interaction and be their product, not the abstract measure by which they are judged. Indeed, a system of law can be challenged to do this in the name of its very own principle—that it be fair, inclusive, comprehensive, genuinely universal.

CONCLUSION TO PART 1

1. See my discussion of similar issues in relation to feminist politics and thought, in Shannon Hoff, "Inheriting Identity and Practicing Transformation: The Time of Feminist Politics," in *Philosophia* 2, no. 2 (2012).

2. Harris, *Hegel's Development*, 342.

3. Law, ethicality, and forgiveness can be shaped in such a way as to reflect acknowledgment of the significance of the other elements. As an example of this kind of dynamic, we can look at Ontario's *Arbitration Act*, which was amended in 2006 by the *Family Statute Law Amendment Act*. The *Arbitration Act* of 1992 allowed civil disputes to be privately arbitrated, and on its basis Jewish and Christian groups produced arbitration boards that relied on religious principles as principles for arbitration (Anna C. Korteweg, "The Sharia Debate in Ontario: Gender, Islam, and Representations of Women's Agency," in *Gender & Society* 22, no. 4 (2008): 436). Under the condition that these arbitrations not violate existing Canadian law, they were legally binding. When Syed Mumtaz Ali announced that the Islamic Institute of Civil Justice would offer private arbitration in family and business disputes on the basis of this Act and in accordance with Islamic legal principles, however, there was intense public reaction. The provincial government responded by commissioning Marion Boyd, a feminist activist, as well as a former attorney general of the Province, to study the use of such arbitration and produce a report. The report recommended that "the Arbitration Act should continue to allow disputes to be arbitrated using religious law, if the safeguards currently prescribed and recommended by this Review are observed." Ministry of the Attorney General of Ontario, "Dispute Resolution in Family Law: Protecting Choice, Promoting Inclusion," prepared by Marion Boyd (December 2004), 133, and recommended the addition of further "institutionalized oversight and education on the principles of religious arbitration and Canadian family law" (Korteweg, "The Sharia Debate," 436). But the government rejected the recommendation, announcing that there would be "one law for all" and introducing the *Family Statute Law Amendment Act, 2006*. The original Act was a powerful example of an attempt to reconcile the equally significant factors of ethical life and law, and the public discussion of the issue, as well as the report's emphasis on ongoing education into principles of religious arbitration, were powerful ways of acknowledging the significance of conscientious interaction, affording space for "multiple normative orders" and supporting interaction among them. Benjamin L. Berger, "Belonging to Law: Religious Difference and the Conditions of Civic Inclusion," unpublished (2012): 7.

4. In this particular complex of issues there is much resonance with Derrida's work—for instance, with *Rogues*, *A Taste for the Secret*, "Of Forgiveness," and "Force of Law." In "Force of Law," for instance, Derrida shows the insufficiency of law when he writes that "there is apparently no moment in which a decision can be called presently and fully just: either it has not yet been made

according to a rule, and nothing allows us to call it just, or it has already followed a rule—whether received, confirmed, conserved or reinvented—which in its turn is not absolutely guaranteed by anything; and, moreover, if it were guaranteed, the decision would be reduced to calculation and we wouldn't call it just" (Derrida, "Force of Law," 24). The possibility of taking responsibility, of acting justly, lies in what Derrida calls an experience of the impossible: "I think that there is no justice without this experience, however impossible it may be, of aporia. Justice is an experience of the impossible. A will, a desire, a demand for justice whose structure wouldn't be an experience of aporia would have no chance to be what it is, namely, a call for justice. Every time that something comes to pass or turns out well, every time that we placidly apply a good rule to a particular case, to a correctly subsumed example, according to a determinant judgment, we can be sure that law (*droit*) may find itself accounted for, but certainly not justice. Law (*droit*) is not justice. Law is the element of calculation, and it is just that there be law, but justice is incalculable, it requires us to calculate with the incalculable; and aporetic experiences are the experiences, as improbable as they are necessary, of justice, that is to say of moments in which the decision between just and unjust is never insured by a rule" (Derrida, "Force of Law," 16). In *Rogues*, he writes that "the responsibility of what remains to be decided or done (in actuality) cannot consist in following, applying, or carrying out a norm or rule. Wherever I have at my disposal a determinable rule, I know what must be done . . . The decision no longer decides anything but is made in advance and is thus in advance annulled. It is simply deployed, without delay, presently, with the automatism attributed to machines. There is no longer any place for justice or responsibility" (84–85). See also Jacques Derrida and Maurizio Ferraris, *A Taste for the Secret*, tr. Giacomo Donis (Cambridge: Polity, 2001); and Jacques Derrida, "On Forgiveness," in *On Cosmopolitanism and Forgiveness*, tr. Michael Hughes (New York: Routledge, 2001).

6. THE IDEAL NATION AND THE REAL NATION

1. "Absolute Freedom and Terror" is the last section of "Culture" in the *Phenomenology of Spirit* (M582–95, S431–41).

2. This chapter resonates especially powerfully with some of Derrida's work on law, democracy, and hospitality, and the reader can consult footnotes for mention of this resonance when it occurs. See especially *Rogues*, "Force of Law," *Politics of Friendship*, and *Of Hospitality*, tr. Rachel Bowlby (Stanford: Stanford University Press, 2000).

3. In *Rogues* Derrida approaches this issue through consideration of the concept of democracy, illuminating its constitutive tension between the founding and foundational democratic principle of inclusion of "whoever comes" and the equally significant need to exclude so as to be able to be constituted as a body capable of exercising concrete democratic concern. See especially section 8: "The Last of the Rogue States: The 'Democracy to Come,' Opening in Two Turns," 78–94.

4. Pinkard illuminates the idea to be developed in this chapter in the following:

> Hegel came to believe that in the wake of the French Revolution and the development of the 'moral worldview,' modern life had (for contingent reasons) developed a set of basic social institutions that created the possibility for a renewal of *Sittlichkeit* (of acting according to norms that are experienced simply as 'the way things are done,' that specify a 'common life,' which count as *authoritative* for modern individuals) which would not only be compatible with the reflective, self-distancing practices of modern life but would make those practices themselves possible as a rational form of self-consciousness. Terry Pinkard, *Hegel's* Phenomenology: *The Sociality of Reason* (Cambridge: Cambridge University Press, 1994).

5. H. S. Harris writes that "no one speaks now for his estate or corporation; everyone participates in National Convention simply as a citizen, making laws for all[,] and in the new, democratic Army too . . . The 'social distinctions' which 'can be founded only on public utility' are no longer seen to have any utility. The social system of the 'spiritual essences or powers' (i.e. the Estates and 'corporations' of all kinds) has collapsed into a homogeneous democratic community" (Harris, *Hegel's Ladder II*, 389).

6. There is an important distinction here between ethical life and revolutionary life: ethical life is grounded in a reality that lies in a sense outside of human affairs and human control (nature and the divine), and revolutionary life is constituted by a system of agents who make the world over into a world that suits their own rational nature. The French Revolution represents recognition of the fact that political life must be reflectively *produced* by human beings in order to be an appropriate environment for them, as beings who are free and self-making. See chapter 2 for further discussion of this issue.

7. Indeed, unlike the Bill of Rights of the United States, the Declaration of the Rights of Man and of the Citizen of 1789 makes no mention of a particular country or system of government.

8. Kant understands by kingdom of ends "a systematic union of different rational beings through common laws." He continues: "Now laws determine ends as regards their universal validity; therefore, if one abstracts from the personal differences of rational beings and also from all content of their private ends, then it will be possible to think of a whole of all ends in systematic connection (a whole both of rational beings as ends in themselves and also of the particular ends which each may set for himself)." Immanuel Kant, *Grounding for the Metaphysics of Morals*, tr. James W. Ellington (Indianapolis: Hackett, 1993), 39.

9. Jean-Jacques Rousseau, "Discourse on Political Economy," in *The Social Contract and Other Later Political Writings*, ed. by Victor Gourevitch (Cambridge: Cambridge University Press, 1997), 6.

10. Rousseau, "On the Social Contract," in *The Social Contract and Other Later Political Writings*, 50.

11. Harris says that "to do a *deed* the community must individualize itself into a head of state. But then all other single citizens are (unjustly) deprived of their share. This means that universal freedom can only produce a fury of annihilation" (Harris, *Hegel's Ladder II*, 394).

12. Harris says that "if the suspicion of opposition to the government is all that there can be, and if this suspicion must be wiped out, then only the death of the embodied singular self-consciousness can secure the triumph of Absolute Freedom. Everything is a faction; so everything is known to be non-identical with general will" (Harris, *Hegel's Ladder II*, 398–99).

13. In the introduction to the *Philosophy of Right*, Hegel comments on the absence of production in the revolutionary context, linking it to the fact that this is a social context built on only one aspect of the will, its "*absolute possibility* of *abstracting* from every determination in which I find myself or which I have posited in myself," in the absence of its other aspect, its transition from indeterminacy to determinacy. "This is the freedom of the void," he writes, which, "if it turns to actuality . . . becomes in the realm of both politics and religion the fanaticism of destruction, demolishing the whole existing social order, eliminating all individuals regarded as suspect by a given order, and annihilating any organization which attempts to rise up anew. Only in destroying something does this negative will have a feeling of its own existence [*Dasein*]. It may well believe that it wills some positive condition, for instance the condition of universal equality or of universal religious life, but it does not in fact will the positive actuality of this condition, for this at once gives rise to some kind of order, a particularization both of institutions and of individuals; but it is precisely through the annihilation of particularity and of objective determination that the self-consciousness of this negative freedom arises. Thus, whatever such freedom believes [*meint*] that it wills can for itself [*für sich*] be no more than an abstract representation [*Vorstellung*], and its actualization can only be the fury of destruction" (*PhR* 5).

14. On the political arena as a "home" for agency, see Kirsten Jacobson, "The Experience of Home and the Space of Citizenship," *Southern Journal of Philosophy* 48 (2010): 219–45.

15. Rebecca Comay captures this ambivalence facing rationality, which can neither assume the world as it is nor leave it behind, for it must both be free from external determination and have a specific terrain upon which to embellish itself: "The entire precipitation into terror is contained in reason's campaign against a world it can neither accommodate nor quite, in the end, give up . . . With an exquisite Nietzschean sensitivity Hegel smells a rat: the stench of the corpse of the abandoned object keeps wafting up from the open grave of the world." Rebecca Comay, *Mourning Sickness: Hegel and the French Revolution* (Stanford: Stanford University Press, 2010), 67–68.

16. Bernstein distinguishes between two different kinds of moral orientation, arguing that Hegel challenges "a vertical relation to a projected externality" (Bernstein, "Love and Law," 399), in which morality is a "question of law and obedience" (Bernstein, "Love and Law," 421), in the name of "horizontal and

so immanent relations of love and life" (Bernstein, "Love and Law," 399), in which morality becomes an issue of "the quality and nature of our relationship with one another" (Bernstein, "Love and Law," 421).

17. According to H. S. Harris, Hegel was convinced throughout his work that "the integrity of human experience and the natural harmony of human existence at its best could not be captured in a conceptual scheme, but was somehow falsified and destroyed by the intellect." Hegel's judgment against the intellect was similarly applicable, says Harris, to the "abstract intellectual character" of the revolution. H. S. Harris, "Hegel and the French Revolution," *Clio* 7, no. 1 (Fall 1977): 10.

18. Hegel's discussion of the condition of right in the *Phenomenology* is similar: the identity of rights-bearing individuals and their detachment from the world render interaction unnecessary and, indeed, problematic (see M477–83, S355–59).

19. The second declaration of the rights of man asserts that "the aim of every political association is the preservation of the natural and imprescriptible rights of man." Frank Maloy Anderson, ed., *The Constitution and Other Select Documents Illustrative of the History of France, 1789–1907* (New York: Russell and Russell, 1908), 59. One way in which to articulate Hegel's critique of the revolutionary nation is to show that its purported support of political *association* actually amounts to a support of political *dissociation* resulting from the isolation and self-absorbed atomism of individuals.

20. Bernstein, "Love and Law," 399.

21. Comay suggests that "absolute freedom *is* terror. It is the infinite melancholia of a self that knows no other. It can recognize no obstacle, no externality, no mediating agency, no local nuance or detour that might delay or dilute the passage from individuality to totality, from part to whole, from citizen to state, and back again: the individual will fuses with the universal will immediately, totally, continuously, without residue" (Comay, *Mourning Sickness*, 68).

22. See M419–28/S311–16 for Hegel's account of law-giving reason, and M429–37/S316–23 for that of law-testing reason. See chapter 5 for a brief discussion of these accounts.

23. Comay also identifies in Hegel a critique of the anonymous rule of abstract law, law dissociated from its substance, when she writes: "Abstract individualism is the principle—the scary link, for Hegel, between the seemingly disparate ideologies of revolutionary decisionism, of social contractualism, of absolutist nationalism, and of free-market liberalism . . . It is in each case, for Hegel, the lost ligature of the social bond which is registered without being acknowledged: the loss of the binding power of religion as *religare*, the splintering of the community into an aggregate of 'volitional atoms,' and the foreclosure of the political . . . within the transparent homogeneity of a civil society sutured together by the anonymous rule of law." Rebecca Comay, "Dead Right: Hegel and the Terror," *The South Atlantic Quarterly* 103: 2/3 (Spring/Summer 2004): 384.

24. In *Politics of Friendship*, *Rogues*, and *Of Hospitality*, Derrida also explores this tension between the demand implicit in the principle of democracy to

delimit itself and the demand to be unconditional. *Rogues* identifies the principle of democracy as demanding it be open to "representing not only the greatest force of the greatest number, the majority of citizens considered of age, but also the weakness of the weak, minors, minorities, the poor, and all those throughout the world who call out in suffering for a legitimately infinite extension of what are called *human* rights"—two demands that carry it in different directions. Jacques Derrida, *Rogues*, tr. Pascale-Anne Brault and Michael Naas (Stanford: Stanford University Press, 2005), 36. *Politics of Friendship* names a limit between the conditional and the unconditional and describes "the duty for democracy itself to de-limit itself" (Derrida, *Politics of Friendship* 105). A democracy must de-limit itself, become and do *something* for *someone*, but the reason behind its doing so is its commitment in principle to a universal responsiveness—its "regulative Idea" and "indefinite perfectibility." *Of Hospitality* also discusses the tension between openness and closedness—the idea that to exercise hospitality and welcome someone one must have a place in which to do so, a place that is circumscribed, delimited, and closed off to the outside world by borders made of walls and locks, self-maintenance and exclusion. Derrida writes there that "one can become virtually xenophobic in order to protect or claim to protect one's own hospitality, the own home that makes possible one's own hospitality" (Derrida, *Of Hospitality*, 53).

25. In "Force of Law" and elsewhere, Derrida writes about this theme, saying, for instance, that

> an address is always singular, idiomatic, and justice, as law (*droit*), seems always to suppose the generality of a rule, a norm or a universal imperative. How are we to reconcile the act of justice that must always concern singularity, individuals, irreplaceable groups and lives, the other or myself *as* other, in a unique situation, with rule, norm, value or the imperative of justice which necessarily have a general form, even if this generality prescribes a singular application in each case? If I were content to apply a just rule, without a spirit of justice and without in some way and each time inventing the rule and the example for each case, I might be protected by law (*droit*), my action corresponding to objective law, but I would not be just. (Derrida, "Force of Law," 17)

26. Joachim Ritter writes that the revolution "excludes all connection with the history of its provenance" (Ritter, *Hegel and the French Revolution*, 51) and excludes from itself and negates the historical substance of human existence (Ritter, *French Revolution*, 60). The political theories of the revolution "are deductive positings of new political forms from principles, and make possible revolutionary emancipation from existing historical institutions and legal forms, and of destroying these in positing the new" (Ritter, *French Revolution*, 69).

27. Giving voice to similar themes, Kenneth L. Schmitz writes, in a review of Joachim Ritter's *Hegel and the French Revolution*, that what Hegel "found inad-

equate in that liberalism, however, was that it seized upon liberty as an individual principle of freedom, lying prior to the actual social life of men; whereas, for Hegel, freedom emerged only in the actual structures of social interaction." Kenneth L. Schmitz, "Hegel and the French Revolution. Essays on the *Philosophy of Right* (review)," *Journal of the History of Philosophy* 22, no. 4 (October 1984): 493.

28. Hegel writes that "blood-relationship therefore supplements the abstract natural movement by adding to it the movement of consciousness, interrupting the work of nature . . . Through this it comes about that the *dead*, the universal *being*, is elevated into a being that has returned into itself, a *being-for-itself*, or the powerless, purely *single* singularity [*reine* einzelne *Einzelheit*] is elevated to *universal individuality* [*allgemeine Individualität*] . . . The Family keeps away from the dead this dishonouring action of unconscious desire and abstract essence, puts its own action in its place, and weds the blood-relation to the bosom of the earth, to the elemental imperishable individuality" (M452, S333). In the French Revolution death looks much different; it is not given significance but has all significance removed. "The sole work and deed of universal freedom is therefore *death*, a *death* too which has no inner significance or filling, for what is negated is the empty point of the absolutely free self. It is thus the coldest and meanest of deaths, with no more significance than cutting off a head of cabbage or swallowing a mouthful of water" (M590, S436).

29. Steven B. Smith, similarly, talks about "the self who is the subject of rights" as not something "given," once and for all, but as "a being in the making, that is, a creature with a history." Steven B. Smith, "Hegel and the French Revolution: An Epitaph for Republicanism," *Social Research* 56, no. 1 (1989 Spring): 244.

7. CRIMINAL ACTION

1. Hegel says of the laws and institutions (*PhR* 144), the ethical powers (*PhR* 145) and substantial determinations (*PhR* 148), that the individual "*stands in a relationship to them* as to his own substantial being" (*PhR* 148) and that they in turn constitute "the objective sphere of ethics, which . . . is substance made *concrete* by subjectivity *as infinite form*" (*PhR* 144).

2. Manfred Baum elegantly captures the constant interpenetration of the elements of universality and particularity in the life of the will when he writes that

> the will is essentially the unity of both these moments, and its freedom consists precisely in this ("speculative") unity. For the apparent transition from the empty freedom of the universality of the will to particularity of the will as an ego that wills this or that determinate content simply meant that determinate willing was already "contained" . . . in the universal willing that was negated. For the universality and indeterminacy of the willing ego arose only

> through the abstraction qua negation of all particular willed content and the return to itself from out of this determinate willing. On the other hand, the determinacy of willing . . . was already implied in the very dependence of the abstracting self on certain determinations of the will from which it was able to abstract in the first place. Thus, Hegel believed he had shown that the universal willing ego essentially finds itself not in a determinacy that is supplied externally but in a determinacy that is a consequence of self-determination, that is to say, of freedom. Manfred Baum, "Common Welfare and Universal Will," in *Hegel on Ethics and Politics*, ed. Robert Pippin and Otfried Höffe (Cambridge: Cambridge University Press, 2004), 128

3. Richard Dean Winfield explores the necessary relationship between the universality of the will and its particular determinations, and what that relationship entails with regard to the wills of others, in "Freedom as Interaction: Hegel's Resolution to the Dilemma of Liberal Theory."

4. This "dialectic of recognition" is famously the subject of the section entitled "Independence and Dependence of Self-Consciousness: Lordship and Bondage," in the *Phenomenology of Spirit* (M178–96, S145–55). See the discussion of this section in chapter 9, "Hegel and the Politics of Recognition."

5. It should be noted that Hegel makes this point in the context of his discussion of morality in the *Philosophy of Right.*

6. As Hegel writes, "the *right of individuals* to their *subjective determination to freedom* is fulfilled in so far as they belong to ethical actuality; for their *certainty* of their own freedom has its *truth* in such objectivity, and it is in the ethical realm that they *actually* possess *their own* essence and their *inner* universality" (*PhR* 153). And "the right of individuals to their *particularity* is likewise contained in ethical substantiality, for particularity is the mode of outward appearance in which the ethical exists" (*PhR* 154).

7. Bernstein, "Love and Law," 420. The topic of this essay is "The Spirit of Christianity and Its Fate," but, as Bernstein himself remarks, "'Spirit of Christianity' provides the most direct and eloquent presentation of the logical structure and moral content of Hegel's ethical vision" (Bernstein, "Love and Law," 393), and is thus helpful in illuminating the further development of that vision.

8. It should be noted that formulating Hegel's account of both crime and punishment demands that one consider Hegel's discussions of action, crime, and punishment beyond "Abstract Right" (*PhR* 34–104), in which the full meaning of action, crime, and punishment is not available. (Later in the chapter I discuss the reasons for this in more detail.) Wolfgang Schild writes about the *Philosophy of Right* that "there are no 'parts' here that could properly be isolated one from another, but only fluid 'moments' of the whole that stand essentially within a context of reciprocal mediation. That is why Hegel presents us not with any concepts that we could simply take away with us like so many fixed and finished items of thought, but rather only with certain *argumentational contexts* that can properly be grasped only as a complex whole." Wolfgang Schild,

"The Relevance of Hegel's Concept of Punishment," in *Hegel on Ethics and Politics*, ed. Robert Pippin and Otfried Höffe (Cambridge: Cambridge University Press, 2004), 151. We can see this, for instance, in the fact that punishment requires a punishing body, one that cannot be found or constructed using only the resources available in the sphere of the person; thus Hegel writes that "in this sphere of the immediacy of right, the cancellation [*Aufheben*] of crime is primarily *revenge*, and its *content* is just so far as it constitutes retribution. But in its *form*, it is the action of a *subjective* will which can place *its infinity* in any infringement [of right] which occurs, and whose justice is therefore altogether contingent, just as it exists *for the other party* only as a *particular* will" (*PhR* 102). Resolution of this contradiction requires "a justice freed from subjective interest and subjective shape and from the contingency of power—that is, a *punitive* rather than an *avenging justice*. *Primarily*, this constitutes a requirement for a will which, as a particular and *subjective* will, also wills the universal as such" (*PhR* 103). In the same vein, Peter G. Stillman argues that "in 'Abstract Right'—and in 'Civil Society,' where the concrete manifestations of abstract rights are discussed—Hegel holds, in their fullness, the central liberal positions" but that the addition of the various "institutions and ways by which the natural man (or the natural child) becomes a civilized man capable of functioning well" show the insufficiency of abstract right as the basis of the state and, I would add, of its function of punishment. Peter G. Stillman, "Hegel's Critique of Liberal Theories of Rights," *The American Political Science Review* 68, no. 3 (1974): 1086. See also Ardis Collins, "Hegel's Critical Appropriation of Kantian Morality," in *Beyond Liberalism and Communitarianism: Studies in Hegel's* Philosophy of Right, ed. Robert R. Williams (Albany: State University of New York Press, 2001), 26.

9. David E. Cooper explains this point in the following: "The crime was, in intention, a demonstration that the victim had no rights. But the victim did have these rights, and so there never was such a thing as the demonstration that he did not have them. So to speak of annulling the crime is to speak of whatever it is that establishes that the victim did have those rights which were implicitly denied by the criminal. What establishes this, of course, is punishment." David E. Cooper, "Hegel's Theory of Punishment," in *Hegel's Political Philosophy: Problems and Perspectives*, ed. Z. A. Pelczynski (Cambridge: Cambridge University Press, 1971), 164.

10. Lewis P. Hinchman says that "the criminal . . . implicitly denies the whole category of mutual recognition, and hence the definition of man as a being whose selfhood is socially mediated . . . to violate one man's rights is to violate the rights of all." Lewis P. Hinchman, "Hegel's Theory of Crime and Punishment," *The Review of Politics* 44, no. 4 (1982): 537.

11. Just as agency is a function of a collective and highly mediated life, and crime does damage to that life, so also is a judge's agency in judgment a function of collective life and the meting out of punishment the sustenance of it. In the context of ethical life, a judge or agent of punishment is not acting merely as the individual person described in "abstract right," for whom the cancellation of crime would be primarily revenge (*PhR* 102), but is acting as

one whose agency is directly and self-consciously derived from the demands of that collective life, or as a collective agent, so to speak.

12. Schild correctly observes that the model of punishment in the *Philosophy of Right* is similar to that described as "punishment as fate" in Hegel's earlier essay, "The Spirit of Christianity and Its Fate." According to that text (treated in chapter 1), to commit a crime is to act against one's own life, in that one's own life cannot be severed from the whole of united life. To commit a crime is to wound the united life in which one's capacity for agency is embedded, and thereby to call upon oneself what Hegel in the "Spirit of Christianity" calls "vengeful fate"—one's own destruction of one's own life. Schild identifies both a difference and a similarity between the two texts. He argues that in "Spirit of Christianity" Hegel looks upon law in the juridical sense as "a dead, alien, external, and abstract principle that, with cold necessity, inevitably demands punishment in response to crime" and that in the *Philosophy of Right* he ceases to look at law in this way. But in the *Philosophy of Right* Hegel develops an account of legal punishment similar to the moral punishment of "Spirit of Christianity": punishment is essentially the criminal's own act, since that act is an injury to the criminal's own life (Schild, "Relevance," 169–70). "Hence punishment as fate is the equal reaction of the trespasser's own deed, of a power which he himself has armed, of an enemy made an enemy by himself" (*ETW* 230). Hinchman also picks up on the organic nature of community in the early Hegel, in which crime damages a united life: "A truly living community—like the *polis*, which Hegel apotheosized—imitated nature by creating a human environment for man to which he responded in just as unconscious and spontaneous a manner as an animal would in its natural environment . . . But if I commit a crime, I destroy this unforced, natural, 'living' bond. And, Hegel adds, since nature is a whole, a unitary existence, the criminal annihilates a part of himself (his being-in-the-community) in doing violence to another" (Hinchman, "Hegel's Theory," 530). Hinchman continues by outlining the consequences of this view of crime for a theory of punishment: "Once crime is interpreted in this way, the role of punishment will undergo a dramatic transformation, too . . . Punishment is intended to heal the wounds in a living community, to reintegrate the community with itself and absorb the criminal back into it. Assuming—as Hegel does—that the community embodies the true 'self' of the individual, the task of punishment is no less than reconciling him to himself" (Hinchman, "Hegel's Theory," 530). This is, as Hinchman notes, not feasible for large, modern communities, but it informs Hegel's development of a theory of punishment more appropriate to the latter (Hinchman, "Hegel's Theory," 533–34).

13. Hegel's critique of the authority of law here has many possible consequences for discussions of his place in the liberal tradition. Instances of such discussions can be found in Drucilla Cornell, Michel Rosenfeld, and David Gray Carlson, eds., *Hegel and Legal Theory* (New York: Routledge, 1991); Abel Garza Jr., "Hegel's Critique of Liberalism and Natural Law: Reconstructing Ethical Life," *Law and Philosophy* 9 (1990–1): 371–98; Michael H. Hoffheimer, "Hegel's Criticism of Law," *Hegel-Studien* 27 (1992a): 27–52; Quentin Lauer, *A Reading of*

Hegel's Phenomenology of Spirit (New York: Fordham University Press, 1993); Adriaan Peperzak, *Modern Freedom: Hegel's Legal, Moral, and Political Philosophy* (Dordrecht: Kluwer Academic, 2001); Gillian Rose, *Mourning Becomes the Law: Philosophy and Representation* (Cambridge: Cambridge University Press, 1996); John Russon, *Reading Hegel's Phenomenology* (Bloomington: Indiana University Press, 2004); Steven B. Smith, *Hegel's Critique of Liberalism: Rights in Context* (Chicago: University of Chicago Press, 1989); Peter G. Stillman, "Hegel's Critique of Liberal Theories of Rights," *The American Political Science Review* 68, no. 3 (1974): 1086–92; Charles Taylor, *Hegel and Modern Society* (Cambridge: Cambridge University Press, 1979); Armin von Bogdandy, *Hegels Theorie des Gesetzes* (Freiburg: Verlag Karl Alber, 1989); Robert R. Williams, ed., *Beyond Liberalism and Communitarianism: Studies in Hegel's* Philosophy of Right (Albany: State University of New York Press, 2001).

14. The constitution, however, also undergoes some kind of change; Hegel writes that "the constitution does undergo further development through the further evolution of the laws and the progressive character of the universal concerns of government" (*PhR* 298). In the Addition it is written that this change "takes place imperceptibly" and does not possess "the form of change" (*PhR* 298A). Some paragraphs earlier, however, he says that the constitution "has being in and for itself, and should therefore be regarded as divine and enduring, and as exalted above the sphere of all manufactured things" (*PhR* 273).

15. The difficulty with law is that it has to be specific enough to speak to actual situations that occur in particular contexts, but that it also has to be general enough to be applicable to various situations of a similar type; it has to be generally authoritative. Here is a full quotation of the Remark to section 299, in which Hegel describes this tension: "a law, in order to be a law, must be more than just a commandment in general . . . , i.e., it must be *determinate* in itself; but the more determinate it is, the more nearly capable its content will be of being implemented as it stands. At the same time, however, so far-reaching a determination as this would give the laws an empirical aspect which would necessarily be subject to alteration when they were actually implemented, and this would detract from their character as laws" (*PhR* 299R).

16. This is also true of the second challenge to law. Decisions about punishing more mildly when society is healthier are made by elements of the legal system, but they are not immediately derivable from formal laws.

17. Additionally, Hegel writes that "thought cannot specify how each crime should be punished" (*PhR* 96A). Reason as such cannot determine the appropriate punishing response to a singular criminal action. It is true that there are different degrees of crime, depending on to what extent "the will's existence [*Dasein*] and determinacy [*Bestimmtheit*] in general is infringed [*verletzt*]" (*PhR* 96), and it is also true that reason can identify the according need for varying degrees of punishment (contrary, as Hegel mentions, to the laws of Draco) (*PhR* 96R). But the subtle judgment of a judge oriented to specificity is needed "to arrive at a finite [*endliche*] and purely positive determination [*rein positive Bestimmung*]" (*PhR* 214R).

18. Peter Steinberger, *Logic and Politics: Hegel's* Philosophy of Right (New Haven: Yale University Press, 1988), 126.

19. A related point of interest here is Hegel's argument in *PhR* 274 regarding the irreducible specificity of national constitutions: "Since spirit is actual only as that which it knows itself to be, and since the state, as the spirit of a nation [*Volk*], is both the law which *permeates all relations within it* and also the customs and consciousness of the individuals who belong to it, the constitution of a specific nation will in general depend on the nature and development [*Bildung*] of its self-consciousness; it is in this self-consciousness that its subjective freedom and hence also the actuality of the constitution lie." In the Remark, he continues: "The wish to give a nation a constitution *a priori*, even if its content were more or less rational, is an idea [*Einfall*] which overlooks the very moment by virtue of which a constitution is more than a product of thought. Each nation accordingly has the constitution appropriate and proper to it" (*PhR* 274).

20. Schild argues that "in the concept of reconciliation . . . we find *the deepest concept of punishment* (and also the deepest concept of right as ethical will)" (Schild, "Relevance," 171). He distinguishes between "the *concept* (the essence) of punishment and the specific *modalities* of conviction and sentencing," arguing that the conceptual perspective of punishment as retribution "implies nothing substantive with respect to any particular punishment. In this regard it is other considerations, which come together in the idea of 'mercy,' that play a decisive role. The criminal should not simply be abandoned but should be given an opportunity for reintegration into society and the community of the state as a whole" (Schild, "Relevance," 173). Schild refers frequently to the untranslated *Vorlesungen über Rechtsphilosophie*, 1818–31 (Stuttgart-Bad Cannstatt, 1973), especially volume 4, in which Hegel seems to refer much more often and explicitly to the necessity of thinking about reconciliation and forgiveness in the context of a theory of punishment.

21. Jankélévitch, *Forgiveness*, 163. His comment here is discussed also in chapter 1.

22. Schild argues that "since general philosophical considerations cannot predetermine precisely how the idea of mercy and the concept of punishment should relate to one another in a particular fashion, this represents a task that must constantly be addressed anew by the individuals who constitute the community of the state. But the continuing tension between these two perspectives cannot itself be eliminated" (Schild, "Relevance," 173). Similarly, "every age is continually called on afresh to find appropriate concrete form for this interplay between (abstract) justice and (concrete) 'mercy' (understood in this context as a specific acknowledgement of the individuality of the agent" (Schild, "Relevance," 176). Two consequences of this continuous interplay are: a) no final or ultimate reconciliation exists; and b) the popular tendency to read Hegel's account of the state as the site of an ultimate reconciliation is misguided.

23. Jankélévitch, *Forgiveness*, 162.

24. Derrida's analysis of forgiveness also leads him to identify the very limits of the politicolegal order, such that forgiveness, while not of that order,

can have political impact by virtue of its transformative impact on that order. The excess to law and politics or the system of exchange, an excess represented by forgiveness, brings us to the heart of its political purpose—to do justice, so to speak, to singularity, to that which cannot be brought under political order, to the free being whose freedom must be made determinate but who in the end cannot be reduced to this or that action. Jacques Derrida, *On Cosmopolitanism and Forgiveness*, tr. Michael Hughes (New York: Routledge, 2001). Paul Ricoeur writes, similarly, that "morality makes a judgement on justice, requiring that it be ever more just, at once more universal and more singular, more concerned with concrete conditions of equality before law and more attentive to the narrative identity of those who appear before it." Paul Ricoeur, *Memory, History, Forgetting*, tr. Kathleen Blamey and David Pellauer (Chicago: University of Chicago Press, 2004), 474.

8. THE POLITICS OF LIBERALISM

1. The discussion of forgiveness upon which I rely is found in the last section of "Morality" called "Conscience. The beautiful soul, evil, and its forgiveness" (M632–71/S464–94).

2. As Allen Wood writes,

> the cause of that [spirit's] freedom is served not only by the structure of a rational social order, but also by the destruction of an order that has lost its rationality. Consequently, the ethical itself has only a limited and conditional justification. Inevitably, Hegel's ethical theory focuses critical attention on prevailing social institutions: Does the existing order actualize its Idea? Is the ethical order itself rational, or has it lost its foundation in spirit's struggle to actualize freedom? Through its conception of the self-actualization of spirit's freedom, Hegel's theory also proposes standards by which those questions are to be answered. Because the *Philosophy of Right* defends the rationality of the modern state, the intent of the theory is supposed to be apologetic, a defense of modern society—and of the existing order to the extent (but only to the extent) that it actualizes the Idea of objective freedom. Allen W. Wood, *Hegel's Ethical Thought* (Cambridge: Cambridge University Press, 1990), 256–57

3. Terry Pinkard says that

> to ask how such an abstract understanding of the unity of the unconditioned and the conditioned—of the unconditional necessity of submitting all our claims to reflective justification together with the fact of our own contingency and the perspectival nature of all our conceptual contents—is to be realized in a way that does not impose

> incompatible commitments or unlivable requirements on those who must live within those institutions and practices. Certainly, Hegel did not think that any political organization could fully live up to that demand (although he clearly thought some were better than others). (Pinkard, "Spirit as the 'Unconditioned,'" 105)

4. Ludwig Siep writes about forgiveness that "it contains different levels or scales, reaching from moral forgiveness to legal pardon and historical oblivion—the spirit's actions leave no scars, as Hegel formulates it" (Siep, "Practical Reason and Spirit," 183).

5. Harris writes that "the process of what Hegel calls *Verzeihung* is not that of ordinary 'forgiveness' at all. In essence, we are dealing with a *logical* forgiveness, exchanged between the agent and the observer, for the inevitable one-sidedness of being agent and observer" (Harris, *Hegel's Ladder II*, 503). We recognize "the universal necessity of forgiveness for our finitude" (Harris, *Hegel's Ladder II*, 521). Concerning the relationship between the individual and the universal, Harris writes that "the judging consciousness is the continuity of the (positive) universal; the agent is the exclusive singular unit" (Harris, *Hegel's Ladder II*, 504).

6. This aspect of forgiveness is at play in Hegel's philosophy of history. In his discussion of the philosophy of history he calls history a "slaughter-bench," observing that individual need, passion, and interest inadvertently become "tools" for the accomplishment of things above and beyond such need, passion, and interest. G. W. F. Hegel, *Introduction to the Philosophy of History*, tr. Leo Rauch (Indianapolis: Hackett, 1988), 24, 28. The idiosyncratic and indeed often destructive character of individual actions is in a sense forgiven because these actions have resulted in or played a part in the constitution of an intelligible process by which freedom has been progressively realized and enacted in human history. It is not my intention, however, to discuss this theme in detail here. For a good indication of the state of contemporary scholarship on these issues, see *Hegel and History*, ed. Will Dudley (Albany: State University of New York Press, 2009).

7. "The forgiveness it extends to the first is the renunciation of itself, of its *nonactual* essence, which it equates with that other that was *actual* action, and it acknowledges to be good the action that was determined by thought to be evil; or rather it abandons this distinction between determinate thought and its determining judgment that is for-itself [*sein fürsichseindes bestimmendes Urteil*], just as the other abandons the determining of action that also is for-itself [das *fürsichseinde Bestimmen der Handlung*]. The word of reconciliation is the *existent* spirit, which intuits the pure knowledge of itself as *universal* essence in its opposite, in the pure knowledge of itself as the *singularity* that exists absolutely in itself [*der absolute in sich seienden* Einzelheit]—a reciprocal recognizing that is *absolute* spirit" (M670, S492–93).

8. Ludwig Siep, "Practical Reason and Spirit, 184.

9. Slavoj Žižek says that the beautiful soul "assumes the position of a judge exempt from what he is passing a judgement on," when in fact he is "involved in the system [he] pretend[s] to reject." He describes the beautiful soul's purity as "the most perfidious form of cheating . . . [that pays] the price for forgetting to include [itself] in the situation into which [it] intervenes" (Butler, Laclau, Žižek, *Contingency*, 228).

10. H. S. Harris says that what is accomplished in forgiveness is "the move to the level of a purely logical recognition that action and judgment are equally necessary moments of free self-conscious being; and that they are equally inadequate and partial taken in isolation. The 'Heart' or the 'Heart's Law' . . . cannot be realized either in action or in judgment, but only in 'comprehension.' That is why the 'word of forgiveness' is (in its logical sense) the foundation of absolute Spirit" (Harris, *Hegel's Ladder II*, 503). The goal of comprehension pulls the conscientious self away from the assertion of its singularity toward an identification with others, toward a broader perspective that recognizes the significance but also the partiality of the fragmented pieces of reality it comprehends.

11. In the *Philosophy of Right*, and with characteristic scorn, Hegel castigates the "particular form of bad conscience" that is found in the celebration of immediate subjective feeling, on the basis of its attitude toward law:

> [T]the distinctive mark which it carries on its brow is its hatred of law. That right and ethics, and the actual world of right and the ethical, are grasped by means of *thoughts* and give themselves the form of rationality—namely universality and determinacy—by means of thoughts, is what constitutes *the law*; and it is this which is justifiably regarded as the main enemy by that feeling which reserves the right to do as it pleases, by that conscience which identifies right with subjective conviction. The form of right as a *duty* and a *law* is felt by it to be a *dead, cold letter* and a *shackle*; for it does not recognize itself in the law and thereby recognize its own freedom in it, because the law is the reason of the thing [*Sache*] and the reason does not allow feeling to warm itself in the glow of its own particularity [*Partikularität*]. (*PhR* 17)

The universal essentially is, in J. M. Bernstein's words, "a matter of recognitional structures" (Bernstein, "Conscience and Transgression," 59.

12. To think of individuality and universality as simply opposed is to think simplistically or superficially; in the *Philosophy of Right* Hegel calls "universal principles" "the substantial source of all deeds" (*PhR* 18). Siep is again helpful here. He writes: "One and the same spirit contains, on the one side, self-consciousness embodied in laws, court decisions, jurisprudence and ethics, common sense moral judgments, and customary moral behavior, and on the other the radically individualized self of personal conscience" (Siep, "Practical Reason and Spirit," 184). Further:

> In the Spirit chapter Hegel tries to prove that reality consists of norms, customs, and institutions that are objective in that they are independent of individual deliberations, wishes, and volitions, but also subjective in two different respects: First of all, as a self-articulating and systematically developing process producing forms of objective knowledge such as codifications, doctrines, reliable jurisdictions, etc. Such a self-differentiating process is for Hegel a form of subjectivity. Secondly, this process is actual through and within the life and actions of individual, self-conscious or subjective human beings. (Siep, "Practical Reason and Spirit," 176)

13. On the relation between law and forgiveness as structures of recognition, and on the idea that forgiveness is the culmination of the *Phenomenology*, see John Russon, "Selfhood, Conscience, and Dialectic in Hegel's *Phenomenology of Spirit*," *Southern Journal of Philosophy* 29 (1991): 533–50, especially 537–44. Russon also powerfully captures the dynamic between singular conscience, on the one hand, and singular others and the social context, on the other, in the following:

> The project of the *Phenomenology* points, ultimately, to the stance of conscience, as the self-conscious embrace of the stance of finite answerability to these infinite claims. It is the conscientious agent who recognizes what we have recognized in this analysis, namely, that what is without is within—we are *intrinsically* called to an answerability to the outside. The conscientious agent knows him- or herself to be a singular desiring self, irreducible to any other, but knows him- or herself to be answerable to others. The conscientious agent knows him- or herself to be a member of a community and answerable to it, but also knows this membership to be finite, and therefore to be guilty of realizing inadequately the imperatives of the other and of the Other. The conscientious agent knows that his or her conscience must be enacted within the demands of the real. In short, the conscientious agent recognizes him- or herself in others and makes his or her finite situatedness a site of hospitality to others within-and-without, while simultaneously forgiving him- or herself for the necessity of his or her limitations and forgiving others for their own. John Russon, "The Project of Hegel's *Phenomenology of Spirit*," in *A Companion to Hegel*, ed. Stephen Houlgate and Michael Baur (Oxford: Blackwell, 2011), 61

14. Maeve Cooke describes this ethical situation by saying that

> each self, if it is to progress towards the realization of moral freedom, must give up its claims to *own* its ethical judgements and actions and release them into the public domain, where they will face the

> criticisms and challenges of other selves. In other words, if it is to progress towards the realization of moral freedom, the individual self may no longer see itself as the sole authority determining the value of its ethical judgements and actions; rather, the value of ethical judgements and actions becomes something to be worked out cooperatively by a plurality of selves in processes of public challenge and response. On such a view, ethical value is not something fixed and given, but rather a property that emerges processually by way of public contestation. Maeve Cooke, "Beyond Dignity and Difference: Revisiting the Politics of Recognition," *European Journal of Political Theory* 8, no. 1 (2009): 88.

15. Siep, "Practical Reason and Spirit," 183 (my italics).

16. Žižek nicely illuminates this point about the self-sundering character of "substance" or social reality in stating that "in Hegel's philosophy, 'reconciliation' does not designate the moment when 'substance becomes subject,' when absolute subjectivity is elevated into the productive round of all entities, but rather the acknowledgment that the dimension of subjectivity is inscribed into the very core of Substance in the guise of an irreducible lack which forever prevents it from achieving full self-identity." Slavoj Žižek, *Tarrying with the Negative: Kant, Hegel, and the Critique of Ideology* (Durham, NC: Duke University Press, 1993), 26. Further, "we are here at the very opposite point of losing the specific dimension of subjectivity, i.e., of reducing the subject to a subordinated moment of the Substance's self-relating . . . insofar as the relationship of the subject to the Substance overlaps with the Substance's self-relating, the fact that Substance appears to subject as an alien-external-inaccessible entity bears witness to a self-splitting of the Substance itself" (Žižek, *Tarrying*, 30).

17. Kelly Oliver describes this dynamic in the following: "The dialectic of forgiveness and confession is an account of the very possibility of subjectivity and intersubjectivity, in which the subject is shown to transgress the community in order to become an individual and through that process realizes the necessity of belonging to the very community that s/he transgresses. For Hegel, consciousness becomes individuated—that is to say we become subjects—through forgiveness and reconciliation." Kelly Oliver, "Forgiveness and Community," *The Southern Journal of Philosophy* 42 (2004): 2. Forgiveness supports the inevitable assertion of singularity, because through it the person's admission back into the fold is presupposed. Further, the social and linguistic codes she transgresses are "modified to incorporate [her] singularity"; the transgression is sublimated by being resignified within these codes (Oliver, "Forgiveness and Community," 10). See also Kelly Oliver, *The Colonization of Psychic Space: A Psychoanalytic Social Theory of Oppression* (Minneapolis: University of Minnesota Press, 2004), for further development of these ideas.

18. Bernstein, "Conscience and Transgression," 56. *Sittlich* should be understood as "ethical," in the sense of customary. What Bernstein calls "*sittlich* constituted forms of action" could be described as forms of action the goal of

which would be to solidify and ensure the continued existence of the society or community, and the inspiration of which would be to express one's identification with and care for the society or community.

19. Bernstein, "Conscience and Transgression," 66.

20. Ludwig Siep, "Practical Reason and Spirit," 184.

21. Bernstein, "Conscience and Transgression," 57. In "Spirit of Christianity" Hegel writes, "Hence punishment as fate is the equal reaction of the trespasser's own deed, of a power which he himself has armed, of an enemy made an enemy by himself" (*ETW* 230).

22. Bernstein, "Conscience and Transgression," 62 (my italics).

23. In *Antigone's Claim*, Judith Butler wrongly claims that Hegel believes in the state's ability to circumscribe all legitimate action and authority and thereby eases the anxiety produced by a critical relation to the law and an openness to transformation. She uses him as an example of why one should challenge political projects that attempt to employ law and the state as allies, since they fail to recognize that the terms that set the debate and the order of hierarchy could never eradicate such hierarchy, for their very existence depends on it. Given his account of the ongoing dynamic between forgiveness and law, however, it is apparent that Hegel does not stand for the will of the state, and in his gradual and persistent circumscription of the operation of law he can hardly be attributed a "desire for the law to be the indisputable law" (Butler, *Antigone's Claim*, 21). The *Phenomenology* presents no "law of laws," but precisely this ambiguity between law, ethicality, and forgiveness. Additionally, Hegel's account could be useful for Butler's purposes—to identify problems with law and the state and imagine forms of agency and identification that do not rely solely on available terms.

24. Siep asks, "Is it possible to conceive of norms and customs that are beyond question and explicit justification, but that can at the same time be examined and criticized by the individual?" He answers: "Hegel's concept of spirit aims at overcoming this alternative. It is meant to include both the unconditionally valid moral and legal laws, on the one hand, and the individual's right of examining every claim to truth and every norm according to its own reason and conscience, on the other" (Siep, "Practical Reason and Spirit," 176). Further, "a concept of ethical spirit enabling such procedures and developments must contain at least three elements, corresponding to the 'moments' of the concept: the universality of rationally justifiable laws, the particularity of customs and traditions of a community based on common historical experiences, and the singularity of a conscience that interprets the laws and applies them appropriately in a specific situation" (Siep, "Practical Reason and Spirit," 179).

25. Bernstein, "Conscience and Transgression," 65.

26. John Gray, "In Theory," *The Nation* (June 5, 2006).

27. Although one can work for a more inclusive regime, there is, on Hegel's account, no form of regime that will not face the problems of injustice and exclusion. While Hegel's discussion of forgiveness has political consequences, it cannot be employed to justify a *particular* political regime, since

it construes the relationship between action and law, and between individuals, to be a relationship that must be continually negotiated. It is a tool by which we can evaluate existing regimes, ensuring that they allow for the practices of recognition characterized by confession and forgiveness. There is no final form of "objective spirit"—no particular political regime—in which such reconciliation could be finally and conclusively achieved. On this theme, see Hegel's philosophy of spirit in the *Encyclopaedia of the Philosophical Sciences*. In section 483 he writes, for instance, "The objective mind is the absolute Idea, but only existing *in posse*: and as it is thus on the territory of finitude, its actual rationality retains the aspect of external apparency." G. W. F. Hegel, *Philosophy of Mind*, tr. William Wallace (New York: Cosimo, 2008).

28. For modern versions of liberalism, see, for instance, the work of Isaiah Berlin, Ronald Dworkin, Will Kymlicka, Martha Nussbaum, and Jeremy Waldron.

29. See Michael Sandel, "The Procedural Republic and the Unencumbered Self," in *Communitarianism and Individualism*, ed. Shlomo Avineri and Avner De-Shalit (Oxford: Oxford University Press, 1992), 18. See also Alisdair MacIntyre, Charles Taylor, and Michael Walzer, among others.

30. Seyla Benhabib, *Situating the Self*, 77. Axel Honneth, Nancy Fraser, Iris Young, and Jim Bohman have also developed similar critiques of liberalism. For a specifically Marxist critique in this vein, see Allen E. Buchanan, *Marx and Justice: The Radical Critique of Liberalism* (Totowa, NJ: Rowman and Allanheld, 1982).

31. David Hollenbach's version of communitarianism seems to be more viable, critical, and dynamic than many others. See especially "Virtue, the Common Good, and Democracy," in *New Communitarian Thinking: Persons, Virtues, Institutions, and Communities*, ed. Amitai Etzioni (Charlottesville, VA: University Press of Virginia, 1995), in which he justifies the idea of civil society from a perspective that is sensitive to issues raised by communitarians. See also "The Common Good Revisited," *Theological Studies* 50 (1989): 70–94; "Contexts of the Political Role of Religion: Civil Society and Culture," *San Diego Law Review* 30 (1993): 877–901; and R. Bruce Douglass and David Hollenbach, eds., *Catholicism and Liberalism: Contributions to American Public Philosophy* (Cambridge: Cambridge University Press, 1994).

32. Benhabib, *Situating the Self*, 77.

33. See, for instance, Patricia Williams, Iris Young, Nancy Fraser, Lisa Schwartzman, Frantz Fanon, Malcolm X, and Charles W. Mills.

34. See Wendy Brown and Janet Halley, eds. *Left Legalism/Left Critique* (Durham: Duke University Press, 2002), 4. See also Michel Foucault, Judith Butler, and Drucilla Cornell, among others.

35. Brown and Halley, *Left Legalism/Left Critique*, 427. I have discussed Wendy Brown's work in detail in "Wendy Brown and the Critique of Tolerance," *Radical Philosophy Review* 11, no. 1 (2008): 35–50.

36. John Rawls, "The Idea of an Overlapping Consensus," *Oxford Journal of Legal Studies* 7 (1987). Rawls also treats the issue of an overlapping consensus

in *Political Liberalism* (New York: Columbia University Press, 1993), where he defends the possibility of a "political liberalism" over a "comprehensive liberalism," asserting that political liberalism can be neutral with regard to other comprehensive doctrines (doctrines involving theories of value and the good or metaphysical views of human nature and purpose).

37. Rawls, "Overlapping Consensus," 12–13.

38. Richard Rorty, "The Priority of Democracy to Philosophy," in *The Virginia Statute for Religious Freedom: Its Evolution and Consequences in American History*, ed. Merrill D. Peterson and Robert C. Vaughan (Cambridge: Cambridge University Press, 1988), 263. Cited in Hollenbach, "Virtue, the Common Good, and Democracy," 144. Rorty makes similar arguments in much of his work. See, for example, *Achieving Our Country: Leftist Thought in Twentieth-Century America* (Cambridge: Harvard University Press, 1998); "Pragmatism as Romantic Polytheism," in *The Revival of Pragmatism: New Essays on Social Thought, Law, and Culture*, ed. Morris Dickstein (Durham: Duke University Press, 1998); and *Contingency, Irony, and Solidarity* (Cambridge: Cambridge University Press, 1989).

39. Bernstein, "Conscience and Transgression," 63.

40. This point is developed nicely by Kimerer Lamothe in "Reason, Religion, and Sexual Difference" and by Carole Anne Taylor, "Positioning Subjects and Objects: Agency, Narration, Relationality," in *Hypatia* 8, no. 1 (Winter 1993): 55–80.

41. In *Discourse on the Origin of Inequality* Rousseau famously argues that the rich initiated law and social organization so as to reduce the instability that led to the loss of their possessions and power to the poor. He says that "the origin of society and law . . . gave new fetters to the weak and new forces to the rich, irretrievably destroyed natural liberty, established forever the law of property and of inequality, changed adroit usurpation into an irrevocable right, and for the profit of a few ambitious men henceforth subjected the entire human race to labor, servitude and misery." Jean–Jacques Rousseau, *Basic Political Writings*, tr. Donald A. Cress (Indianapolis: Hackett, 1987), 70. Marx exposes what he thinks to be the particular side of rights that are supposed to be universal: they presume, and aid in producing, a certain kind of subject with very specific characteristics. This makes other kinds of subjectivity unavailable to people and hence is a deep restriction on, not protection of, freedom. See Karl Marx, "On the Jewish Question," *The Marx-Engels Reader*, ed. Robert C. Tucker (London: W. W. Norton, 1978), 26–52.

42. Brown and Halley, eds., *Left Legalism/Left Critique*, 430.

9. HEGEL AND THE POLITICS OF RECOGNITION

1. Indeed, the two who engage in the struggle to the death implicitly posit that their physical bodies are dispensable in comparison with their desire for recognition. "And it is only through staking one's life that freedom is won;

only thus is it proved that for self-consciousness, its essential being is not being, not the *immediate* form in which it appears, not its submergence in the expanse of life, but rather that there is nothing present in it which could not be regarded as a vanishing moment, that it is only pure *being-for-self*" (M187, S149).

2. David Ciavatta calls this the "inherently ecstatic nature" of identity: "Spirit is what ultimately accounts for what we can call the inherently *ecstatic* nature of my identity, for the fact that I am myself even outside myself: it is what accounts for the fact that my identity is not simply contained within the untroubled sphere of my own 'internal,' intentional consciousness, or within the boundaries of my skin, but is rather to be found equally in the active, expressive bodies of others, in the *actual words and deeds* of other selves" (Ciavatta, *Spirit, Family, Unconscious*, 38).

3. As John Russon writes, "since to be a self-conscious agent is to be a center of desire involved with other self-conscious centers of desire, we cannot ever succeed in being ourselves by ourselves, since our identity is in the hands of these other centers" (Russon, *Reading*, 89).

4. Ciavatta writes that others "exist, from Hegel's phenomenological point of view, . . . as conditions *through which* I experience the world in general, rather than *simply* as particular objects occurring *in* my experience. In this respect, therefore, we can still understand the whole range of our concrete relations with others as functioning in the role of a priori conditions of experience, for they constitute the element *through which* our experience of the objective world, as well as our concrete experience of ourselves, becomes possible in the first place" (Ciavatta, *Spirit, Family, Unconscious*, 27).

5. My discussion of the first aspect of recognition, the "fact of recognition," is at least partially compatible with Axel Honneth's treatment of love, the first stage of reciprocal recognition, through which subjects develop a sense of basic self-confidence and independence. Axel Honneth, *The Struggle for Recognition: The Moral Grammar of Social Conflicts* (Cambridge: MIT Press, 1995). The second and third stages of reciprocal recognition that he identifies—respect and esteem—resonate with the second aspect of recognition that I will call the "demand for recognition," tied as they are to legal rights on the one hand and singular identity and achievement on the other.

6. Simone de Beauvoir gives the name "apprenticeship of freedom" to this formative process. See Simone de Beauvoir, *The Ethics of Ambiguity*, tr. Bernard Frechtman (New York: Citadel, 1948), 37.

7. Discussing Hegel and the centrality of recognition to self-formation, Frantz Fanon also employs this language of certainty and truth, saying, "I go beyond life toward an ideal which is the transformation of subjective certainty of my own worth into a universally valid objective truth." Frantz Fanon, *Black Skin, White Masks*, tr. Richard Philcox (New York: Grove, 2008), 193.

8. R. D. Laing, *The Divided Self* (London: Penguin Books, 1969), 41. I am grateful to John Russon for directing me to Laing's work; Russon himself has drawn the parallel between Laing's notion of ontological security and Hegel's

dialectic of recognition in "Recognition and Narrative," chapter 8 of *Infinite Phenomenology: The Lessons of Hegel's Science of Experience* (Evanston: Northwestern University Press, forthcoming).

9. Laing says that "if the individual does not feel himself to be autonomous this means that he can experience neither his separateness from, nor his relatedness to, the other in the usual way," with "a sense of relatedness and attachment to [an other] based on genuine mutuality" as opposed to either "complete isolation or complete merging of identity" (Laing, *Divided Self*, 52–53). If a person has "a sense of his presence in the world as a real, alive, whole, and, in a temporal sense, a continuous person . . ." then "he can live out into the world and meet others: a world and others experienced as equally real, alive, whole, and continuous" (Laing, *Divided Self*, 39).

10. Axel Honneth states that "the conceptual model of a 'struggle for recognition' had lost its central position within Hegel's theory" already in the *Phenomenology* (Honneth, *Struggle*, 5). But from the above passage (M177) we can see that the phenomenon of recognition is not simply explicated in sections dedicated explicitly to it and then dropped. With the idea of a struggle for recognition we have the concept of spirit, but what remains to be explored in the *Phenomenology* will be the experience of that concept, the experience of recognition that is absorbed and embedded in a way of life (esssentially the subject matter of chapter 6). What I call the "fact of recognition," for instance, is addressed by Hegel's discussion of ethical life, and what I call the "demand for recognition" is addressed by Hegel's discussion of forgiveness—and is arguably the single most important norm governing human interaction. David Ciavatta nicely describes the way in which our self-relation is inherently mediated by our concrete involvements with other selves, stating that Hegel's phenomenological approach is

> alive to the fact that my experience as a concrete, living self is always and inescapably intertwined with the actual experience of other concrete, living selves, and that my very openness onto the experiential world is essentially mediated *from the start* by my relationship to the actual and possible experiences of others . . . For Hegel, then, understanding the precise nature of the self's concrete relations with other selves—the relations whereby each self actually finds itself, qua self-consciousness, reflected in the other—proves to be crucial for understanding what it is to experience the world in general, and so the proper subject matter of phenomenology turns out to be, not simply the autonomous "I," but just as much a "we." (Ciavatta, *Spirit, Family, Unconscious*, 18)

Ciavatta, that is, explores the fact that the basic reality of recognition constitutes what it is to experience a world in general and hence that all explanation of such experience must take its lead from that basic truth.

11. Terry Pinkard implicitly identifies the ambivalence of this inheritance in the following: "For the individuals brought up within these basic social institutions, they generate not only a determinate set of desires and needs, but also a sense of what is and is not really possible in their own lives, and in leading their lives in terms of the desires, hopes and expectations engendered by these institutions, individuals develop a concrete sense of what they are to do in terms of 'the way things are done'" (Pinkard, *Sociality*, 295).

12. Maeve Cooke argues that struggles for recognition are not simply oriented toward the goal of recognition of human dignity, or of human difference, but also toward recognition of "the value of a concrete good," a good that will *not* be shared but the goodness of which does not rest simply in its difference (Cooke, "Beyond Dignity," 81). Some examples she gives are Welsh-language initiatives, the concept of eco-gastronomy advocated by the "Slow Food" movement, and a campaign in London for the protection of *hijab*, all of which are concrete goods that are a significant aspect of human flourishing and human traditions and attention to which avoids "what we might call the privatization of ethical concerns" (Cooke, "Beyond Dignity," 84). What is key here is to recognize that it is *universally true* that human beings adopt particular ways of life, even though the particular ways of life will never be universally shared; we are *all* recognized by particular communities and inducted into particular ways of being human; we are all dependent on goods that we do not create.

13. Hegel represents both Antigone and Creon as attached to one-sided ethical commitments, when the substance they unwaveringly support falls apart around them because of their inherited, engrained, and unquestioned ways of taking up the project of being human. "This ruin of the ethical Substance and its passage into another form is thus determined by the fact that the ethical consciousness is directed on to the law in a way that is essentially *immediate*" (M476, S354).

14. As an example, consider the case of our development of habits of speaking. I may grow up in a context in which I am only listened to if I speak aggressively and if I prevent others from interrupting me through the force with which I use words. I thus develop habits of speaking that make it difficult for me to participate in and hence benefit from contexts that require different kinds of speaking or participation in order to function. For insightful treatment of these and related issues, see John Russon, *Human Experience: Philosophy, Neurosis, and the Elements of Everyday Life* (Albany: State University of New York Press, 2003), especially chapter 4.

15. Nancy Fraser makes a similar distinction as that between specificity and transformation when she distinguishes between what she calls "affirmative" and "transformative" remedies for the absence of recognition. An affirmative remedy for political injustice involving the absence of recognition or misrecognition would be to affirm the value of previously devalued group identities, whereas a transformative remedy would be to challenge and destabilize the cultural-valuational structure that underlies "existing group identities and

differentiations" and hence destabilize these identifications and differentiations. Nancy Fraser, *Justice Interruptus: Critical Reflections on the "Postsocialist" Condition* (New York: Routledge, 1997), 24.

16. Seyla Benhabib treats the tension between the idea that we belong somewhere in particular, immersed in relations of recognition, and the idea that we are situated also in contexts of universality in a chapter of *Situating the Self* called "The Generalized and the Concrete Other." On the one hand, "the standpoint of the generalized other requires us to view each and every individual as a rational being entitled to the same rights and duties we would want to ascribe to ourselves . . . Our relation to the other is governed by the norms of *formal equality* and *reciprocity*: each is entitled to expect and to assume from us what we can expect and assume from him or her. The norms of our interactions are primarily public and institutional ones." On the other hand,

> the standpoint of the concrete other . . . requires us to view each and every rational being as an individual with a concrete history, identity, and affective-emotional constitution . . . Our relation to the other is governed by the norms of *equity* and *complementary reciprocity*: each is entitled to expect and to assume from the other forms of behaviour through which the other feels recognized and confirmed as a concrete, individual being with specific needs, talents and capacities . . . The norms of our interaction are usually, although not exclusively private, noninstitutional ones. They are norms of friendship, love and care . . . In treating you in accordance with [them], I confirm not only your *humanity* but your human *individuality*. (Benhabib, *Situating the Self*, 158–59)

What is missing here, however, is discussion of the idea of human transformation that neither the idea of our specificity nor the idea of our commonality adequately captures.

17. Hegel writes that

> the simple "I" is this genus or the simple universal, for which the distinctions are no distinctions, just since it is the *negative essence* of the shaped independent moments. Self-consciousness is thus only certain of itself through the superseding [*das Aufheben*] of this other that presents itself to self-consciousness as an independent life; self-consciousness is *desire*. Certain of the nothingness of this other, it posits *for itself* the other's nothingness as its truth, negates the independent object, and gives itself thereby the certainty of itself as *true* certainty, as certainty that has come to be for it in an *objective way*. (M174, S143)

Or, "there is nothing in it [the other] that does not exist through it" (M182, S146). Russon explains this idea in the following:

> such agents . . . are, *qua* desiring, engaged in specifying what they take to be the significance of things in the world and of themselves . . . Desire begins precisely by refusing "objectivity" and by specifying itself as that which determines the nature, the significance, of things: desire is purely "subjective." Unlike what is the case for other things, for such desiring beings their own being is an issue, and they mark themselves as the defining powers within that world. (Russon, *Reading*, 87)

18. "The object of self-consciousness, however, is equally independent in this negativity of itself, and thus it is *for itself* genus, universal fluidity in the idiosyncrasy of its seclusion; it is living self-consciousness" (M176, S144). And:

> In this way, this movement of self-consciousness in relation to another self-consciousness has been represented as *the action of the one*, but this action of the one has itself the twofold significance of being just as much *its action* as *the action of the other*. For the other is just as independent and self-enclosed, and there is nothing in it that does not exist through it. The first does not have the object in front of it as it was initially merely for desire, but rather has an object that exists for itself, independently, and it can do nothing about that object for itself if that object does not do in itself what it does in the object. (M182, S146)

19. Hegel writes that "the other consciousness supersedes itself as being-for-self, and in so doing itself does what the first does to it" (M191, S152).

20. "In the cultivating [of the thing], being-for-self becomes for him *his own* being-for-self, and he comes to the consciousness that he himself is in and for himself. The form, in being *posited externally*, does not become for him something other than himself, for even it is his pure being-for-self that thereby comes to truth for him. It becomes so through this retrieval, on his own, of his *own significance*, accomplished precisely through work, which seemed initially to have a merely *alien significance*" (M196, S154).

21. The condition of slavery will become, "in its accomplishment, the opposite of what it immediately is; as consciousness *forced back* into itself, it will commune with itself and will turn itself around into true independence" (M193, S152).

22. Robert Pippin writes that

> one cannot coerce [the desire of the other], merely trick the other into granting it, Jacob and Esau like, or be indifferent to the issue without losing one's own hold on the claim as a claim to authority, one with genuine normative force. So the only condition in which the authority of one's self-constituting self-construals can be "true" is the condition of genuine mutuality. This means that

> those normative considerations that emerge from the imagined *Kampf* must be in some clear sense genuinely accepted by the other, something only the other can manage and which I cannot coerce; and vice-versa with respect to the other's claims on me. They must be claims and considerations that can be shared. (Pippin, *Hegel on Self-Consciousness*, 91–92)

23. Charles Taylor says, similarly, that "the discourse of recognition has become familiar to us . . . on two levels: First, in the intimate sphere, where we understand the formation of identity and the self as taking place in a continuing dialogue and struggle with significant others. And then in the public sphere [with] a politics of equal recognition." Charles Taylor, "The Politics of Recognition," in *Multiculturalism: Examining the Politics of Recognition*, ed. Amy Gutmann (Princeton: Princeton University Press, 1994), 37. He then distinguishes between two kinds of recognition at work in the public sphere or "the politics of equal recognition": a politics of equal dignity ("a politics of universalism, emphasizing the equal dignity of all citizens") and a politics of difference ("the unique identity of this individual or group, their distinctness from everyone else") (Taylor, "Politics," 37–38). But there are significant differences between his account and mine. His characterization of the politics of difference should address the fact that the significance of these differences is not simply inwardly generated; his politics of equal dignity is not sensitive enough to the risk that naming universal human qualities or capacities can take a specific and particular shape and foreclose the transformation of which human beings are capable and to which the ideal of equal dignity is mobilized to respond; and his account of the difference between the two should consider the fact that they are actually an expression of the same idea—the idea that singularity must take on a particular content.

24. To borrow Hannah Arendt's terms, we could call this the "what" of recognition, a set of concrete qualities rather than an open determinacy, qualities that we are not free to define on our own but to which we thereby have the benefit of others' contributions. Hannah Arendt, *The Human Condition* (Chicago: University of Chicago Press, 1998). For Arendt, the "who" or the *unique* identity of the human being is revealed in action and speech, whereas the "what" or the set of traits that can be *shared* by human beings is associated with labor and work. This should remind us of the determinate aspect of free action delineated in Hegel's *Philosophy of Right* and discussed in chapter 7—"the translation from undifferentiated indeterminacy to differentiation, determination" (*PhR* 6).

25. Craig Calhoun says that "we face problems of recognition because socially sustained discourses about who it is possible or appropriate or valuable to be inevitably shape the way we look at and constitute ourselves, with varying degrees of agonism and tension." Craig Calhoun, *Critical Social Theory: Culture, History, and the Challenge of Difference* (Oxford: Blackwell, 1995), 213.

26. Again, following Arendt we could call this the "who" of recognition—an empty and infinitely determinable capacity rather than a concrete

and determinate quality. This should remind us of the indeterminate aspect of free action discussed in the *Philosophy of Right*—"the element of pure indeterminacy . . . in which every limitation . . . is dissolved" (*PhR* 5).

27. Charles Taylor, "Politics of Recognition," 36.

28. It can invoke an already operative conception of human being and parade it as the goal of social justice, such that recognition's "difference-consciousness" and law's "difference-blindness," to invoke Patchen Markell's formulations, are separately complicit in perpetuating "deep-seated structures of inequality and relations of power." Patchen Markell, *Bound by Recognition* (Princeton: Princeton University Press, 2003), 4. Markell argues that the ideal of mutual recognition is impossible and even incoherent because of "the practical limits imposed upon us by the openness and unpredictability of the future" (Markell, *Bound*, 4–5), but if we take seriously the possibility of recognition of indeterminacy (which I discuss as the second aspect of recognition), then this openness is something that can in a certain way be attested to in practices of recognition.

29. Kelly Oliver gives voice to this criticism in the following: "If recognition is conceived as being conferred on others by the dominant group, then it merely repeats the dynamic of hierarchies, privilege, and domination. Even if oppressed people are making demands for recognition, insofar as those who are dominant are empowered to confer it, we are thrown back into the hierarchy of domination" (Oliver, *Witnessing*, 9).

30. Fanon writes that "as long as he [man] has not been effectively recognized by the other, it is this other who remains the focus of his actions. His human worth and reality depend on this other and on his recognition by the other. It is in this other that the meaning of his life is condensed." Frantz Fanon, *Black Skin*, 191; Frantz Fanon, *Peau noire, masques blancs* (Paris: éditions du Seuil, 1952), 176 (hereafter *PN*). But, further, "he who is reluctant to recognize me is against me" (Fanon, *Black Skin*, 193; *PN* 177), and the need for recognition becomes a burden: I need recognition from one who is against me, and in needing that recognition express my attachment to that which opposes me. Oliver also discusses the critical aspect of the approach that Fanon takes to struggles for recognition—how they "are caught up in the logic of colonialism and oppression that made them necessary in the first place" (Oliver, *Witnessing*, 26–27), how "the trap of recognition" with its "powerful jaws . . . sprawls out the body and psyche of the oppressed," and how "colonization has soldered his self-identity to the recognition of his oppressor" (Oliver, *Witnessing*, 27).

31. Fanon, *Black Skin*, 194–95, translation modified (*PN* 178–79).

32. In *The Wretched of the Earth* Fanon argues that the colonist produces a Manichaean society in which the colonized is a thing without value, and the only way that the value of the colonized can be asserted is by "the creation of new men . . . through the very process of liberation." Frantz Fanon, *The Wretched of the Earth*, tr. Richard Philcox (New York: Grove, 1994), 2; Frantz Fanon, *Les damnés de la terre* (Paris: éditions La Découverte & Syros, 2002), 40 (herafter *DT*). This creation, however, is only possible if the Manichaean

world of the colonist is destroyed. "One does not disorganize a society with such an agenda if one has not decided from the very start—that is, from the very formulation of this agenda—to smash all the obstacles one will encounter in the process" (Fanon, *Black Skin*, 3, translation modified; *DT* 41). He writes, further, that "in Indochina, Madagascar, and the colonies, the 'native' has always known he can expect nothing from the other side. The work of the colonist is to make even dreams of liberty impossible for the colonized. The work of the colonized is to imagine every possible method for annihilating the colonist. On the logical plane, the Manichaeanism of the colonist produces a Manichaeanism of the colonized . . . For the colonized, life can only materialize from the rotting cadaver of the colonist" (Fanon, *Black Skin*, 50; *DT* 89).

33. Fanon, *Black Skin*, 187 (PN 171).

34. Fanon, *Black Skin*, 193 (PN 177).

35. Our response to this demand for recognition is essentially akin to what Kelly Oliver, in the context of a critique of the idea of recognition, calls "witnessing," which involves, as she writes, "testifying to that which cannot be seen, in other words, bearing witness" (as well as "seeing with one's own eyes," or testifying) (Oliver, *Witnessing*, 16). The demand for recognition is the demand to testify to that which cannot be seen—the infinite *possibility*, which characterizes any determinate human self, to define itself differently. This is one aspect of Hegel's version of recognition; it is recognition of the essential fact and presence of unfamiliarity, of the human being as essentially open to the future.

36. Catherine MacKinnon's attempts to justify legal protection for women with regard to pornography, harassment, and gender-related violence have been identified as problematic in these terms. See, for instance, her *Feminism Unmodified: Discourses on Life and Law* (Cambridge: Harvard University Press, 1987), *Only Words* (Cambridge: Harvard University Press, 1993), and *Women's Lives, Men's Laws* (Cambridge: Harvard University Press, 2007).

37. Wendy Brown and Janet Halley, eds., *Left Legalism/Left Critique* (Durham: Duke University Press, 2002), 430.

38. See Wendy Brown's criticism of the operation of tolerance in liberal discourse in *Regulating Aversion: Tolerance in the Age of Identity and Empire* (Princeton: Princeton University Press, 2008).

39. This theme is especially at play in chapter 5 of Fanon's *Black Skin, White Masks*, and in "On Violence" of his *The Wretched of the Earth*.

40. Christopher Zurn describes the relation between the issue of recognition and law in the following: "Recognition theory gives a distinctive twist to the analysis of the institutions securing equal civic autonomy by understanding them as legal realizations of the intersubjective conditions required for self-respect, that is, those conditions of consociation necessary for persons to understand themselves as free and equal legal subjects and political citizens amongst other subjects and citizens." "[L]egal rights [and] political democracy . . . are rather understood as the outcomes of historical struggles that can be rationally reconstructed." Hans-Christoph Schmidt am Busch and Christopher Zurn, eds., *The Philosophy of Recognition: Historical and Contemporary Perspectives* (Lanham, MD: Lexington Books, 2010), 5.

41. Karin de Boer writes that Hegel's remarks on democracy are "not directed against the state as such" but "might be used to argue that *any* government—whether elected or not—seeks to establish itself as the universal will of the society by effacing its proper particularity. If this is the case, then its effort to extricate itself from this particularity might well turn into the repression of modes of particularity it finds over against itself." Karin de Boer, "Hegel's Account of the Present: An Open-Ended History," in *Hegel and History*, ed. Will Dudley (Albany: State University of New York Press, 2009), 60.

42. In the *Philosophy of History* Hegel writes:

> Not satisfied with the establishment of rational rights, with freedom of person and property, with the existence of a political organization in which are to be found various circles of civil life each having its own functions to perform, and with that influence over the people which is exercised by the intelligent members of the community, and the confidence that is felt in them, "*Liberalism*" sets up in opposition to all this the atomistic principle, that which insists on the sway of individual wills; maintaining that all government should emanate from their express power, and have their express sanction. Asserting this formal side of Freedom—this abstraction—the party in question allows no political organization to be firmly established. The particular arrangements of the government are forthwith opposed by the advocates of Liberty as the mandates of a particular will, and branded as displays of arbitrary power. The will of the Many expels the Ministry from power, and those who had formed the Opposition fill the vacant places; but the latter having now become the Government, meet with hostility from the Many, and share the same fate. Thus agitation and unrest are perpetuated. G. W. F. Hegel, *The Philosophy of History*, tr. J. Sibree (Buffalo: Prometheus Books, 1991), 452; G. W. F. Hegel, *Vorlesungen über die Philosophie der Geschichte*, ed. E. Moldauer and K. M. Michel (Frankfurt am Main: Suhrkamp, 1986), 534–35

43. Taylor, "Positioning Subjects," 74.

CONCLUSION. THE ETHICS AND POLITICS OF CONSCIENCE

1. Émile Durkheim, in speaking of the power the social affords to the individual, writes:

> We speak a language we have not created; we use tools we have not invented; we invoke rights we have not instituted; each generation inherits a treasure trove of knowledge it did not amass itself. We owe these various benefits of civilization to society, and if we

> do not generally perceive their source, at least we know they are not of our making. Yet this is what makes man distinct among all creatures; for man is man only because he is civilized. He could not escape the feeling that outside him there are powerful causes which are the source of his characteristic nature, benevolent powers that aid him, protect him, and assure him a privileged fate. Émile Durkheim, *The Elementary Forms of Religious Life*, tr. Carol Cosman (Oxford: Oxford University Press, 2001), 159

2. In a discussion of the resonance between Hegel and Derrida in relation to the notion of legacy or inheritance, Rocío Zambrana writes that "inheritance requires making decisions that irrespective of intentions, aims, and outcomes involve violence. Indeed, carrying a legacy forward means negotiating a *logic* of inclusion-exclusion." Zambrana, "Hegel's Legacy," 274.

3. My analysis here draws on Hegel's discussion of law-giving reason in the section of the *Phenomenology* titled "Individuality, Which to Itself Is Real in and for Itself" (M425, S314). The upcoming example of "loving one's neighbor" is also taken from this section.

4. We should be reminded here of the ambivalence of Hegel's claim that "the wounds of the spirit heal and leave no scars behind" (M669, S492): such healing and erasure of scars signify not simply reconciliation but also a losing and a forgetting of what is valuable and meaningful. Zambrana writes, similarly, that "gathering is an act of memory that determines a legacy *as* a legacy, a history *as* a history. Gathering determines an event, norm, idea, or institution as something to be passed on for a future to come. This determination, however, is also a form of forgetting, since a legacy is determined *as* a legacy, a history *as* a history, according to commitments authoritative in the present" (Zambrana, "Hegel's Legacy," 276).

BIBLIOGRAPHY

Arendt, Hannah. *The Human Condition*. Chicago: University of Chicago Press, 1998.

Avineri, Shlomo. *Hegel's Theory of the Modern State*. Cambridge: Cambridge University Press, 1974.

Avineri, Shlomo and Avner de-Shalit. *Communitarianism and Individualism*. Oxford: Oxford University Press, 1992.

Baum, Manfred. "Common Welfare and Universal Will." In *Hegel on Ethics and Politics*, ed. Robert Pippin and Otfried Höffe. Cambridge: Cambridge University Press, 2004.

Baur, Michael, and John Russon, eds. *Hegel and the Tradition: Essays in Honour of H. S. Harris*. Toronto: University of Toronto Press, 1997.

Beiser, Frederick C., ed. *The Cambridge Companion to Hegel*. Cambridge: Cambridge University Press, 1993.

Benhabib, Seyla. *The Rights of Others: Aliens, Residents, and Citizens*. Cambridge: Cambridge University Press, 2004.

———. *Situating the Self: Gender, Community and Postmodernism in Contemporary Ethics*. New York: Routledge, 1992.Benhabib, Seyla, ed. *Democracy and Difference: Contesting the Boundaries of the Political*. Princeton: Princeton University Press, 1996.

Berger, Benjamin L. "Belonging to Law: Religious Difference and the Conditions of Civic Inclusion." Unpublished manuscript, 2012.

Bernasconi, Robert. "Persons and Masks: The Phenomenology of Spirit and Its Laws." *Cardozo Law Review* 10, no. 6 (March/April 1989): 1695–1711.

Bernstein, J. M. "Confession and Forgiveness: Hegel's Poetics of Action." In *Beyond Representation: Philosophy and Poetic Imagination*, ed. Richard Eldridge. Cambridge: Cambridge University Press, 1996, pp. 34–65.

———. "Conscience and Transgression: The Persistence of Misrecognition." *The Bulletin of the Hegel Society of Great Britain* 29 (Spring/Summer 1994): 55–70.

———. "Love and Law: Hegel's Critique of Morality." *Social Research* 70, no. 2 (Summer 2003): 393–432.

Bradley, F. H. *Ethical Studies*. London: Henry S. King, 1876.

Brandom, Robert. "The Structure of Desire and Recognition: Self-Consciousness and Self-Constitution." *Philosophy and Social Criticism* 33, no. 1 (2007): 127–150.

Bowra, C. M. *Sophoclean Tragedy*. Oxford: Oxford University Press, 1970.

Brod, Harry. *Hegel's Philosophy and Politics: Idealism, Identity and Modernity*. Boulder: Westview, 1992.

Brown, Wendy. *Edgework: Critical Essays on Knowledge and Politics*. Princeton: Princeton University Press, 2005.

———. *Regulating Aversion: Tolerance in the Age of Identity and Empire*. Princeton: Princeton University Press, 2008.

Brown, Wendy, and Janet Halley, eds. *Left Legalism/Left Critique*. Durham: Duke University Press, 2002.

Brunkhorst, Hauke. *Solidarity: From Civic Friendship to a Global Legal Community*. Boston: MIT Press, 2005.

Buchanan, Allen. *Marx and Justice: The Radical Critique of Liberalism*. Totowa, NJ: Rowman and Littlefield, 1982.

Burbidge, John. *Hegel's Systematic Contingency*. New York: Palgrave Macmillan, 2007.

———. *The Logic of Hegel's Logic: An Introduction*. Peterborough: Broadview, 2006.

Butler, Judith. *Antigone's Claim: Kinship between Life and Death*. New York: Columbia University Press, 2000.

———. *Giving an Account of Oneself*. New York: Fordham University Press, 2005.

Calhoun, Craig. *Critical Social Theory: Culture, History, and the Challenge of Difference*. Oxford: Blackwell, 1995.

Caputo, John D. *The Prayers and Tears of Jacques Derrida*. Bloomington: Indiana University Press, 1997.

Caputo, John D., Mark Dooley, and Michael J. Scanlon, eds. *Questioning God*. Bloomington: Indiana University Press, 2001.

Changfoot, Nadine. "Hegel's *Antigone*: A Response to the Feminist Critique." *The Owl of Minerva* 33, no. 2 (Spring/Summer 2002): 179–204.

Chanter, Tina. *Ethics of Eros: Irigaray's Reading of the Philosophers*. New York: Routledge, 1995.

Ciavatta, David V. "The Event of Absolute Freedom: Hegel on the French Revolution and Its Calendar" Unpublished paper.

———. *Spirit, the Family, and the Unconscious in Hegel's Philosophy*. Albany: State University of New York Press, 2009.

Comay, Rebecca. "Dead Right: Hegel and the Terror." *The South Atlantic Quarterly* 103, no. 2/3 (Spring/Summer 2004): 375–395.

———. *Mourning Sickness: Hegel and the French Revolution*. Stanford: Stanford University Press, 2010.

Cooke, Maeve. "Beyond Dignity and Difference: Revisiting the Politics of Recognition." *European Journal of Political Theory* 8, no. 1 (2009): 76–95.

Cornell, Drucilla. *At the Heart of Freedom*. Princeton: Princeton University Press, 1998.

———. *Beyond Accommodation: Ethical Feminism, Deconstruction, and the Law*. Lanham, MD: Rowman and Littlefield, 1999.

———. *Defending Ideals: War, Democracy, and Political Struggles*. New York: Routledge, 2004.

Cornell, Drucilla, Michel Rosenfeld, and David Gray Carlson, eds. *Deconstruction and the Possibility of Justice*. New York: Routledge, 1992.

Dahlstrom, Daniel O. "Die Quelle der Sittlichkeit in Hegels *Phänomenologie des Geistes*." *Hegel-Jahrbuch* (1987): 256–261.

Dallmayr, Fred R. *G. W. F. Hegel: Modernity and Politics*. Lanham, MD: Rowman and Littlefield, 2002.

de Beauvoir, Simone. *The Ethics of Ambiguity*, tr. Bernhard Frechtman. New York: Citadel Press, 1948.

de Boer, Karin. "Hegel's Account of the Present: An Open-Ended History." In *Hegel and History*, ed. Will Dudley. Albany: State University of New York Press, 2009.

———. "Hegel's *Antigone* and the Dialectics of Sexual Difference." *Philosophy Today: SPEP Supplement* (2003): 140–146.

———. "Tragedy, Dialectics, and Difference: On Hegel and Derrida." *Southern Journal of Philosophy* 39 (2001): 331–357.

Derrida, Jacques. Jacques Derrida, "Force of Law: The 'Mystical Foundation of Authority.'" In *Acts of Religion*, ed. Gil Anidjar. New York: Routledge, 2002.

———. *Glas*, tr. John P. Leavey, Jr. and Richard Rand. Lincoln: University of Nebraska Press, 1986.

———. *Of Hospitality*, tr. Rachel Bowlby. Stanford: Stanford University Press, 2000.

———. *On Cosmopolitanism and Forgiveness*, tr. Mark Dooley and Michael Hughes. London: Routledge, 2001.

———. *Politics of Friendship*, tr. George Collins. London: Verso, 2005.

———. *Rogues: Two Essays on Reason*, tr. Pascale-Anne Brault and Michael Naas. Stanford: Stanford University Press, 2005.

Derrida, Jacques, and Maurizio Ferraris. *A Taste for the Secret*, tr. Giacomo Donis. Cambridge: Polity, 2001.

Donougho, Martin. "The Woman in White: On the Reception of Hegel's *Antigone*." *The Owl of Minerva* 21, no. 1 (Fall 1989): 65–89.

Dudley, Will. "Ethical Life, Morality, and the Role of Spirit in the *Phenomenology of Spirit*." In *Hegel's* Phenomenology of Spirit, ed. Dean Moyar and Michael Quante. Cambridge: Cambridge University Press, 2008.

Dudley, Will, ed. *Hegel and History*. Albany: State University of New York Press, 2009.

Durkheim, Émile. *The Elementary Forms of Religious Life*, tr. Carol Cosman. Oxford: Oxford University Press, 2001.

Dworkin, Ronald. *The Philosophy of Law*. Oxford: Oxford University Press, 1977.

Ebert, Teresa. "Writing in the Political." In *Legal Studies as Cultural Studies*, ed. Jerry Leonard. Albany: State University of New York Press, 1995.

Etzioni, Amitai. *New Communitarian Thinking*. Charlottesville: University Press of Virginia, 1995.

Fanon, Frantz. *Black Skin, White Masks*, tr. Richard Philcox. New York: Grove, 2008.

———. *Les damnés de la terre*. Paris: Éditions La Découverte and Syros, 2002.

———. *Peau noire, masques blancs*. Paris: Éditions du Seuil, 1952.

———. *The Wretched of the Earth*, tr. Richard Philcox. New York: Grove, 1994.

Fichte, J. G. *Foundations of Natural Right*, tr. Michael Baur. Cambridge: Cambridge University Press, 2000.

Finlayson, J. G. "Conflict and Reconciliation in Hegel's Theory of the Tragic." *Journal of the History of Philosophy* 37, no. 3 (July 1999): 493–520.

Fish, Stanley. *The Trouble with Principle*. Cambridge: Harvard University Press, 1999.

Flay, Joseph. *Hegel's Quest for Certainty*. Albany: State University of New York Press, 1984.

Forst, Rainer. *Contexts of Justice: Political Philosophy beyond Liberalism and Communitarianism*, tr. John M. M. Farrell. Berkeley: University of California Press, 2002.

Foucault, Michel. *Society Must Be Defended*, tr. David Macey. New York: Picador, 2003.

Franco, Paul. *Hegel's Philosophy of Freedom*. New Haven: Yale University Press, 2002.

Fraser, Nancy. *Justice Interruptus: Critical Reflections on the Postsocialist Condition*. New York: Routledge, 1997.

Fraser, Nancy, and Axel Honneth. *Redistribution or Recognition?: A Political-Philosophical Exchange*. London: Verso, 2003.

Furth, Peter. "Antigone—Oder zur Tragischen Vorgeschichte der Bürgerlichen Gesellschaft." *Hegel-Jahrbuch* (1984/5): 15–29.

Garza Jr., Abel. "Hegel's Critique of Liberalism and Natural Law: Reconstructing Ethical Life." *Law and Philosophy* 9 (1990–1991): 371–398.

Gray, John. "In Theory." *The Nation* (June 5, 2006).

Grene, David, and Richmond Lattimore, eds. *Greek Tragedies: Volume 1*, 2nd ed. Chicago: Chicago University Press, 1991.

Habermas, Jürgen. *Between Facts and Norms*, tr. William Rehg. Cambridge: MIT Press, 1998.

———. *The Inclusion of the Other: Studies in Political Theory*. Boston: MIT Press, 2000.

———. *The Theory of Communicative Action*, vols. 1 and 2, tr. Thomas McCarthy. Boston: Beacon, 1985.

Hampton, Jean and Jeffrie G. Murphy. *Forgiveness and Mercy*. Cambridge: Cambridge University Press, 1998.

Harris, H. S. *Hegel's Development: Towards the Sunlight 1770–1801*. Oxford: Oxford University Press, 1972.

———. *Hegel's Ladder I: The Pilgrimage of Reason*. Indianapolis: Hackett, 1997.

———. *Hegel's Ladder II: The Odyssey of Spirit*. Indianapolis: Hackett, 1997.

———. *Hegel: Phenomenology and System*. Indianapolis: Hackett, 1995.

Hegel, G. W. F. *Aesthetics*, 2 vols., tr. T. M. Knox. Oxford: Clarendon, 1975.

———. *Early Theological Writings*, ed. R. Kroner, tr. T. M. Knox. Philadelphia: University of Pennsylvania Press, 1971.

———. *Enzyklopädie der philosophischen Wissenschaften*, in Werke in zwanzig Bänden, vol. 8–10. Frankfurt am Main: Suhrkamp Verlag, 1970.

———. *Elements of the Philosophy of Right*, ed. Allen W. Wood, tr. H. B. Nisbet. Cambridge: Cambridge University Press, 1991.

———. *Hegel's Phenomenology of Spirit*, tr. A. V. Miller. Oxford: Oxford University Press, 1977.

———. *Introduction to the Philosophy of History*, tr. Leo Rauch. Indianapolis: Hackett, 1988.

———. *Lectures on the Philosophy of Religion: The Lectures of 1827*, ed. Peter C. Hodgson, tr. R. F. Brown, P. C. Hodgson, and J. M. Stewart. Berkeley: University of California Press, 1988.

———. *Natural Law*, tr. T. M. Knox. Philadelphia: University of Pennsylvania Press, 1975.

———. *Phänomenologie des Geistes*. Frankfurt am Main: Suhrkamp Verlag, 1970.

———. *The Philosophy of History*, tr. J. Sibree. Buffalo: Prometheus Books, 1991.

———. *Philosophy of Mind*, tr. William Wallace. Oxford: Oxford University Press, 1971.

———. *Political Writings*, tr. T. M. Knox. Oxford: Clarendon, 1964.

———. *Science of Logic*, tr. A. V. Miller. Atlantic Highlands, NJ: Humanities Press International, 1989.

———. "Two Fragments of 1797 on Love," tr. H. S. Harris. *Clio* 8 (1978–9): 258–265.

———. "Two Hegel Texts on Law," tr. Michael H. Hoffheimer. *University of Toledo Law Review* 24 (1993): 933–942.

———. *Vorlesungen über die Philosophie der Geschichte*, ed. E. Moldauer and K. M. Michel. Frankfurt am Main: Suhrkamp, 1986.

Heidegger, Martin. *Basic Writings*, tr. David Farrell Krell. New York: Harper Collins, 1993.

———. *Being and Time*, tr. John Macquarrie and Edward Robinson. New York: Harper and Row, 1962.

Helmick, Raymond G., and Rodney L. Petersen. *Forgiveness and Reconciliation*. Radnor, PA: Templeton Foundation, 2001.

Hinchman, Lewis P. *Hegel's Critique of the Enlightenment*. Tampa: University of South Florida Press, 1984.

Hoff, Shannon. "Inheriting identity and practicing transformation: The time of feminist politics." *Philosophia* 2, no. 2 (2012).

———. "Wendy Brown and the Critique of Tolerance." *Radical Philosophy Review* 11, no. 1 (2008): 35–50.

Hoffheimer, Michael H. "Hegel's Criticism of Law." *Hegel-Studien* 27 (1992a): 27–52.

———. "The Idea of Law (*Recht*) in Hegel's *Phenomenology of Spirit*." *Clio* 21, no. 4 (1992b): 345–367.

Honneth, Axel. *The Struggle for Recognition: The Moral Grammar of Social Conflicts*. Cambridge: MIT Press, 1996.

Houlgate, Stephen. *Freedom, Truth and History: An Introduction to Hegel's Philosophy*. London: Routledge, 1991.

———. *The Opening of Hegel's Logic: From Being to Infinity*. West Lafayette: Purdue University Press, 2006.

Hutchings, Kimberly. *Hegel and Feminist Philosophy*. Cambridge: Polity, 2003.

Hyppolite, Jean. *Genesis and Structure of Hegel's* Phenomenology of Spirit, tr. Samuel Cherniak and John Heckman. Evanston: Northwestern University Press, 1974.

———. "L'Etat du Droit (La Condition Juridique)." *Hegel-Studien*, Beiheft 3. Bonn: H. Bouvier u. Co. Verlag (1996): 181–185.

Ignatieff, Michael. *Human Rights as Politics and Idolatry*. Princeton: Princeton University Press, 2003.

Inwood, Michael. *A Hegel Dictionary*. Oxford: Blackwell, 1992.

Irigaray, Luce. *An Ethics of Sexual Difference*, tr. Carolyn Burke and Gillian C. Gill. Ithaca: Cornell University Press, 1993.

———. *Democracy Begins between Two*, tr. Kirsteen Anderson. New York: Routledge, 1996.

———. *I Love to You*, tr. Alison Martin. London: Athlone, 2001.

———. "Sexes and Genealogies." In *The Irigaray Reader*, ed. Margaret Whitford. Oxford: Basil Blackwell, 1991.

———. *Speculum of the Other Woman*, tr. Gillian C. Gill. Ithaca: Cornell University Press, 1985.

———. *This Sex Which Is Not One*, tr. Catherine Porter. Ithaca: Cornell University Press, 1985.

Jacobs, Carol. "Dusting Antigone." *MLN* 111, no. 5 (1996): 890–917.

Jacobson, Kirsten. "The Experience of Home and the Space of Citizenship." *Southern Journal of Philosophy* 48 (2010): 219–245.

Jankélévitch, Vladimir. *Forgiveness*. Chicago: University of Chicago Press, 2005.

Jurist, Elliot L. "Recognition and Self-Knowledge." *Hegel-Studien* 21 (1986): 143–150.

Kain, Philip J. "Hegel, Antigone, and Women." *The Owl of Minerva* 33, no. 2 (Spring/Summer 2002): 157–177.

Kant, Immanuel. *Grounding for the Metaphysics of Morals*, tr. James W. Ellington. Indianapolis: Hackett, Inc., 1981.

———. *Political Writings*, ed. H. S. Reiss. Cambridge: Cambridge University Press, 1991.

Kellogg, Catherine. "Mourning the Law: Hegel's Metaphorics of Sexual Difference." *Philosophy and Social Criticism* 29, no. 4 (2003): 361–374.

Kelly, George Armstrong. "Notes on Hegel's Lordship and Bondage." *Review of Metaphysics* 19 (1965/6): 780–802.

Kojève, Alexandre. *Introduction à la Lecture de Hegel*, ed. R. Queneau. Paris: Gallimard, Hachette, 1947.

Korteweg, Anna C. "The Sharia Debate in Ontario: Gender, Islam, and Representations of Women's Agency." *Gender and Society* 22, no. 4 (2008): 434–454.

Kymlicka, Will. *Politics in the Vernacular: Nationalism, Multiculturalism, and Citizenship*. Oxford: Oxford University Press, 2001.

Laing, R. D. *The Divided Self*. London: Penguin Books, 1969.

Lamothe, Kimerer L. "Reason, Religion, and Sexual Difference: Resources for a Feminist Philosophy of Religion in Hegel's *Phenomenology of Spirit*." *Hypatia* 20, no. 1 (Winter 2005): 120–149.

Lauer, Quentin. *A Reading of Hegel's* Phenomenology of Spirit. New York: Fordham University Press, 1993.

Levinas, Emmanuel. *Otherwise Than Being*, tr. Alphonso Lingis. Pittsburgh: Duquesne University Press, 1998.

———. *Totality and Infinity*, tr. Alphonso Lingis. Pittsburgh: Duquesne University Press, 1969.

Locke, John. *Two Treatises of Government and Letter Concerning Toleration*, ed. Ian Shapiro. New Haven: Yale University Press, 2003.

MacIntyre, Alasdair. *After Virtue: A Study in Moral Theory*, 3rd ed. South Bend, IN: University of Notre Dame Press, 2007.

MacKay, L. A. "Antigone, Coriolanus, and Hegel." In *Transactions and Proceedings of the American Philological Association* 93, ed. Donald W. Prakken. Ithaca: Cornell University Press, 1962.

MacLachlan, Alice. "Practicing Imperfect Forgiveness." In *Feminist Ethics and Social and Political Philosophy: Theorizing the Non-Ideal*, ed. Lisa Tessman. New York: Springer Books, 2009.

Maclaren, Kym. "The Role of Emotion in an Existential Education: Insights from Hegel and Plato." *International Philosophical Quarterly* 48, no. 4/192 (December 2008): 471–492.

Markell, Patchen. *Bound by Recognition*. Princeton: Princeton University Press, 2003.

Marx, Karl, and Friedrich Engels. *The Marx-Engels Reader*, ed. Robert C. Tucker. London: W. W. Norton, 1978.

Menke, Christoph. *Tragödie im Sittlichen: Gerechtigkeit und Freiheit nach Hegel*. Frankfurt am Main: Suhrkamp Verlag, 1996.

Miller, Elaine P. "The 'Paradoxical Displacement': Beauvoir and Irigaray on Hegel's Antigone." *The Journal of Speculative Philosophy* 14, no. 2 (2000): 121–137.

Mills, Patricia. "Feminist Sympathy and Other Serious Crimes: A Reply to Swindle." *The Owl of Minerva* 24, no. 1 (Fall 1992): 55–62.

———. "Hegel's *Antigone* Redux: Woman in Four Parts." *The Owl of Minerva* 33, no. 2 (Spring/Summer 2002): 205–221.

Milne, Drew. "The Beautiful Soul: From Hegel to Beckett." *diacritics* 32, no. 1 (Spring 2002): 63–82.

Ministry of the Attorney General of Ontario. "Dispute Resolution in Family Law: Protecting Choice, Promoting Inclusion." Prepared by Marion Boyd, December 2004.

Minow, Martha. *Between Vengeance and Forgiveness: Facing History after Genocide and Mass Violence*. Boston: Beacon, 1998.

Moyar, Dean, and Michael Quante, eds. *Hegel's* Phenomenology of Spirit. Cambridge: Cambridge University Press, 2008.

Murphie, Jeffrey. *Getting Even: Forgiveness and Its Limits*. New York: Oxford University Press, 2004.

Norman, Richard. *Hegel's* Phenomenology: *A Philosophical Introduction*. Brighton: Sussex University Press, 1976.

Nussbaum, Martha. *The Fragility of Goodness*. Cambridge: Cambridge University Press, 1986.

Oliver, Kelly. "Antigone's Ghost: Undoing Hegel's *Phenomenology of Spirit*." *Hypatia* 11, no. 1 (Winter 1996): 67–89.

———. *The Colonization of Psychic Space: A Psychoanalytic Social Theory of Oppression*. Minneapolis: University of Minnesota Press, 2004.

———. "Forgiveness and Community." *The Southern Journal of Philosophy* 42 (2004): 1–15.

———. "Forgiveness and Subjectivity." *Philosophy Today* 47, no. 3 (Fall 2003): 280–292.

———. *Witnessing: Beyond Recognition*. Minneapolis: University of Minnesota Press, 2001.

Ormiston, Alice. "'The Spirit of Christianity and Its Fate': Toward a Reconsideration of the Role of Love in Hegel." *Canadian Journal of Political Science* 35, no. 3 (Sept. 2002): 499–525.

Peperzak, Adriaan. *Modern Freedom: Hegel's Legal, Moral, and Political Philosophy*. Dordrecht: Kluwer, 2001.

Pinkard, Terry. *Hegel's Phenomenology: The Sociality of Reason*. Cambridge: Cambridge University Press, 1994.

Pippin, Robert. *Hegel on Self-Consciousness: Desire and Death in the* Phenomenology of Spirit. Princeton: Princeton University Press, 2011.

———. *Idealism as Modernism: Hegelian Variations*. Cambridge: Cambridge University Press, 1997.

Pritchard, Annie. "Antigone's Mirrors: Reflections on Moral Madness." *Hypatia* 7, no. 3 (Summer 1992): 77–94.

Raaflaub, K. A. "Freiheit in Athen und Rom: ein Beispiel divergierender politischer Begriffsentwicklung der Antike." *Historische Zeitschrift* 238 (1984): 529–567.

Rasmussen, David, ed. *Universalism vs. Communitarianism: Contemporary Debates in Ethics*. Cambridge: MIT Press, 1990.

Ravven, Heidi Miriam. "Further Thoughts on Hegel and Feminism: A Response to Philip J. Kain and Nadine Changfoot." *The Owl of Minerva* 33, no. 2 (Spring/Summer 2002): 223–249.

———. "Has Hegel Anything to Say to Feminists?" *The Owl of Minerva* 19, no. 2 (Spring 1988): 149–168.

———. "A Response to 'Why Feminists Should Take the *Phenomenology of Spirit* Seriously.'" *The Owl of Minerva* 24, no. 1 (Fall 1992): 63–69.

Rawls, John. "The Idea of an Overlapping Consensus," *Oxford Journal of Legal Studies* 7 (1987): 1–25.

———. "Kantian Constructivism in Moral Theory. *The Journal of Philosophy* 77, no. 9 (September 1980): 515–572.

———. *Political Liberalism*, 2nd ed. New York: Columbia University Press, 2005.

———. *A Theory of Justice*. Cambridge: Harvard University Press, 1971.

Ricoeur, Paul. *Memory, History, and Forgetting*, tr. Kathleen Blamey and David Pellauer. Chicago: University of Chicago Press, 2006.

Ritter, Joachim. *Hegel and the French Revolution: Essays on The Philosophy of Right*, tr. Richard Dean Winfield. Boston: MIT Press, 1984.

Rorty, Richard. *Achieving Our Country: Leftist Thought in Twentieth-Century America*. Boston: Harvard University Press, 1999.

———. *Philosophy and Social Hope*. New York: Penguin, 2000.

Rose, Gillian. *The Broken Middle: Out of Our Ancient Society*. Oxford: Blackwell, 1992.

———. "The Comedy of Hegel and the Trauerspiel of Modern Philosophy." In *Hegel's* Phenomenology of Spirit: *A Reappraisal*, ed. G. K. Browning. Dordrecht: Kluwer, 1997.

———. *Hegel Contra Sociology*. Atlantic Highlands, NJ: Humanities, 1981.

———. *Mourning Becomes the Law: Philosophy and Representation*. Cambridge: Cambridge University Press, 1996.

Russon, John. *Bearing Witness to Epiphany: Persons, Things, and the Nature of Erotic Life*. Albany: State University of New York Press, 2009.

———. *Human Experience: Philosophy, Neurosis, and the Elements of Everyday Life*. Albany: State University of New York Press, 2003.

———. *Infinite Phenomenology: The Lessons of Hegel's Science of Experience*. Evanston, IL: Northwestern University Press, forthcoming.

———. *Reading Hegel's* Phenomenology. Bloomington: Indiana University Press, 2004.

———. *The Self and Its Body in Hegel's* Phenomenology of Spirit. Toronto: University of Toronto Press, 1997.

Sandel, Michael, ed. *Liberalism and Its Critics*. New York: New York University Press, 1984.

Schild, Wolfgang. "The Relevance of Hegel's Concept of Punishment." In *Hegel on Ethics and Politics*, ed. Robert Pippin and Otfried Höffe. Cambridge: Cambridge University Press, 2004.

Schmidt am Busch, Hans-Christoph, and Christopher Zurn, eds. *The Philosophy of Recognition: Historical and Contemporary Perspectives*. Lanham, MD: Lexington Books, 2010.

Schmitz, Kenneth L. "Hegel and the French Revolution. Essays on the *Philosophy of Right* (review)." *Journal of the History of Philosophy* 22, no. 4 (October 1984): 493–494.

Shklar, Judith N. *Freedom and Independence: A Study of the Political Ideas of Hegel's* Phenomenology of Mind. Cambridge: Cambridge University Press, 1976.

———. "Hegel's *Phenomenology*: An Elegy for Hellas." In *G. W. F. Hegel: Critical Assessments* III, ed. Robert Stern. London: Routledge, 1993.

Siep, Ludwig. "Practical Reason and Spirit in Hegel's *Phenomenology of Spirit*." In *Hegel's* Phenomenology of Spirit*: A Critical Guide*, ed. Dean Moyar and Michael Quante. Cambridge: Cambridge University Press, 2008.

Smith, Adam. *An Inquiry into the Nature and Causes of the Wealth of Nations*. Chicago: University of Chicago Press, 1977.

Smith, Steven B. "Hegel and the French Revolution: An Epitaph for Republicanism." *Social Research* 56, no. 1 (Spring 1989): 233–261.

———. *Hegel's Critique of Liberalism: Rights in Context*. Chicago: University of Chicago Press, 1989.

Solomon, Robert. *In the Spirit of Hegel: A Study of G. W. F. Hegel's* Phenomenology of Spirit. Oxford: Oxford University Press, 1983.

Speight, Allan. *Hegel, Literature, and the Problem of Agency*. Cambridge: Cambridge University Press, 2001.

Steinberger, Peter J. *Logic and Politics*. New Haven: Yale University Press, 1988.

Stepelevitch, Lawrence S., and David Lamb, eds. *Hegel's Philosophy of Action*. Atlantic Highlands, NJ: Humanities, 1983.

Stillman, Peter G. "Hegel's Critique of Liberal Theories of Rights." *The American Political Science Review* 68, no. 3 (1974): 1086–1092.

Stone, Alison. "Hegel's Dialectic and the Recognition of Feminine Difference." *Philosophy Today: SPEP Supplement* (2003): 132–139.

Swindle, Stuart. "Why Feminists Should Take the *Phenomenology of Spirit* Seriously." *The Owl of Minerva* 24, no. 1 (Fall 1992): 41–54.

Taylor, Carole Anne. "Positioning Subjects and Objects: Agency, Narration, Relationality." *Hypatia* 8, no. 1 (Winter 1993): 55–80.

Taylor, Charles. *Hegel*. Cambridge: Cambridge University Press, 1977.

———. *Hegel and Modern Society*. Cambridge: Cambridge University Press, 1979.

———. "The Politics of Recognition." In *Multiculturalism: Examining the Politics of Recognition*, ed. Amy Gutmann. Princeton: Princeton University Press, 1994.

Tutu, Desmond. *No Future without Forgiveness*. New York: Random House, 1999.

Unger, Roberto Mangabeira. *The Critical Legal Studies Movement*. Cambridge: Harvard University Press, 1986.

von Bogdandy, Armin. *Hegels Theorie des Gesetzes*. Freiburg: Verlag Karl Alber, 1989.

Walsh, Lisa. "Her Mother Her Self: The Ethics of the Antigone Family Romance." *Hypatia* 14, no. 3 (Summer 1999): 96–122.

Westphal, Kenneth R. *Hegel's Epistemology: A Philosophical Introduction to the* Phenomenology of Spirit. Indianapolis: Hackett, 2003.

Westphal, Merold. *History and Truth in Hegel's* Phenomenology, 3rd ed. Bloomington: Indiana University Press, 1998.

Wildt, Andreas. *Autonomie und Anerkennung. Hegels Moralitätskritik im Lichte seiner Fichte-Rezeption*. Stuttgart: Klett-Cotta, 1982.

Williams, Patricia. *The Alchemy of Race and Rights*. Cambridge: Harvard University Press, 1992.

Winfield, Richard Dean. "Freedom as Interaction: Hegel's Resolution to the Dilemma of Liberal Theory." In *Hegel's Philosophy of Action*, ed. Lawrence S. Stepelevitch and David Lamb. Atlantic Highlands, NJ: Humanities, 1983.

Wirszubski, Chaim. *Libertas as a Political Idea at Rome*. Cambridge: Cambridge University Press, 1960.

Wood, Allen. *Hegel's Ethical Thought*. Cambridge: Cambridge University Press, 1990.

Wylleman, A., ed. *Hegel on the Ethical Life, Religion, and Philosophy*. Leuven: Leuven University Press, 1989.

Zambrana, Rocío. "Hegel's Legacy." *The Southern Journal of Philosophy* 50, no. 2 (June 2012): 273–284.

———. "Hegel's Logic of Finitude." *Continental Philosophy Review* 45 (2012): 213–233.

Žižek, Slavoj. *Less Than Nothing: Hegel and the Shadow of Dialectical Materialism*. London: Verso, 2012.

———. *Tarrying with the Negative: Kant, Hegel, and the Critique of Ideology*. Durham: Duke University Press, 1993.

Žižek, Slavoj, Judith Butler, and Ernesto Laclau. *Contingency, Hegemony, Universality*. London: Verso, 2000.

INDEX